The Infiltrators

The Infiltrators

PHILIP ETIENNE & MARTIN MAYNARD

With Tony Thompson

MICHAEL JOSEPH
LONDON

MICHAEL JOSEPH

Published by the Penguin Group
Penguin Books Ltd, 27 Wrights Lane, London w8 5tz, England
Penguin Putnam Inc., 375 Hudson Street, New York, New York 10014, USA
Penguin Books Australia Ltd, Ringwood, Victoria, Australia
Penguin Books Canada Ltd, 10 Alcorn Avenue, Toronto, Ontario, Canada m4v 3b2
Penguin Books India (P) Ltd, 11, Community Centre,
Panchsheel Park, New Delhi – 110 017, India
Penguin Books (NZ) Ltd, Cnr Rosedale and Airborne Roads, Albany, Auckland, New Zealand
Penguin Books (South Africa) (Pty) Ltd, 5 Watkins Street,
Denver Ext 4, Johannesburg 2094, South Africa

Penguin Books Ltd, Registered Offices: Harmondsworth, Middlesex, England

First published 2000
1

Set in 12/14.75 pt Monotype Bembo
Typeset by Rowland Phototypesetting Ltd, Bury St Edmunds, Suffolk
Printed in England by Clays Ltd, St Ives plc

A CIP catalogue record for this book is available from the British Library

Hardback ISBN 0-718-14319-1
Trade paperback ISBN 0-718-14441-4

To all the SO10 officers, past, present and future. For their courage.

Prologue

We'd been waiting nearly an hour for the deal to go down. It was the last week of October, there'd be a frost later. We'd turned off the car's engine and, with the stereo draining the battery as it pumped out street sounds, we had to lose the heating too. Within ten minutes the temperature had dropped enough for my breath to form little clouds which appeared pale orange as they soaked up the glow from the street lights.

We were parked in a slip road directly opposite a row of small shops and fast-food restaurants in the run-down Birmingham suburb of Handsworth. Just around the corner, the third member of our team sat in a second car with £10,000 in carefully folded notes stuffed into a supermarket carrier bag. As soon as the dealers turned up, we'd make the buy and get the hell out of there.

There were lots of people about, most of whom seemed to be trooping in and out of the Kentucky Fried Chicken restaurant across the road so when two rough-looking guys in combats, Timberlands and hooded tracksuit tops walked by the front of the car, I didn't pay any attention. Their appearance didn't mark them out. Even when they came up, tapped on the driver's side window and asked for a light, I wasn't fazed. They weren't our guys and that's all I needed to know. But then things went shit-shaped. Quick as a flash two pairs of hands darted in through the window past my partner and made a grab for the car keys. It was all going wrong. I knew I mustn't get trapped in the car and made to get out as quickly as possible as I grabbed the latch and pushed open the passenger door. Out of nowhere appeared another man, dressed like the first two, filling the gap and blocking my escape. In his pocket, pressed against the fabric, I could make out the outline of an automatic pistol pointing directly at my head, his finger on the trigger.

I didn't know who he was: it was too dark to see his face clearly, all I could make out were the pale whites of his eyes floating in the shadows inside the hood of his jacket. His voice, a harsh mix of Birmingham street slang and Jamaican patois, was loaded with raw aggression. 'Get back in the car bumba clot,' he screamed. 'Back in the car, get back in the fucking car bwoy before I shoot you down.'

I tried to speak but no words came out. My throat had dried up in an instant, the tightness silencing me. Somewhere behind me I could hear the sounds of my partner struggling violently with the other attackers. I knew he was in trouble and taking punishment but I couldn't turn around, I couldn't even blink.

The hooded gunman took a step towards me. He wasn't going to take any chances, he couldn't risk missing. He believed I was this bigshot crack dealer from south London, in Birmingham to source a major new supplier. He'll have assumed that I was tooled up too because that's just how business gets done. In this game the only people without guns in their pockets are the police. Although he was on his own I felt surrounded and without options. If I stayed in the car, even for a split second longer, I was a dead man for sure. I knew that if I got out I might have some chance, some room for manoeuvre at least.

I pushed the door of the Mondeo back and forced myself to stand up to face him. We were so close our noses were almost touching. I could feel his hot, caustic breath on my face and the hard metal of the gun against my ribs. He stepped back in surprise – me coming forward was the last thing he expected. 'You stupid fuck, get back in the car,' he barked. 'Back in the car right now!'

I gingerly raised both my hands high in the air. I wanted to tell him that it was over, that I quit, that I wasn't going to play the game any more, but I still couldn't speak. Overcome with fear, I knew what was coming and I just wanted to get it over with.

Behind me: the harsh snap of a gunshot cut through the cold air, its report echoing around the surrounding brickwork.

It's nothing like the movies: when someone fires a gun in real life the sound stops people in their tracks. Deafeningly crisp, it's the sharp crack of a giant Guy Fawkes banger. And immediately you're surrounded by smoke, a genie swirling out of its bottle.

The gunshot startled us both. Neither of us could place the shot or its target. I looked round, but stumbled forward, bouncing into my assailant, forcing him to lurch back a step. I then saw his eyes clearly for the first time and like mine they were wide with fear. At once we both ditched our private battle and broke away for cover, nearly clambering over each other in our rush to escape.

I made for the parade of shops across the road, their lights offering the promise of safety. But after only a couple of steps, a subconscious instinct for survival turned me round, to keep one eye on the place where the shot seemed to have come from. I ended up running awkwardly backwards away from the car, trying to work out what the fuck was going on.

Under the dull glow of the street lights, I could make out the outlines of two heavy-set men in pale hooded tracksuits, both bent over, furiously punching and kicking at something on the ground. The muffled sound of each blow conveyed the damage it was inflicting. Above the sickening thuds of the impacts, I could hear them raging: 'Where's the money you blood clot, where's the fucking money?' My heart was pounding and I was no longer making conscious decisions. I just wanted the police to ride to the rescue but there was no sign of them. I was less than halfway across the road when one of the men I was watching broke off his attack, twisting on the balls of his feet as he stood up and came after me.

'Get back here you fucking bitch, get back here now.'

I was about forty feet away when he raised his right arm, tracking me as I staggered back.

Time seemed to slow down then. I saw the gun barrel as the light picked up the metal and I watched as his finger tightened on the trigger. There was a whipcrack as smoke followed a small spit of flame from the muzzle. I felt the air bend, filling the vacuum the bullet created as it ripped past me.

And I turned away in slow motion, no longer able to panic.

I

Martin: I never wanted to be a policeman.

I left school at sixteen and quite frankly didn't give a monkey's about anything that didn't have four wheels and an engine. All I knew was that I wanted my life to revolve around cars and, after a bit of faffing around, I got a five-year toolmaking apprenticeship with a small engineering firm close to my home in Hatch End. The company made parts for classic sports and racing cars so the workshop was always jammed full of Maseratis, Alfa Romeos and Ferraris and I had loads of opportunities to take them apart and play around with them. It was as if I'd died and gone to heaven.

I couldn't get enough. Most nights I'd stay behind after work and help my boss rebuild his beautiful jet black Lotus Esprit. He was probably having me over – getting me to do overtime for nothing – but I was young and keen and really didn't care. I was doing a job that I loved, learning a trade, building a career and getting paid to boot. It couldn't have been better.

Three fabulous years later my whole world fell apart: the company lost a key contract and the boss was forced to scrap half the workforce. Being one of the last to join, I was one of the first to be made redundant, and in the space of twenty-four hours I went from having a good job with prospects to being in a worse position than when I started.

No other firm was willing to take me on because I hadn't finished my apprenticeship so I mooched around at home for a couple of months before taking a filler job as an animal ambulance driver for the RSPCA. It sounds a million times more glamorous than it actually was – mainly the work involved driving around dodgy council estates at 2 a.m. in a little van, looking for whatever was left over after some bloke had come home drunk, got into a row and ended up throwing the family puppy out of a window, twenty floors up. The hours were long and the pay was crap but I figured it was better than doing nothing.

All the other staff were vegetarians or vegans and whenever they saw an animal in pain or even just a bit under the weather, they would pretty much fall to pieces. I was the only meat eater in the whole building and while I really loved animals, I could manage to be a lot more practical about things. Every day we'd get dozens of adorable new-born kittens coming in for which it was impossible to find homes. No one else had the heart to do what had to be done, so it always came down to me.

I'd sit in a quiet corner of the surgery with a box of cute fluffy kittens on one side, a bucket on the other and a dirty great syringe full of Imobolin – a drug that causes instantaneous, painless death – in my hand. I'd pick up a kitten, flip it over, stab it in the breastbone with the syringe and inject it, then toss it in the bucket and move on to the next one. Sometimes I'd be at it for hours.

In the rare quiet moments I'd don my thinking cap and try to work out what I really wanted to do for a living. It was almost a year before I finally made up my mind: I decided that I wanted a job that commanded respect and admiration. I wanted a job where no two days would ever be the same, where I'd be part of a team but still encouraged to use my initiative and think on my feet, to work within the community and help people. Most of all I wanted something that would give me enormous job satisfaction.

So I decided to join the fire brigade.

To qualify, you had to have a minimum 36-inch chest with a two-inch expansion. I was in good shape at the time – I played a lot of football – but I was quite a slim build. When they slipped the tape around me, they found that I had the expansion but not the chest. 'Sorry, mate,' the recruitment officer told me. 'You're just not big enough.' I took it on the chin, went away and signed up for the nearest gym. Starting that day I pumped iron every spare minute I had, switched to a high-protein, high-carbohydrate diet and watched my body start to grow.

By the time I reapplied to the brigade six months later I had arms like Popeye, legs like tree trunks and a perfect six-pack for a stomach. But when they measured me up, they found my chest was exactly the same bloody size it had been before. 'You want to get down the gym,' the recruitment officer told me. 'Build yourself up and then try again. And maybe switch to a high-protein diet.'

This time I couldn't hide my disappointment. 'Sod that for a game of soldiers,' I thought. 'I'll join the police instead.'

They welcomed me with open arms.

I wanted to get out on the streets and start doing real police work as soon as possible, but first I had to get through eighteen weeks at the training college in Hendon, a sixty-four-acre prison-like complex of beige and brown buildings that becomes temporary home to every new recruit to the capital. I hated it right from the word go: the second I arrived, on a Sunday evening, I was handed a slip of paper with a long and complex definition of the word 'police' on it and told to learn it word perfect for 9 a.m. the following morning. 'But I've only just got here,' I protested.

The man behind the reception desk gave me a sarcastic smile. 'And you're learning stuff already. Good here, ain't it?'

It was all downhill from there. There were endless lessons about different types of paperwork, hours spent marching up and down the drill square doing left turns, right turns and about turns until my head was spinning and my feet covered in blisters. Then there was more paperwork, pointless exercises like bulling your boots – using melted polish to produce a mirror-like sheen on the toe cap – or whitening your plimsolls before every PE lesson. Finally there were lectures on points of law, rules and regulations, endless technical procedures and all the paperwork that went with them.

I learned about the various street drugs and their many names from heroin (brown, scag) and cocaine (Charlie, nose candy), to amphetamine (speed, Billy Whizz), crack (rock, wash) and cannabis (puff, spliff), but the only examples I ever saw were in pictures on posters. The exercise wasn't so much about learning to identify stuff as knowing which law, act and section to charge someone under and how to fill out the accompanying paperwork.

And every Monday morning, just to make sure everything I was being taught had really sunk in, there would be a lengthy assessment. Failure meant having to repeat that entire stage.

The whole time I was at Hendon the only thing I enjoyed was the role-playing exercises. Every now and then one of us from the class would be picked to play the part of a mugger, drunk or someone accused of theft or some other crime, and another one would have to play the part of the officer arresting or interrogating them. I always excelled at those exercises, but other than that it felt as if I'd been sent back to school, never my favourite place. There was nothing to do but see it as a means to an end, so I gritted my teeth, worked hard and managed to come through it with flying colours.

I got posted to Plaistow, right in the heart of the old East End. The police station itself, a four-storey red-and-white brick monstrosity on Barking Road, was nearly a hundred years old and looked more like a Victorian mental hospital than a centre of law and order. Fanning out from the station were seemingly never-ending roads of tiny two-up, two-down terraced houses, more often than not home to at least three generations of the same family. The combination of poverty, unemployment and urban decay made it the perfect breeding ground for petty crime.

From day one I put my knowledge of motors to good use and set about becoming the scourge of the local joyriders and professional car thieves. I tracked down all their hiding places, uncovered their favourite hunting grounds and would lie in wait for them to come along. After only a few months, the drivers of the area cars – the fast ones used for high-speed chases – were nearly fighting among themselves to see who would get to go out on patrol with me because they knew there was a good chance they'd see some action.

When I wasn't chasing stolen cars, I was chasing stolen car radios. Plaistow seemed to be a magnet for the heroin addicts in the East End, most of whom funded their habits by constantly breaking into cars. At least once a week I'd be on street patrol in full uniform, walk round a corner and catch someone right in the act. I'd stop, they'd look over, we'd make eye contact and the chase would be on.

It never ceased to amaze me: these guys would pump themselves full of heroin every day, their skin looked as if it was made of grey tissue paper, they'd be covered in spots, their hair would be lank and falling out and they were always so skinny you'd think they'd snap in a strong breeze. But when they were in the shit, they'd suddenly turn into Linford Christie. Boy, could they run; like bullets out of a gun. I'd chase them through people's back gardens, through shops, over fences and walls, up and down the stairs in council flats. And every time I got close enough, I'd bring them down with a rugby tackle or body slam.

Pretty soon it was happening so often it became second nature, almost routine. One night I was out on patrol with my friend Ray in a standard Panda car when an urgent call about an assault at the new red-brick housing estate on Clegg Street came over the radio. We raced to the scene on 'blues and twos' – blue lights flashing and two-tone sirens blaring – and got there barely two minutes later. The call had come from a flat on the first floor and we arrived to find the front door open and a woman sitting in the middle of the living room holding a bath towel to her face and crying hysterically.

The towel was soaked with blood, so much so that it was dripping on to the carpet and running down the side of her face on to her clothes. There were arcs of blood across the walls. During a heated row with her alcoholic boyfriend, who had wrongly accused her of having an affair, he had suddenly produced a large lock knife and attacked her, slashing her face from behind one ear all the way across her cheek.

While Ray administered first aid and called for an ambulance, I moved through the flat to the little balcony at the back which looked out over the High Street. Under the glow of the street lights I saw a shadowy figure running past the Black Lion pub towards the Broadway. I bolted down the stairs as fast as I could, barking instructions into the radio as I went. When I hit street level the man I was after had slowed to walking pace, thinking he had got away. By the time he saw me, just at the top of Balaam Street, and had it on his toes, it was too late.

I lined him up as he went past a wall and body slammed him,

sending him spinning out of control to the ground. I jumped on top of him and fought to hold him down as he wriggled around like a snake, until the back-up finally arrived. It was only when my colleagues manhandled him into the police van that we realized he still had the lock knife in his hand. It was sheer luck that I'd made him hit the wall so hard that he had been stunned and unable to use it. I later received a commendation for my bravery that night, presented by the Commissioner himself.

After five years in uniform I moved to the Criminal Investigation Department – CID. Before I joined the police, I always assumed that becoming a detective was a promotion. It's not. Although there's a little bit of friendly antagonism between CID and uniformed officers (the former are affectionately referred to as 'brains' or 'suits' by their opposite numbers, the latter as 'lids', 'woodentops' or 'buttons'), a detective constable earns exactly the same wage as a police constable. The only difference is that detectives specialize in actively pursuing criminals rather than just responding to their crimes.

Detectives are taught, through a combination of on-the-job training and a series of short courses, to investigate everything from money laundering and sexual offences to fraud and homicide. Further classes cover evidence-gathering and techniques of mobile surveillance. The best thing about being a detective for me, however, was that I got to go around in plain clothes. Maybe I'd just watched too many episodes of *Starsky and Hutch* when I was a kid but that was the one thing I was really itching to do. I thought it would mean that I'd be able to blend into the background, move around undetected, even work undercover – but that couldn't be further from the truth. The problem is that a police officer in plain clothes is not trained to act as anything other than a police officer and that means that, uniform or not, they still stick out like a sore thumb.

So while CID officers might get to drive around in unmarked cars, every local villain with half a brain has memorized the registration number of all the vehicles in the pool so the detectives can't go anywhere without being spotted. And even though they are out of uniform, they still have to carry one of those big radio units. In theory they have three volume settings but all the ones I've ever used have only had two – very loud or off. Stealth was out of the question.

Once a week a plain clothes officer from my station would be sent down to Rathbone market to try to catch pickpockets. They were lucky if they didn't get pickpocketed themselves. They would patrol up and down the stalls all day and before too long, all the market traders would be saying hello to them and offering them cups of tea. The crooks knew who they were and would simply wait until they were out of sight before striking. As far as I could see, working in plain clothes was mostly a waste of time.

Not that I had much time to dwell on it. At an East End CID office, there was always plenty of work coming through and plenty of variety: shootings, stabbings, stranglings, poisonings, beheadings, drownings, bludgeonings, suicides, double suicides, hit and runs, electrocutions and suffocations. Sometimes the victims were elderly men, sometimes they were young women, sometimes they were new-born babies, but mostly they were blokes who found them-selves caught up in the inter-gang warfare that had plagued the area ever since the time of the Krays.

In Ronnie and Reggie's days the battles were about the spoils of armed robbery, protection rackets and burglaries. By the time I got there all the old so-called gentleman crooks had vanished. The drug dealers had replaced them.

One rainy afternoon, as I sat in the canteen of Plaistow nick, Ray, who had followed me into CID and was now working with the drug squad, started telling me how some of the smarter, more enterprising drug dealers had set up shop in abandoned flats in the tower blocks off Pelly Road up towards West Ham.

'It's a nightmare to try and deal with. What they do is take off those council-issue wooden doors and replace them with these solid steel contraptions that wouldn't look out of place in a bank vault. I've even seen some fitted with heavy duty security shutters, the kind you get on shops,' Ray explained. 'They usually have some kind of peephole – a little eye-level flap the size of a small letterbox – and most of the time they do the deals through that. Customers come along, say what they want, hand over the money and get given the stuff. If it's a regular, they open up and let them inside so they can smoke their crack or whatever inside. Save them being caught for possession when they come out. We've tried using crowbars and jemmies to get into a couple of places but you're fighting a losing battle. It takes so long and makes so much noise that by the time you get inside, any drugs have been flushed down the khazi or bunged out the window and there's nothing left to nick them for.'

One dealer, a stocky Rastafarian called Rudy, was becoming a real nuisance, openly selling large quantities of crack, cannabis and speed from his fortified flat off Brooke Road. 'This geezer's a scrote of the first order,' said Ray. 'He's got loads of form but we just can't get to him. It's like Fort bleeding Knox. If there's ever a nuclear war, I want to be on the other side of his door. That's how fucking solid it is.'

A couple of plain clothes drugs squad officers had tried to get the jump on the dealer by simply going up, knocking on the door and asking if they could buy some spliff. After being scrutinized through Rudy's peephole flap for a few seconds, they were sent on their way with a curt 'Fuck off, copper.'

After that experience Ray's boss decided to call in the 'Ghostbusters', the nickname of the specialist police division that break into houses in double quick time. Their main weapon is a device called the 'enforcer', a two-handled hydraulic cylinder which is swung against a door and packs a punch equivalent to a quarter of a ton. Used effectively, just one or two strikes will separate even the sturdiest door from its frame. In extreme situations, such as a hostage rescue, the Ghostbusters will step up a league and use pump-action shotguns loaded with 'Hatton' rounds. These fire a burst of compacted lead powder which disintegrates anything it hits. Fired at the hinge of a door, a single Hatton round will instantly reduce it to dust.

Two of the Ghostbusters came down to Plaistow and spent a few minutes inspecting the outside of Rudy's flat. When they returned to the office where most of CID was anxiously waiting for them, it was plain from their faces that it was not going to be good news. 'Sorry lads, can't do it for you,' said one. 'This guy's obviously been raided before and worked out the best way of keeping us out. The enforcer's no good because the door opens outwards and we can't get to the hinges because they're covered with sheet steel. It would take us at least half an hour to get it open. It would be quicker to hire a couple of sledgehammers and knock a hole in the bloody wall. You'll just have to find some other way to get in.'

It was just as the Ghostbusters were leaving that I had a brainwave. I put it to the other members of the team and, after a brief discussion about whether or not it would work, we decided to give it a go.

A week later, just after 9 a.m., I found myself nervously walking down the covered concrete walkway that led to Rudy's fourth-floor flat. I was wearing a full postman's uniform, borrowed from a friend who was having a day off, and holding an old shoebox stuffed with newspapers and wrapped in brown paper that I'd prepared the night before. I had carefully stencilled Rudy's full name and address neatly on the front and used the office franking machine to make the parcel look as though it had really been through the Royal Mail.

The dozen or so members of the arrest team, made up of the drug squad, a dog handler (Rudy was said to have a pit bull) and a handful of uniformed officers from the Territorial Support Group, were hiding at the far end of the corridor in a recess by the rubbish chute. The plan could not have been simpler. If I could get Rudy to open the door, then everyone would rush in behind me.

The corridor had a low ceiling and filthy brown carpet that stank of urine. All the flats were on the left-hand side and on the right was a bare brick wall and a series of broken louvre window panes. There were graffitied tags everywhere, even on the ceiling, and most of the flats I passed were abandoned, burnt out or boarded up.

I arrived at number 47 and instantly saw what the Ghostbusters had meant. The doorway was nearly four feet wide and seemed to be a solid expanse of steel. It was almost impossible to see where the door ended and the wall began and it was fitted so tightly there was no space left for a sheet of paper let alone the end of a crowbar. Apart from the peephole there were only two large key sized gaps at the top and bottom. I knocked loudly on the flap, not knowing what to expect. A few seconds later I heard the internal door open, then the flap slid back and Rudy's bloodshot eyes filled the space.

'What?' he said in a strong east London accent.

'Postman, got a delivery for you,' I said.

'Shit man. Just put it through the fucking slot. That's what it's there for.'

'Too big. It's a parcel.'

'Parcel? I ain't expecting no fucking parcel. What is it?'

'Well, how the hell am I supposed to know?' I had to think fast, I could feel Rudy's suspicions rising and I needed to allay them as quickly as possible. I lifted the shoebox up so it was out of his line of sight. 'It's some foreign thing. Looks like it's been sent from Amsterdam,' I said. 'Do you want me to open it and have a look for you?'

'No, no, no,' said Rudy, a touch of panic in his voice. 'It's OK. Just hang on.'

It was an obvious choice but a good one. Amsterdam is the drug capital of Europe with softer drugs like cannabis on open sale. It's common for British holidaymakers to attempt to smuggle stuff back by simply posting it. Whether Rudy received his drugs like that or not I didn't know but his reaction seemed to prove it was at least a possibility. His eyes glanced left and right through the flap, checking the coast was clear, then it snapped shut.

As I listened to the locks being undone and bolts and chains being unattached, my heart started to pound. Rudy had fallen for my deception hook line and sinker. It was actually going to work. I had an almighty urge to look across at the back-up team and give them a smile and a thumbs-up or something, but I had to resist. With a creak, the heavy door finally swung open and I saw Rudy properly for the first time.

He was bare-chested, with a tattoo of the Jamaican flag on his left shoulder. Half his body was obscured by waist-length dread-locks which hung over his shoulders. A smoking joint drooped from his lips and a blue canvas bum bag was tied around his middle. When he spoke, I could see one of his front teeth was made of gold. The air that wafted out of the flat was thick with the cloyingly sweet smell of cannabis.

To my left, I could sense the arrest team sneaking up the corridor. In a few moments it would all be over. I couldn't believe it had been so easy. I was stunned into silence.

'So,' said Rudy impatiently. 'You gonna give me the parcel or you gonna take a fucking picture?'

As I opened my mouth a pair of gloved hands grabbed the edge of the door and pulled it back further. With a loud cry of 'Go, go, go!' the arrest team pounced. Someone dived forward and tackled Rudy round the neck, bringing him to the ground while the others almost fell over themselves to get into the flat as quickly as possible. Inside I could hear more shouting, screaming and the sound of glass breaking. I stepped to one side and let them get on with it.

A few minutes later calm had returned and the drug squad were celebrating a result. Rudy's flat turned out to be an Aladdin's cave of drugs. Everywhere you looked, you found something. He had hidden stuff in all the usual places – in the toilet cistern, under the mattress and at the bottom of drawers – but also in lots of unusual places. It was in the saucepans on the stove, in bags behind the radiator, behind the videos on the shelf, in corners under the carpet. We found every drug I had ever heard of, a haul worth tens of thousands of pounds. Rudy crumbled. In the end he even meekly handed over his personal stash from his bum bag.

Once we'd established that the system worked, I started helping out the drug squad on a regular basis. The postman's outfit worked every time and after a couple of months I got so confident, I even started to play around.

One time we were raiding a house in Hayday Road and the entire back-up team had sneaked into an empty house opposite the target property. I knocked on the door, told the guy I had a parcel for him and he opened up right away. Knowing the back-up team were watching my every move, I handed over the shoebox and walked away, letting the guy close the door behind me.

I knew that all my colleagues on the squad would be thinking that I'd lost my mind but I was just having a little bit of fun. A second later I turned and went back to the door and knocked again. 'Sorry mate,' I said, 'I forgot. You need to sign for it.'

'OK, no problem. You got a pen?'

'Actually no, but I have got a warrant to search your house.'

I didn't just pose as a postman, I also had a gas man's uniform and a BT engineer's uniform, both of which worked just as well. I guess playing all those different roles really helped mould me for undercover work. My only worry was that once word got around, a lot of postmen in the East End probably ended up getting their heads kicked in every time they tried to call at the house of a local villain.

A few months later, my guvnor called me into his office one day, sat me down and slid an internal job application form across the desk. 'You know, Martin, you should think about joining SO10. They're always looking for good people.'

I listened carefully, picked up the form and flicked through it, then sat back in my chair. 'I'm quite happy to apply,' I said, 'just so long as you can answer one question: who are SO10 and what do they actually do?'

Scotland Yard, the headquarters of the Metropolitan Police Service, has two principal operation departments – Specialist Operations and Territorial Operations. The latter is charged with providing specialist support to officers on the ground: TO18 provides public order training, TO26 is the Air Support Unit, while other elements deal with prisoner transportation (TO10), horses and dogs (TO27, TO28) and Community Affairs (TO31).

The Specialist Operations unit is currently split into twenty distinct divisions: SO4 is the National Fingerprint Office, SO13 the Anti-Terrorist Branch, SO6 the Fraud Squad, SO19 the Firearms Unit, SO8 the armed robbery specialists of the Flying Squad and SO11 the Criminal Intelligence Branch, a specialist unit which employs a small team of officers to carry out high-tech surveillance operations.

SO10, known simply as the Crime Operations Group, is one of the most secretive units within the whole of the police force. Even SO12, Special Branch (the group which works hand in hand with MI5, the internal secret service), is relatively open about the nature of its work. But the brochures and information packs about the Met, and even its new flashy website, all fail to give any mention of SO10 at all.

The chief consequence of this is that not only have most of the public never heard of the division but the vast majority of serving police officers have absolutely no idea what SO10 is, what it does or how it operates. In fact the division has four main areas of responsibility: hostage negotiation, witness and jury protection, the organization of informants and, most importantly, undercover operations, the latter being the field my guvnor was recommending I try out for.

The application form was surprisingly sparse, with boxes for bog standard, routine information about how long I'd served on the force, what training I'd undertaken and what experience I'd gained. I would later learn that SO10 places far more emphasis on what kind of person you are than on your actual track record. New recruits are taken from both uniform and CID, sometimes they have years of experience, sometimes almost none at all. There was one box where I had to list my special skills and interests. I drew a total blank. The only thing I could think of was that I occasionally acted as a DJ at parties and weddings and had my own turntables so I spent a lot of time doing mixes and playing records. I couldn't see that there was anything particularly special about me so I sent the form off and promptly forgot all about it.

Four months later I received a call out of the blue from Detective Sergeant Chris Taylor. 'Martin. Hi, how you doing today? I'm calling from SO10. We got your application and we'd like you to come in for an interview.'

'Oh. Right. OK then. When were you thinking of?'

'Friday morning.'

It was just after 4 p.m. on Wednesday. 'Right. Fine. I'll be there.'

I put the phone down and tried to stop myself from getting too overexcited. As I was soon to discover, one of the key qualities SO10 look for in any potential recruit is the ability to think on their feet, use their initiative. Arranging the interview at short notice is part of that assessment process. I got back on the phone and started calling round all my friends in the force, trying to find someone who knew something, anything about SO10, someone who could give me a few hints on what to expect.

I finally tracked down a DC from Woolwich called Charlie, a friend of a friend who while not a member of SO10 himself had at least been through the interview process, having applied a couple of years earlier and been turned down. It was a long way from being ideal but Charlie was the nearest thing I had to an inside man and that made him worth his weight in gold. We met up for a drink that same evening.

'I have to wish you the best of British, Martin. SO10 is the most amazing place,' said Charlie, chugging long and deep on a pint of frothy bitter. 'I was gutted when I didn't get in. Do you know all about the sort of things they get up to, the kind of undercover jobs they do?'

'Well, drugs and guns, I guess,' I replied.

'Yeah, drugs and guns are part of it, but there's a lot more to it than that. A whole lot. They get involved in so many different areas it's untrue. They have people who are specialists in just about every single field you can think of. They do jobs where their blokes pose as lorry drivers helping to smuggle immigrants into the country, they infiltrate companies where they think the workers are on the take; they've had people pretend to be football hooligans, nazis, solicitors, bus drivers, doctors, council workers – you name it, they've done it.

'They love it if you've got some special skill. They've got guys with a professional pilot's licence and they end up going undercover all over the world, getting into flying clubs and stuff or joining drugs gangs who are looking for someone to import for them. Then they have people who know everything about boats, HGV drivers. People with degrees in chemistry who offer to mix drugs or make up batches of explosives for terrorists. I tell you, they've even got one bloke whose skill is that he is really brilliant at snooker, could be a world champion. Whoever he plays, he just cleans up. And they took him on just because of that.'

I was genuinely impressed. 'Sounds amazing, but what sort of things do they look for when it comes to new recruits?'

'Well, I'm probably not the best person to ask because whatever it is, I obviously don't have it. But I'll tell you as much as I can. You have to know your law because a lot of the time you're trying to avoid doing anything illegal while you're undercover. I know they also like people who look a bit bland, are able to blend into the background. You can't work undercover if you stand out from the crowd. But mostly it's about having some special skill. What did you put down on your form?'

'Just that I play music . . .'

'Oh, you'll be fine,' said Charlie, not letting me finish my sentence. 'I'm sure they'll have a million uses for someone like you. Oh, and another thing you need to know. At the interview they'll ask you about stated cases, SO 10 jobs that have now become law. They'll expect you to know them all backwards. That's really important.'

Charlie had given me a taste of what was to come but I decided that, what with having to get all the guff on the stated cases in a single day, there was only one way to get the information I needed – straight from the horse's mouth.

The SO 10 office is based on the fifth floor of New Scotland Yard, home of the famous revolving triangle, just off St James's Park. I arrived early the following morning and opened the plain wooden door to find there was a counter in my way, a bit like a makeshift bar. A man in a suit was standing there, counting a bundle of £20 notes and eyeing me suspiciously. Beyond the counter were several standard police issue desks piled high with files, papers, computers and typewriters. A series of smaller offices led off from the main room. Any wall space was filled with a line of filing cabinets.

A softly spoken middle-aged guy from the nearest desk ambled over. Hanging jowls and pallid skin showed he spent far too much time indoors and on his backside. He wore a nice suit and tie, and his dark hair, in which the first signs of grey were just beginning to show, had a neat side parting. His large oval glasses with metallic silver frames covered most of his face and distorted his blue-grey eyes. He asked if he could help.

'Yeah. My name is Martin Maynard. I'm from CID at Plaistow. I've got an interview here tomorrow and I was hoping to get a bit of information. I understand I need some stuff on stated cases and whatever else you've got that I can take away.'

The guy cocked his head slightly to one side and looked me up and down for a second. 'Sure, Martin. Wait right there and I'll see what I can find for you.' He turned and began rummaging around in one of the filing cabinets in the far corner.

Despite the vast amount of ground that its work covers and the large number of officers attached, the actual SO10 office is relatively small. The reason is that there is no such thing as a full-time undercover officer – most of the time they are just engaged on routine police work like everybody else. It is only when they are given an assignment that they switch to undercover mode. Apart from picking up their expenses or attending the odd briefing, undercover officers rarely visit the SO10 office at all.

However, its small staff at Scotland Yard still perform many vital roles. As I stood at the counter, just looking around, I overheard the voice of a woman in a small office ahead of me to the right. I could see that she was sitting on a swivel chair next to a large bank of telephones. Every now and then one of the phones would ring and she would reach over and answer it with a cheery 'Hello, DOP Holdings' or 'Good morning, Conkax Limited' or 'GXPX, can I help you?' The initial response seemed to vary according to which phone she picked up. The follow-up line, however, would always be the same: 'Trying to connect you', followed by a short pause and 'I'm sorry caller, they're in a meeting right now. I understand it's likely to go on for some time. Can I take a message?'

That woman in her tiny office, I would later discover, single-handedly ensured the safety of dozens of undercover officers out in the field. SO10 has a number of fake companies which have been established purely to provide cover for its operatives. It enables officers to pose as anything from international investment bankers and double-glazing salesmen to architects and plumbers, complete with business cards, headed notepaper and even company credit cards. When they are posing as sole traders, officers simply give a mobile phone number. In the case of larger companies, operatives are able to give out a variety of telephone and fax numbers, all of which are automatically diverted to the SO10 call centre. When a call comes through, a message is taken and the officer concerned is then contacted and told to phone the target as soon as possible.

A few minutes later the man who had first greeted me came back to the counter with a small bundle of papers. 'OK, Martin. Here are the bits of case law that you need to know and I've also put in some stuff about *agents provocateurs* for you. There's a bit of bumf on the history of the unit and some general bits and pieces. Should be all you need.'

'Thanks,' I said, reaching across to shake the man's hand. 'I really appreciate this.'

'No problem. And good luck for tomorrow.'

I got up even earlier on the Friday morning than I had on Thursday. I'd read through all the paperwork the night before and went through it again in the morning. The information about *agents provocateurs* was particularly complex and is probably the biggest pitfall for any undercover officer. Learning how to be part of the planning of a crime without ever actively encouraging anyone to do something they would not do of their own accord is a key skill. I was still struggling to get my head round it all as I put on my best suit and made my way down to Scotland Yard, battling my growing nerves every step of the way. Interviews within the Metropolitan Police are always highly formalized, demanding affairs. The applicant sits on a chair facing anything up to eight senior officers behind a long table who then fire questions continually for up to an hour. It's as much an endurance test as it is a test of suitability for a job,

and as the tube train neared St James's Park I did my best to prepare mentally for the ordeal that was to come.

I arrived back on the fifth floor and saw the friendly face of the man who had given me the information the day before standing by the counter. He held out his hand. 'Martin. Nice to see you again. I'm DS Chris Taylor. Come on through.'

I was so surprised I could hardly speak, and what came next surprised me even more. DS Taylor led me to one of the offices off the main room with three armchairs inside. He sat in one and motioned for me to sit in another. An older, serious-looking Detective Chief Inspector with grey hair and a dark suit, the then acting head of SO10, came in and sat in the other, completing our cosy little circle. It was the absolute opposite of what I had been expecting.

We spent a short time talking about my record of service, before the DCI asked me if I knew of the legal precedents under which SO10 operated. I reeled off the stated cases, word perfect.

'So how do you know about them then?' asked DS Taylor with a big grin.

'Er. Well. I came up here yesterday and asked for some information and you gave it to me.'

'Good answer,' said the DCI also grinning.

I allowed myself the faintest hint of a smile. I couldn't help thinking it was all going rather well.

'So what kind of things do you think we get up to at SO10?' asked the DCI.

'Well, drugs and guns obviously. But I know that you do much more than that. I know you have HGV drivers, chemists and professional pilots on your books. I hear you've even got a snooker player.'

There was an uncomfortable silence as DS Taylor and the DCI turned and looked at each other then back at me. 'What?' they said in unison.

'Er. A snooker player. You know, to go undercover as, er, a snooker player.'

The DCI sat back in his armchair and scratched his head. 'I have to say, Martin, all the other stuff you said was fine but a snooker player? That's the biggest load of crap I've ever heard. Where on earth did you hear that from?'

DS Taylor cut in straight away, not giving me time even to try to answer. 'What on earth would we need a bloody snooker player for?' he asked, trying to hold back his giggles. 'I can't believe you've just said that. Don't tell me you came here because you want to play snooker all day. You're in the wrong bloody job if that's what you want.'

By now they were both chuckling. With any luck they'd remember it as amusing rather than stupid. Perhaps I was still in with a chance.

'Moving swiftly on,' said DS Taylor. 'Now let's talk about your own special skills. And for fuck's sake don't say snooker. It says here on your form that you play music. Could be handy. Tell me, what instrument do you play?'

Now it was my turn to pause. 'Turntables,' I said softly.

'I'm sorry?' said the DCI.

'Turntables, sir. I work as a DJ, just for fun, friends, parties and little events.'

'Oh. So you don't play an instrument. At all.'

'No, nothing. Just turntables.'

I bit my lip as I watched the DCI cross out something he had written in his notebook. I wanted to kick myself for having given up piano lessons as a kid. I was sure that when he believed I was a musician, he had some mission in mind where I would be going undercover inside a rock and roll band or something to expose massive cocaine deals within the music business. As a DJ I clearly wasn't going to be up to the grade.

The interview finished pretty quickly after that ('Thanks for coming in Martin, we'll let you know') and I had a miserable journey back to East London, convinced that I'd blown it. Back at the CID office at Plaistow, Ray and the others were eager to know how it had gone, what questions they had asked and what answers I had given. I recounted the whole story and at the end of it everyone in the room was shaking their heads. Ray spoke for them all: 'You prat. You bloody idiot. You didn't say that, did you? I don't believe it. You've got no chance. You've totally and utterly cocked that one up, mate. I don't think you'll be going anywhere.'

Three days later, SO 10 called up again. 'Martin. It's Chris Taylor. We were very impressed when you came in. We'd like to book you on the next course.'

For those who get past the initial assessment, the only way to qualify to work for SO 10 is to go through what is widely considered to be the most difficult and demanding training course the police force has to offer. Based at the Peel Centre in Hendon, the same place where raw recruits are put through their paces, the course starts at 7 a.m. on a Monday morning and runs straight through until 4 a.m. the following morning. If they're lucky, students manage to grab a couple of hours' sleep before starting again at 7 a.m. on Tuesday. And so it goes on, day after day, night after night, for two solid weeks.

The monthly course, which takes just twelve students at a time, is so highly thought of that it is used by all the other forty-two police forces in the country to train their own undercover operatives. Each new intake is always massively over-subscribed at the start and each course is always a few people short by the time it ends.

On our first day, the main instructor, Ken, took the opportunity to remove any preconceptions we might have about what we were getting into. We sat lining two sides of a narrow white-walled room, while Ken perched on a desk at one end next to a flip chart. 'So, you're here to learn how to work undercover? Well, the first thing I have to say is that not everyone here is going to be right. In the next two weeks there will be some of you who discover that this game isn't for you. And there will be some of you who I decide aren't right. Either way, I want you to know that you can leave at any time. No questions, no retribution, no shame.'

Ken smiled revealing a row of nicotine-stained teeth between his thin lips. He had a big round face with a pudgy nose and tiny eyes topped with a mop of sandy hair that made him look a bit like a potato in a wig.

'So what does going undercover mean?' Ken slowly looked around the room at each of his students. No one dared to answer so he carried on. 'OK. Forget everything you've seen on TV, forget every airport novel you've ever read. It's not just about hanging about in dodgy pubs and clubs and it's certainly not for everyone. You have to be supremely disciplined. You can never forget who you are, not even for a minute. You have to be happy to work alone, I mean *really* alone. You might have back-up at the start of a job and it will certainly be there in abundance when it comes to the final raid but all those times in between, you'll be on your tod. Not even a radio for company.

'Pretending to be someone else is a huge challenge. When you're out in the field you're going to come across the same personality conflicts you get everywhere else in life. You'll be sent into places that you can't stand but you'll have to convince everyone you're having the time of your life. You'll spend hours talking to people whom you don't like and have nothing in common with but they have to believe you like them more than anyone you've ever met.

'Whatever happens, you have to keep your head. You have to be able to deal with the pressure of knowing that if you make just one mistake, you could mess up months, even years of work.'

By now some of the students were starting to look at each other nervously. It was only the first day and already it was sounding far more daunting than any of us had expected.

Ken could sense the growing unease but continued without missing a beat. This was his way of sorting the wheat from the chaff. 'When you're out in the field, deep undercover, there's no one telling you what to do, what to wear or what time to get up. And what you're going to be exposed to is what real crime is all about. We're not talking about kids nicking tins of beans out of Tesco's, we're not talking about Mrs Smith down the high street having her car nicked, we're not talking about some geezer on a street corner with fifty quid's worth of dope in his back pocket.

'Real crime is about always having a couple of grand in your pocket. It's about having the car of your dreams parked outside the house of your dreams. It's about eating in the best restaurants, getting into the best clubs without having to wait in line, it's about being treated with respect by everyone around you. It's about never hearing the word "no".'

At the end of that first day, two of the recruits decided they didn't want to come back. They were both still in uniform and the idea of dealing face-to-face with top level criminals was simply too much for them.

Over the following two weeks, along with the remaining students, I was subjected to constant exams, assessments and exercises. There were lectures about points of law including how to avoid being an *agent provocateur*, detailed role-playing sessions where I practised dealing with every conceivable situation, hands-on instruction in using hidden tape recorders, transmitters and other technical equipment. I was taught the art of dealing with informants, reading body language, striking drug deals, talking my way in to a gang and talking my way back out again. I covered how to dress, how to speak, how to act and how to react once I was on a job. I learned about arrest teams, firearms divisions, surveillance squads and all the other back-up units that would be at my disposal. But most of all, I learned how to stay sharp and think on my feet when I was dog-tired and would rather have been somewhere else.

Every scenario was taken right through from the initial planning to meetings with the informant to going undercover with the gang to presenting the case at court. There is a replica courthouse at the Hendon training school and we would take it in turns to present evidence before a selection of real judges and barristers who would be brought in to make the experience even more realistic – and even more terrifying.

It was incredibly hard graft but, unlike during my first time at Hendon, there was no drill, no bulling my boots and precious little paperwork. It was just pure graft. I worked harder than I've ever worked in my life and absolutely loved every minute of it.

The other students were a real mixed bag. There was Helen, a detective from north London with whom I became quite friendly, Colin and Jamie, a couple of good old South London boys whose career paths seemed pretty similar to my own, and one guy with whom most of us found it hard to get on. Hailing from the West Midlands force, Floyd was instantly unforgettable. He was of mixed race with a large mole-like growth in the centre of his right cheek and soon picked up the nickname 'foul-mouthed Floyd' by virtue of the fact that he could barely utter more than a few words at a time without swearing. Having been told that SO10 avoided recruiting anyone who was too physically distinctive, I could never work out how he had made it on to the course.

One day Ken was teaching us the importance of always sticking to what we knew, not straying too far outside our patterns of behaviour. 'Just because they are criminals, it doesn't mean they are stupid. And just because you're undercover, it doesn't mean you have to try to be something that you're not. If you've never smoked a cigarette in your life, then don't do it when you're undercover. You'll stand out a mile. If you don't drink, then don't drink. If you normally wear glasses don't think, well I'd better take them off. There's no point in being as blind as a bat.

'It's the same when it comes to talking about your background because at some point someone is going to ask you what you've done. Let's say I'm sitting down with a few members of my gang and Floyd is the undercover who has got into us. Floyd, we're a gang from down south, you're from up north, and we've been talking about the time we spent in prison in Parkhurst. Everyone in my gang has done time. Then we turn to you and ask if you've ever done time. What do you say?'

Floyd thought for a moment. 'I think I'd say yeah I had, but I'd choose a different prison.'

'OK,' continued Ken. 'Which one?'

'I don't fucking know,' said Floyd. 'I guess I'd say Wormwood Scrubs, say I did some time there.'

'All right. You say that. Then one of my boys, he's been around a bit. He says he's done time in the Scrubs. Says he was there just a few months before you were. He calls over: "Hey Floyd, what's the name of the head screw on G-wing, it's slipped my mind."'

Floyd thought again. 'I'd say I couldn't remember, that I spent a lot of time in solitary, didn't mix with people. Something like that.'

'Nice try, Floyd,' said Ken. 'Trouble is, there ain't no G-wing in Wormwood Scrubs. It only goes up to E. You just got yourself busted.

'It's like that famous bit in *The Great Escape*, when the two Brits have forged passports and uniforms and they are about to get on the bus to freedom. The guard looks them over and they exchange pleasantries in perfect German and you think they're going to get away with it. Then just as they get on the bus, the guard says in English, "Good luck" and one of the guys turns back and says in his stupid English accent, "Oh, ta very much."

'So what's the lesson? You never say you've been to prison. Not unless you actually have. And if you have, then stay behind and see me afterwards because you shouldn't fucking be here. And the ladies among us, the one thing you never say is that you're a tom. If you pose as a prostitute and some bloke takes a fancy to you, he's going to ask you to pop round the back and give him one. And then what you gonna say? The lesson is simple. Don't do it. Don't ever try to be anything that you're not.'

Floyd wasn't the only one who made mistakes. We all did, and that was the best way to learn.

One scenario involved meeting a target in a pub. It seemed straightforward enough and to make it more real, Ken chose a quiet pub just round the corner from the training school. He and the rest of the students sat inside, one posing as the target and the rest as customers, while I made my way in from the street.

I opened the door, saw the man I was supposed to be meeting and started walking straight over towards him, ignoring everyone else. I had only just reached halfway when Jamie, obviously briefed by Ken, suddenly stepped out in front of me, greeting me like a long-lost friend. 'Martin. Good to see you, mate. You still in the police then?'

After the laughter had died down, Ken gathered us together in a corner and talked us through it. 'OK. Pubs. Believe you me, you're gonna be spending a hell of a lot of time in pubs. I know most of you will be pretty happy about that, but you've got to learn to change your behaviour if you want to work undercover. First thing. Any police officer in a pub. Where do they sit? With their back to the wall facing the door so they can see people coming in. And what do they do every time the door opens? They look up to see who it is. Both of them habits that you need to drop.

'But these are minor things. What you did, Martin, is much more serious. Whenever you meet someone at a pub or anywhere like a pub, never go straight up to them. Have a quick scan around to see if there's anyone you know. It might happen one day and you can't take that chance. If there is, you can stop them halfway, have a quick chat then leave. You call the target later and tell them you spotted Old Bill or some enemy, whatever.'

 By the end of the first week I felt as though my brain was going to explode. There just didn't seem to be any way to cram any more information in. I started to worry that I might not make it. But during week two it started getting a little easier. So much had sunk in from the first week that I started to see a logic in the way that undercover officers were expected to operate. 'You know why that is, don't you, Martin,' Ken said to me after I confessed that I felt it was getting a little easier. 'That's because your true undercover personality is starting to develop. You'll do fine.'

On the last night of the course we all went out to celebrate at a club. Ken tried to get the men to pick up a woman as part of their first undercover assignment but no one wanted to play, mostly because we were just too exhausted. After half an hour or so, Chris Taylor turned up. He had come along to congratulate the latest intake. 'So,' I asked him, 'I've done the course. What happens now?'

Chris took a long sip on the bottle of beer he was drinking then rested his hand gently on my shoulder. 'What happens now is that you just go back to your CID office and get on with your work. If something comes up that we think you're right for, we'll give you a call. Could be weeks, could be months. To be honest Martin, some people do the course but never get called up. All you can do is go off and wait.'

2

Philip: I did my first undercover job long before I'd ever even heard of SO 10.

I was pretty green at the time, just a couple of months out of police training school, still finding my feet and, to be honest, a bit pissed off with the whole job: I wasn't sure I'd made the right career choice and the idea of jacking it in was playing heavily on my mind.

I'd come to the Met after a brief stint as a haematologist, something I'd got interested in while studying A level biology at school. The summer after my exams I took a placement at a lab close to my home in Ealing so I could get a proper feel for the work. Almost instantly, I realized it wasn't at all what I'd expected. I'd spend all day, every day, looking down a microscope, examining different samples of bile, blood, snot, hair, ear wax, body fluids and, most of all, shit.

There was baby shit, old people's shit, pale shit, dark shit, runny shit, dried up shit, shit with bits in it, shit from people with sickle cell anaemia, with hepatitis and with haemophilia. There was shit everywhere and the smell was hideous – I felt as if I was working in a toilet bowl. The day I discovered I could tell the different types of shit apart just by looking at them was the day I realized that, after just two weeks, I'd already been there way too long. I quit that afternoon.

I didn't fancy going to university – I wanted to earn money – so I got a job in the finance department of British Gas. The work was monotonous and the pay was rubbish but the other people in the office were a really good laugh. No one there saw it as anything more than a filler so we just larked about most of the time. I was still looking around for other career ideas but nothing had caught my eye until I'd been there almost a year. One lunchtime I was flicking through a copy of the *Daily Mail* someone had left in the canteen and saw a big advertisement at the back: 'Want to make a difference? Become a Police Officer.'

Until then, the idea of joining the police had never even occurred to me. I'd never been in any trouble with them but, as far as I was concerned, they were a pain, kicking me and my mates out of football matches when we got a bit too rowdy or stopping our souped-up cars every time we tried to drive anywhere. But as I looked at the advert and read about putting something back into the community, the career structure and the benefits, joining the police suddenly seemed like the best idea in the world.

The eighteen weeks at Hendon were a real ordeal. I could understand why they made us do things that taught discipline, but I couldn't see how making sure my PE shorts had a perfect crease at the start of every lesson or staying up until the small hours bulling my boots until I could see my face in them would make me a better policeman. Things improved once I got on division but I still wasn't completely happy: I hated the shift system, starting work at some ridiculous hour in the morning or not finishing until the middle of the night.

I knew I was doing a good job and building a reputation for being efficient and reliable – as one of the few black PCs on my division I'd been called in to help out the drug squad a few times, posing as a buyer and knocking on the doors of drug dens so they could be raided – so I put my reservations to one side and made up my mind to see out the two-year probationary period and then decide whether to stick with it.

When a call came through from DCI Brian Cooke in Stoke Newington saying that there was a job he wanted me to help him with, I expected it to be nothing more than another door-knocking caper. But as I sat down on the full-length leather swivel chair in his large oak-panelled office, I quickly realized there was a very different game he wanted me to play.

'Thanks for coming in at such short notice, Philip. How's it going? Enjoying the job?'

'Well,' I said cautiously, 'it's quite different from what I'd expected.'

'Excellent,' said DCI Cooke who had joined the force after a career in the military and had the clipped voice and all the manner-isms associated with a man used to ordering his troops into suicidal missions. 'Variety, unpredictability. Who'd want to be stuck in some boring nine to five rut when they can have what we have to offer? You've got the right stuff, Philip. I can tell.'

I took no notice. 'So you wanted to see me, sir. About some kind of job?'

DCI Cooke settled back in his chair and gently pressed his fingertips together under his chin. 'Basically, Philip, we've got an illegal drinker, a speakeasy if you will, operating down at the bottom of the Sandringham Road. It's been there for a couple of months now and we're getting a steady stream of complaints from shop-keepers, residents and, surprise surprise, the local publican. They all want to know when we're going to do something about it. And that's what this is about. What we need is for one of our chaps to go along, get inside and report back on everything they see.'

'Why not just raid the place?' I asked.

'Good question, Philip. I'm glad you asked me that. The reason is quite simple. To be perfectly honest, we don't have the foggiest idea of what's going on inside there. Could be drug dealers planning to flood the streets with crack cocaine, could be a gang of armed robbers setting up some big job. Could even be terrorists planning to blow up Buckingham Palace. Or it could just be a bunch of chaps having a few drinks without paying the duty. Point is, we don't know until we send someone in. And I'd like that someone to be you.'

As DCI Cooke reached into a drawer at the front of his desk and pulled out a wad of black-and-white surveillance photographs, I found myself wondering how long it had been since he had ventured outside his office, let alone on the streets.

'We've had an observation point close to the club for the last couple of weeks. It seems that a number of local faces are starting to use it as a regular meeting place. Who knows what they're planning?

'What we need before making a strike is solid, first-hand evidence. We need to know the best time to go there, the best day of the week, what kind of security they have, and that's where you come in. It's a bit more involved than knocking on a door, Philip. Do you think you can handle it? There's no pressure, I just wanted to run it up your flagpole and see if you salute.'

The truth was I had no idea if I could handle it or not, but there was no way I was going to turn down the opportunity to find out. For the first time since I had joined, the police service was offering me the chance to do something other than just walking up and down the streets.

'I'd love to give it a go,' I said, trying to sound relaxed about it. 'But you're not expecting me to go in there on my own, are you? I think I'll need someone else with me otherwise I'll stick out like a sore thumb. If I go into a place like that on my tod and start trying to make conversation with people I don't know, they'll think I'm some kind of weirdo.'

The look on the DCI's face told me that he had indeed expected me to do it alone but thought better of saying so. 'Fair enough. Who do you have in mind?'

I knew that another black PC, a guy called Clive, had recently joined the division, working out towards Haringey. He had even less experience than I did and when I phoned him up and explained the basics he was less than keen to say the least.

'So let me get this right, Philip. Here I am, I've just finished my training. For the last six months I've been living the police, breathing the police, sleeping the police. I've got the police in my blood now. I know who I am and what my job is. Now you're saying you want me to pretend that I'm not a policeman, to walk into some shithole of a drinking club, packed full of killers, drug dealers, pimps, toms and God knows what else and then just start chatting away to them. You must be off your head.'

It didn't take Clive long to come round to the idea. The fact that we would have fairly unlimited expenses and be released from our usual police duties for up to a month, that we would be provided with a flashy car to drive around in (to complete our image) and that we would be on overtime for the majority of the time helped to swing it. So did the fact that it was bound to look good on our service records.

Everything was new to me. The first step was a trip in a 'nondy', the term given to unmarked observation vehicles. They all vary but this one was a standard Transit van with the back windows blacked out. There was a wooden panel behind the driver and anyone looking in the back would see nothing but their own reflection. A series of peepholes were built into the side, covered with strips of Velcro that could be peeled back to observe what was going on outside.

Although such surveillance operations are generally pretty safe, there have been times when it has all gone pear-shaped and people's lives have been put in danger. Before a drugs raid on the notorious Broadwater Farm estate in Tottenham, two plain clothes detectives spent an afternoon in a nondy in a corner of the main car park next to a couple of burnt-out cars, watching the dealers go about their business. The estate was a pretty lawless place and after an hour or so a couple of bored young kids on bicycles started kicking stones at the van which clearly didn't belong to anyone on the estate.

Then, to the horror of the guys inside, they siphoned off some petrol from a nearby abandoned car and began sprinkling it around. Neither man had a radio – the risk of being overheard was simply too great – so they could do nothing but sit there and watch as the laughing kids tried to find some matches to finish the job. It was only the intervention of a passing patrol car, aware of the nondy's presence, that saved their lives.

Thankfully Clive and I were in no such danger. Secreted in the back of the van, we bounced around on the journey to the club. Our driver parked on the main road almost opposite, then went off to a local pub for a couple of hours. After waiting a few minutes, we gently peeled back the Velcro strips and looked outside.

There wasn't all that much to see. The club was in the basement flat of a four-storey white terraced house and the entrance was well below street level, reached only by a narrow wrought-iron spiral staircase. The reason we were there was to see the kind of people who were going in, the kind of clothes they were wearing and the kind of cars they were driving. That way, we'd be able to mould our undercover image to ensure we blended in. After a couple of hours, our driver returned and took us back to Stoke Newington. The following morning we had a debriefing with DCI Cooke.

'Well chaps, how did it go? What do you think?' he asked, brightly.

Clive and I smiled at each other. 'Yeah. I don't think there will be any problem getting in,' I said. 'We need to get some new street clothes and a car but apart from that, no problem.'

'Excellent news. Excellent,' DCI Cooke replied with a huge smile before leaning forward and speaking more softly. 'I want the two of you to know that I'm going to be doing everything I can to ensure your safety when you go in there. I have prepared a task force of the finest officers who, at a moment's notice, will tear down those doors with their bare hands to get you out. You have nothing to worry about.'

I glanced over at Clive who was now looking very worried indeed. From the way DCI Cooke was talking it was as if we were trying to penetrate a serial killers' convention rather than a shebeen. I spent the rest of the afternoon reassuring Clive that he was just out of touch, not hiding something from us.

Since we were totally untrained in undercover work and no one from Stoke Newington had any real experience in it either, we simply had to make things up as we went along. The shebeen was on the corner of a block that had a parade of shops and cafés on one side, a pub on the other and a place selling discount tyres on the other. The pub and shops seemed to be a magnet for the local community so we decided the best place to start was there.

We spent every night for a week just walking round, eating in a couple of the cafés, drinking in the pub and popping in and out of the off licence and the newsagents, in the hope that some of the people who went to the shebeen might notice us in the area and therefore recognize us as locals when we went in for the first time.

Once Clive and I felt ready, we told DCI Cooke. He arranged a briefing to introduce us to the forty-strong back-up team – almost the entire Stoke Newington relief – who, according to Clive, were there to 'drag our lifeless bodies out before the people in the shebeen start eating us'.

At just after 7 p.m. we all squeezed into the station's conference room and DCI Cooke took the floor. 'We have two back-up teams who will be secreted in four unmarked vans spread around Sandhurst Road. The undercovers are going to go in for half an hour, no longer. If they do not emerge after that time, then Harry's team will go in through the front, Frank's team in through the back. There's also a dog unit on its way to provide extra cover. I want you all to know that, while we expect great things to come out of this, I'm quite happy to blow the whole operation to ensure the safety of Clive and Philip. If they're not back outside at 10.30 p.m., then I want everyone . . .'

My hand shot up in the air almost automatically. ''Scuse me, guv. Ten-thirty. Are you saying that we're going in at ten o'clock?'

'Twenty-two hundred hours,' he replied, 'that is to be your time of entry.'

My eyes widened and my brain raced as I desperately tried to think of a diplomatic way to tell him what a huge mistake that was. 'Twenty-two hundred hours? No offence guv, but in my experience, I don't think there will be many people there at that time. My understanding is that this sort of place only really heats up after midnight, sometimes not even until 1 a.m. We'll be the only people there, we'll stick out a mile if we go in then.'

'Good. That also means you'll be less likely to run into trouble. Now let's all synchronize our watches.'

At two minutes to ten, Clive and I rounded the corner of the block the shebeen sat on and walked in. Clive's nerves were proving infectious and I was beginning to wonder just what kind of horrors might be waiting for us inside. As we arrived at the spiral staircase, two young black women in mini skirts and boob tubes appeared and began descending the steps to the front door so we hurried up and walked in right behind them. No problem.

The steel-reinforced double door and the fact that it was a basement flat did a good job of dampening the noise that was coming from the sound system, but the second we entered Clive and I developed instant pounding headaches from the noise and vibration. The hardcore ragga music was so loud and the bass turned up so high that we could feel our bones shaking in time with the beat.

The club itself was nothing more than a standard one-bedroom flat that had been adapted to hold a large number of people. All the furniture and fittings had been ripped out. From the hallway you walked into the main living room, a large rectangle with the DJ diagonally opposite the door in a small alcove. At the far end of the room, a semicircular hatch led to the kitchen just beyond. The only person in there was the barman who would serve drinks through the hatch.

I felt unsteady underfoot until I realized the carpets had been pulled up leaving a chipped concrete floor. At the far left-hand corner of the main room, a small corridor led off to the bathroom and bedroom. There were about ten other people there, standing alongside the left-hand wall and slowly swaying in time to the music. The air was thick with the smell of cannabis – it seemed that everyone there apart from myself and Clive was smoking a joint – and the only lights were the flashing red and orange bulbs alongside the DJ's turntables.

We headed straight for the bar. The most popular drink seemed to be a tiny bottle of wine liqueur called Caneye. Deciding it was better to fit in, especially on our first night, than try and get away with orange juice or coke, Clive and I got a Caneye each, then found a space on the wall to lean against. People had formed themselves into small groups and were talking but it was much too early for there to be any real activity. The two girls we had come in with hooked up with a few others and began chatting animatedly, two Rastafarians squatted in a corner smoking king-size spliffs and a few others of mixed ages just walked around. After twenty-five minutes we were more than happy to leave.

As we reached the front door, I said to the stocky bald-headed black man who was acting as the club's doorman, 'See you tomorrow.'

The bloke looked at me as if to say 'Who the fuck are you?'
'Whatever,' he replied.

At the top of the stairs, I looked at my watch and saw it was 10.29. Clive and I started jogging the two blocks to where the back-up team was waiting. When we got to the corner where two of the vans were parked we saw the back doors were open and everyone was out stretching their legs and limbering up for the assault. We had got there just in time.

The following morning it was time to meet with DCI Cooke again. 'Well chaps, you've broken the ice. If you feel confident that you can fit in without arousing suspicion, then I'll authorize the two of you to go there as often as you like. Remember, information is the name of the game. I need to see those reports on my desk each and every morning. I want to know this place so well that I feel like a regular myself.'

During the following three weeks Clive and I went to the club three or four times a week, usually after 1 a.m. at which time it would be packed to the rafters and absolutely buzzing. We soon became well-known faces and spent our time talking to the regulars. Because everyone was smoking dope the whole time, we knew we had to do something to fit in, even though neither of us actually smoked. In the end, we made up a couple of fake joints – giant Rizlas and tobacco, nothing more – and stuck them behind our ears each time we went down there.

I thought about pretending to smoke, or taking it up for the duration of the job – asking someone for a light is a good way of opening a conversation – but having talked it over with a couple of more experienced officers, I decided against it. If something doesn't come naturally, you're bound to stand out when you do it.

One of the most flamboyant regulars was a colossal Rastafarian called Lester. I met him one night while I was standing at the bar and he accidentally brushed against me. 'Sorry man,' he said with a heavy patois twang. 'Hey, you looking to buy some draw?'

I pointed to the joint tucked behind my ear. 'I'm sorted.'

'What ya smoking?'

The question confused me for a second until I realized he was asking what type of cannabis I had in my roll-up. I pulled out of the air the first name that I could think of. 'Moroccan black,' I said. I'd arrested someone with a lump of the stuff a couple of months earlier so it was still fresh in my mind.

Lester's heavy jaw fell open in shock. 'Resin? You're smoking resin?' His accent became even more intense. 'Bwoy, you may as well take the tyres off your car and smoke them instead. Brother, you should be smoking weed. You should be smoking sinsemilla.'

Lester pulled a little square plastic envelope from the folds of his jacket and held it up in front of my face. In the half-light I could just make out a leafy green substance inside. I recognized it from training school as sinsemilla, a form of herbal cannabis sought after because of its high level of THC, the active ingredient which produces a high.

'Maybe later,' I said, 'when I've smoked this.' I knew Lester was going to be more insistent so I was relieved when a young blonde girl wearing a gold mini skirt and white furry bomber jacket came running over, grabbed Lester's face with both her hands, kissed him full on the lips then ran off. It was a welcome chance to change the subject.

'Is that your girlfriend?'

'Nah man, that's one of my girls,' he said, roaring with laughter. He called her back over. 'Ere Gail, go through the list for the benefit of my friend here.'

The girl looked at me. She was probably about twenty years old but could easily have passed for younger. 'It's £30 for a straight fuck, £25 for hand relief, £15 for oral and for a tenner I'll toss you off with my tits.'

'Thanks Gail, now be a good girl and fuck off will you,' said Lester.

As soon as she was out of earshot he leaned towards me and whispered, 'That's what she charges, but most of it's mine. I just let her suck on my dick once in a while, give her a bit of sensi and she's happy. I tell you man, you've got to get into this business. It's so sweet. I must be making four hundred a week and I don't have to do Jack Shit.'

A couple of nights later I bumped into Gail again and we got chatting. She was actually quite beautiful. 'What do you do, Philip?'

'As little as possible,' I said. 'Just a bit of buying and selling. It gets me by. So how did you get on to the game? Was it through Lester?'

'Nah, I was doing it long before I met him. He just looks after me now. I don't know what I'd do without him. He's lovely, isn't he?'

I bit my tongue. 'Yeah, seems like a right good bloke.'

By the end of our second week in the club, Clive and I couldn't help but enjoy ourselves. It was a real insight into another world that, even as police officers, we had no idea existed. The local burglars would offer us cut-price videos or televisions, the local car thieves would offer us a choice of luxury motors at a fraction of the retail price, Lester would continually offer us various high-potency brands of cannabis, while Gail and the other girls would occasionally try to increase their earnings by offering us their bodies. We quickly learned that the one bedroom at the back of the flat worked as a makeshift brothel with the owner and the girl splitting the fee for its use.

I knew that such things went on in society and I had arrested people like Lester and Gail dozens of times, but as a policeman you only ever get one side of the story, people never really open up to you and you never allow yourself to get too close. Working undercover, I was talking to these people as an equal. They treated me as one of their own. I picked up tips on how to get round some of the alarm systems on houses, how to break into cars with minimal damage, where the best fences lived and who was behind most of the local trade in everything from heroin and speed to crack and dope. I was offered fake driving licences, stolen credit cards, bootleg beer and cigarettes, counterfeit designer clothes and stolen designer clothes.

One group of lads was going around offering counterfeit currency – £50 notes for a fiver each. 'What you need to do,' one explained, 'is find shops where they will let you buy things that cost fifteen or twenty quid with one of these. Has to be at least fifteen pounds, anything less and they get a bit suspicious. Then for your fiver, you end up with thirty-odd quid real money. Not a bad little earner.'

The offers never stopped. Jewellery, stolen MOT certificates, tax discs and every kind of drug under the sun. One man even told me that if I ever needed a gun, he could get me one in less than an hour. I learned more about crime in the few weeks I spent at the club than I did in the six months I spent at Hendon. And it was a hell of a lot more interesting.

Once we felt there was little more to gain from continuing to visit the club it was time to plan the raid. In order to protect our cover, DCI Cooke decided the best thing to do was to arrest both Clive and myself along with everyone else. To prevent any confusion during the chaos of the raid, two members of the arrest team would become our personal designated arresting officers. That meant that they would ignore everyone and everything else, make their way straight to us and take us away.

'Now chaps,' said DCI Cooke at the pre-raid briefing. 'You need to make it look realistic, kick up a bit of a fuss, do a bit of struggling, but for God's sake don't get carried away. Did a job last year where the designated arresting officer ended up with a concussion. The officer he was trying to arrest pushed him over then everyone else in the place jumped on him.'

We chose a Thursday, by far the most popular night at the club. Clive and I arrived just after midnight with the raid planned for 2.30 a.m. The reason we wanted to be there so early was just in case there was any sign of trouble, then there would still be time to call it all off.

For me, this night was the apex of my criminal double life. Although I had been involved in dozens of raids myself, I had never seen it from this perspective. I had to constantly fight the urge to look at my watch during the course of the evening, but as I felt it get closer I could not help letting a little smile creep across my lips, realizing that I knew what was coming but no one else did.

Just before 2.30 a.m., the electricity to the flat was cut, the lights went out and the music wound down. Almost immediately there was the sound of thunder, the sound of wood and metal splintering and tearing, the sound of glass being broken. The women began screaming, the men, most of whom were too stoned to react quickly, started gathering their things. Everyone was trying to work out if they were coming in the front or the back, trying to work out which way to run. The truth was the raid was taking place from both ends at the same time. Everyone was trapped. The only light was from the raiding team's torches and the ends of people's joints.

As the hinges and windows gave way, the first arrest team, dressed in full riot gear and holding batons, burst into the main living room. They ordered everyone to stand against the door. Clive and I had separated to make things look more convincing: he was down at the bar and I was up by the DJ along with Lester.

Some people went quietly, a few tried to get away and were tackled to the ground by the ever increasing number of officers rushing into the room.

I played the role of the calm, easy-going villain and continued to lean against the wall while the mayhem went on around me, waiting for my designated arresting officer. I finally spotted him through the mêlée but, as he got to within a few feet, Lester suddenly launched himself at him, pinning him to the ground and starting to slap him around the head. 'Get away man,' he yelled to me. 'Go, run, bwoy.'

My instinct was to go and help but I couldn't. I just had to wait until two other members of the back-up team dragged Lester away and I could finally be arrested in peace. Clive and I were handcuffed like all the others and taken outside in groups of four to be loaded into police vans. When it came to our turn, Clive and I were placed in a separate Transit van on our own and driven to a different station to be debriefed. Our adventure had come to an end.

The intelligence we gathered helped secure more than thirty convictions ranging from living off immoral earnings and drug possession to theft and fraud. And, of course, the shebeen was finally shut down.

It meant much more than just a job well done. For the first time I could see there was more to police work than just walking up and down the streets. Suddenly my career choice made sense. Over the next few years I worked my way up out of uniform, through the

Crime Squad into CID, gaining valuable experience along the way.

But even after the shebeen job, it was still several years before I discovered that SO10 existed and that opportunities to do that kind of work were far more common than I thought. When I did, I applied at once and, having passed the training course and learned how to work undercover properly, I couldn't wait to get started. I knew I wanted to do as much work for SO10 as I possibly could.

3

Martin: Only three days after finishing the SO 10 training course, I was put to work and found myself in a plush Bayswater flat with two bigshot drug dealers.

I could hardly take it all in. I just sat there in silence while Patrick, the undercover policeman whose fictitious gang I was supposedly working for, set up a deal to buy £200,000 worth of high-quality cocaine. 'Now unfortunately,' Patrick was saying, 'I've got some other business to attend to tomorrow so Martin here is gonna be running things. He'll be the one looking at the merchandise and, if it all checks out OK, he'll be the one that calls in the readies.'

I smiled weakly as the older of the two dealers, Abdul, nodded his head, sank back on his big leather sofa and stretched out his arms. He was a Middle Eastern guy in his early forties, well built, immaculately tailored and impeccably groomed. He looked as if he'd just come back from a night at the opera or some society ball – a real class act. The flat was amazing too: it took up two floors of a big white Edwardian house, the type that has columns outside, and was filled with antiques, jewelled ornaments and every kind of luxury. These guys were a world away from the street level druggies I came across when I was pounding the pavements in full uniform or even when I was working with the CID. If we could take them out of the game, it would have a major impact on supplies in the capital. But if they figured out who we really were, they'd slit our throats without a moment's hesitation.

'OK Patrick, my friend,' said Abdul in his strong Arabic accent. He was looking straight at me, trying to suss me out. 'If you are willing to vouch for this man, then that is good enough. Martin, I will meet you here tomorrow afternoon. Two o'clock. And then we will make a deal.'

'Sure thing. Sounds good to me,' I said, trying to seem as though I'd done this kind of thing a thousand times before.

Patrick let out a little chuckle, reached over and slapped me on the shoulder. 'You won't have any problems, Abdul. Martin's a good guy. We've done a lot of work together over the years. I trust him all the way – he's like a brother to me.'

In actual fact I'd met Patrick for the first time only twenty minutes earlier.

I'd spent the day in the CID office at Plaistow investigating a particularly nasty rape case. Three young lads had met a seventeen-year-old hairdresser at a club out towards Epping, separated her from her friends then repeatedly raped her in the back of a car. It was harrowing stuff but totally absorbing to work on. I was trying to track down the driver of the taxi that had taken her friends home when my new covert mobile phone began ringing for the first time.

After graduating from the training course, all SO10 officers are issued with second mobile phones to be used only for undercover work. Registered in false names to fake addresses, they are completely untraceable. It means officers are able to give the villains they meet a contact telephone number without fear of being compromised. And because they know that any incoming call on the covert phone needs to be answered in their undercover guise, there is no risk of them slipping up.

I picked it up and answered, not knowing what to expect. 'Hello?'

'Martin. Great. This is Patrick from SO10. I've got a drugs job running and I've been told that you're the man to call,' he said. 'There's a big meeting tonight. I'll pick you up outside Marble Arch tube station at 2200 hours. Don't be late. Bye.'

It was just after four in the afternoon. I'd been planning to knock off work at six then head straight home for what was meant to be a special evening. I hadn't seen much of my girlfriend Kathy during the course and she was getting more and more pissed off with me not being around. As a way of making amends, I'd sent her a big bunch of flowers and booked a table for dinner at her favourite restaurant. But now I was going to have to call it off. Worse still, I was going to have to do it over the phone – she lived out in Surrey and there just wasn't time for me to get there and back.

I gingerly dialled her number. 'Hi darling,' I said softly.

'Martin. Hello, what a surprise . . .' I could hear the delight in her voice trail off as she quickly read the situation. 'Oh hang on a minute,' she said, her voice harsher and more abrupt than before. 'You're not going to cancel tonight, are you? You promised.'

'I'm sorry, darling. It's an SO10 job. There's nothing I can do about it.'

'Of course you can do something about it. You can say no. Go and tell them you can't do it. I just don't believe you sometimes . . .'

The more I tried to explain that I had no choice, the more upset Kathy got. She hung up, seething. I walked down the corridor to the station locker room and looked at myself in the full-length mirror. I was wearing a pair of blue jeans, a pale grey T-shirt and a dark blue overshirt. I'd never pass for a bank manager, but as a drug dealer I reckoned I'd be OK. The final touch was a piece of gear I'd picked up at a market the day I finished the course. It was a black baseball cap with 'NUFF RESPECT' printed in bold white letters across the front.

What I liked about it most was that it wasn't the kind of thing I would usually wear. Putting it on made me look and feel like a totally different person. It was like a cue to get into my new character. When it comes to working undercover, most people expect we use all kinds of fancy technical kit. Sometimes we do but mostly it just comes down to having the right look.

People tend to take things at face value. If you see an unshaven man wearing filthy clothes sitting in a shop doorway, you'll believe he's homeless. If you see a guy in a flash suit, dripping with gold and driving a Porsche, you'll believe he's anything from a drug dealer to a footballer. Once you have the right look, people will respond to you in a certain way and that makes it easier to stay in character. My hat made me look and feel streetwise and confident – that was how I would come across to others.

There were still a couple of hours to go before I had to leave so

I tidied my desk, caught up on paperwork and rearranged my filing cabinet – anything to keep my mind distracted. I also took a fair bit of flak from some of my colleagues – 'Nice hat Martin, bit old to go raving, aren't we?' – which helped me relax. I was so nervous about making a hash of my first assignment, I was desperately trying to forget about it. It worked for all of three minutes and then I had to give up. I couldn't fight it any longer. I found myself a comfy chair, sat back and carefully thought through everything that Ken had taught me about working undercover.

I got to Marble Arch with a few minutes to spare and made my way to the rendezvous point. Patrick had called me back after remembering that the tube station had fourteen exits and told me exactly where to go. I took exit number one and emerged into the cold night air on the edge of Oxford Street, opposite Park Lane, and turned right until I got to the late-night chemist which Patrick had mentioned. I stood alongside a set of railings next to a phone box and waited. And waited.

It was a mild night but standing around meant I soon started to feel chilly so I began pacing up and down to keep warm. Half an hour went by and there was still no sign of anyone. There were plenty of false alarms. Every now and then a car would stop on the double red lines and someone would vault the railings and run into the chemist. I'd given up looking and was beginning to think that the whole thing was a wind-up when a brand-new silver BMW 3-series convertible pulled up. The driver was a big, bald black guy with a slightly battered, clean-shaven face that made him look like a boxer or nightclub bouncer. He wore a heavy leather jacket which was open at the neck to allow the copious amounts of gold jewellery he had on – inch-thick rope chains and necklaces – to be seen. He was bobbing his head up and down in time with some hardcore rap track that he was playing so loud it was making the windows of the chemist shop rattle. I could tell straight away that he was a nasty piece of work. A real thug, pure low life. He scanned the pavement until his eyes met mine. 'You Martin?'

I nodded, slowly.

'Great. I'm Patrick. Come on, get in, we're late.'

As we set off through the streets, Patrick filled me in on the background. The Regional Crime Squad had been targeting this particular gang for nearly two months and had come to SO10 for help in making the final bust. 'These villains are very sophisticated, very clever and extremely careful,' Patrick explained. 'It's taken us more than a month to get on good speaking terms with the chiefs. The main players are both from somewhere like Kuwait or one of the other Gulf states. They're big friends of Charlie and Billy Whizz. Major dealers. Most of their customers are the rich kids in the Marble Arch and Edgware Road area.' He looked around outside the car windows and smiled. 'Little Arabia. It's another world. All the women are covered up, all the signs are in Arabic and all the blokes just sit around outside cafés smoking and drinking coffee.' Patrick was revelling in its exoticism.

'There's so much money, so many rich men that the place is teeming with high-class brasses but it's all backwards here. It's the clients who stand on the street corners while the toms drive around in sports cars and pick them up. That way the blokes don't get done for kerb crawling.'

I'd driven up the Edgware Road a thousand times before but I'd never really paid all that much attention. This time, as we crawled along in a queue of traffic from one set of lights to the next, I had a good look around. It was easy to see what had caught Patrick's eye: there were newsagents with pavement racks of Arab newspapers and magazines, greengrocers with displays piled high with figs, dates and other tropical fruits, many restaurants whose interiors were decorated with mirrors and elaborate chandeliers – one even had a gigantic golden urn in the window – and the air around them was filled with the scent of roasting meat and pungent spices.

Patrick continued his running commentary. 'It's split up according to nationality: the Kuwaitis work in finance, the Iraqis run the estate agents, the Lebanese are restaurant or hotel managers and the video shops and cab offices are run by Egyptians. When it comes to drugs, well everyone does drugs, but the guys we're after today are Moroccan. They used to deal only to other Arabs – bored princesses and rich kids of oil sheikhs over here as students – but now they're starting to expand. I guess they are getting greedy. They were making loads of money but now they want to make even more.'

As we headed towards Bayswater, Patrick explained that the initial introduction to the gang had come through an informant called Rashid, a playboy character from a wealthy Arab family who got a big thrill out of playing an incredibly dangerous game. He wasn't a criminal himself but he knew lots of people who were and, for no other reason than that he got a kick from the thrill of the chaise and seeing villains get locked up, had decided to become a police informer. Rashid had introduced the first undercover officer, Mark, to the gang. Once he had become accepted, Mark had introduced another undercover officer who in turn introduced another and so on.

It's a painfully slow process – penetrating a major gang can take months, even years – but it's standard SO10 practice designed to protect informants like Rashid and make sure that, when the targets are eventually arrested, they can never be certain who it was that sold them out. If the informant gets a grilling, he can always say, 'Hey, I introduced you to Mark because I know him and trust him. If you dealt with anyone else after that, hell, it's nothing to do with me.'

The technique is so effective at disguising the source of a breach that it is not unknown for the undercover officers introduced at the start of the operation to still be completely trusted by the gang after they've ended up inside. They will go and visit them in prison and sit there bold as brass trying to help them work out who it was that grassed them up and promising to look after their wife and kids for them.

As part of the infiltration into Abdul's gang, the other SO10 officers had made a series of test purchases of small amounts of drugs, a few hundred or a couple of thousand pounds at a time. That was to make sure the gang were telling the truth about what they had on offer. More importantly, it built up our credibility as no drug buyer worth his salt would set up a large deal without first getting a sample, and it helped dilute any suspicion among the targets that they were being set up.

Patrick told me that on this particular job I was to be the last man in, the one who would set the gang up for the big bust. 'Actually I had someone else in mind for tonight,' he confessed, 'but then I spoke to the guy who was running your undercover course. He told me how much you'd impressed him and said to give you a shot. So here you are. Don't let me down,' he said with a mischievous grin.

I tried to reply but the most I could manage was a weak croak. A part of me was hugely flattered but mostly I just felt under even more pressure to perform. 'Once we've got the introductions out of the way, I'll be doing most of the talking,' said Patrick. 'So you can just observe and learn. Are you ready?'

With a jolt it dawned on me that we were going straight there, straight round to the dealer's house. Shit. I'd assumed that we were going to a police station for a proper briefing and to plan our strategy. I still had my warrant card on me, papers from work and loads of other stuff that showed I was a policeman. I even had my wedding ring on. Inexperienced as I was, I still knew it wouldn't do.

On the training course they go to great lengths to teach you that working undercover is completely unpredictable. You cannot take a chance because you never know what might happen. Leave a warrant card in your jacket pocket and it will be the one time you forget your jacket behind at someone's house. Stick it in your shoe for safekeeping and the dealer will ask you to take your shoes off because he's got new carpets. When I decided to come clean, Patrick was really cool about it. 'Just stick it all in the glove compartment,' he said as we arrived at the flat. 'Don't worry, it'll be fine. Just relax.'

At the target's address we found a parking space, in between a large Mercedes and a Ferrari. When I first saw Patrick I thought the BMW was a bit over the top but as we pulled up I realized it was absolutely vital to the success of our operation. He was posing as one of the leading members of a drug gang with up to a quarter of a million pounds to spend on merchandise. If he had turned up in a battered old Vauxhall Cavalier the illusion would have been shattered in an instant and his cover would have been blown. For that reason, SO 10 maintains a sizeable fleet of prime motors from Range Rovers and Saabs to BMWs and Porsches which undercovers can make use of.

Abdul's flat was in an imposing four-storey townhouse that sat on the edge of a quiet square with its own tree-filled private garden in the middle. The door was answered by a tall blonde woman wearing too much make-up and not enough clothing who offered us a drink then took us through to the lounge. I looked on as Abdul and his partner Mohammed greeted Patrick with a big hug as if he was an old friend and invited us both to sit down. 'Good to see you my friend,' Abdul said. 'Looking good. Looking very good. I can see that life is treating you well.'

There were a couple of other people in the room – a big Oriental bear of a man who never said a word the whole time I was there and another Arab bloke with wild hair who seemed to be Abdul's minder. Neither was introduced. There was clearly a pecking order in the gang and the two of them didn't rank high enough to warrant names.

I didn't want to sit on one of the sofas because I would have been right next to Mr Wild Hair so I casually pulled out a wooden chair from under the dining table and sat on that. We got straight down to business: Patrick and Abdul started throwing figures around about how much it was going to cost and whether we wanted to take three kilos of amphetamine along with the coke and then reverse it the next time or one of dozens of other combinations. 'You know it makes sense,' said Abdul, trying his level best to inflate the size of the deal. 'The more you buy, the better the price I give you, the more money you make. Everybody goes home happy.'

Patrick pulled out a calculator and started punching in a few numbers. 'Come on Abdul,' he said. 'Play the game. If we go up to five kilos of speed along with the coke, you've got to drop the price. I'm doing you a favour taking that much in one go. I know you know that.'

Abdul smiled and waved his hand around the room, indicating

all the wealth that surrounded him. 'What can I say, Patrick? I have overheads. I agree the price is perhaps a little higher than what you might pay in, say, South London, but then so is the quality. And you can't tell me you'd rather be in some tower block than in my beautiful home. I'll tell you what. If you take, say, ten kilos of cannabis as well, then maybe I can do something.'

And so it went on. To be honest, I was getting a bit lost. I tried to chip in with the odd comment – 'ha ha', 'that's right' and 'good idea' – to show that I had a part in the deal too but Patrick was really flowing so I just let him get on with it. It was a masterclass.

At one point I was idly looking round the room when I caught sight of the wild-haired guy reaching into his jacket pocket. He casually pulled out a lump of cannabis resin the size of a house brick. My jaw dropped open. I could hardly take my eyes off it. It was the biggest lump of dope I'd ever seen. For a split second I almost fell back into usual police mode. My instinctive reaction was to jump up and arrest him but I caught myself just in time, sank back into my seat and watched as he produced a flick knife, began chipping bits off and expertly rolled himself a huge spliff. Then he passed the block to me. 'Nah, I like to keep a clear head when I'm doing business,' I said, 'but when this is all over, we'll have a good smoke together then, OK?' I took the block and handed it to Patrick who made his own excuses and passed it on once more.

It wasn't a problem. People imagine that big drug dealers are always big drug users but that simply isn't the case. There's just too much money at stake for people to risk making a bad decision and losing it for the sake of a quick high. A surprising number of the most vicious, ruthless and frightening gangsters I have ever met have been strictly teetotal and drug-free. It means there's never any pressure for an undercover to have to indulge just to fit in, which is just as well. If a defendant could prove that an SO10 operative had been taking drugs on the job, that officer's credibility would collapse and the villain would almost certainly walk free. The Oriental guy and the blonde woman both rolled joints but Mohammed and Abdul didn't touch it either.

After twenty-odd minutes in the flat, I started to relax and settled back in my chair. That's when I felt something sticking out of the back pocket of my jeans, digging me in the kidney. I instinctively reached round for it. Big mistake. As soon as my fingers touched it I knew what it was – my Metropolitan Police diary. 'Shit,' I muttered to myself. In my haste to put all my stuff in the car's glove box, I'd forgotten it was there. My heart started racing. I could hear it pumping inside my chest. I felt completely exposed. Gently I pushed the diary back down, took a deep breath and looked up. Abdul was giving me a hard stare but turned away the second our eyes met.

Soon after that the meeting came to an end with a final deal firmly in place. We would buy five kilos of cocaine and six kilos of amphetamine this time round – a pretty hefty deal by anyone's standards and one which put Abdul firmly in the upper echelons of the London crime scene – and then increase the amount of coke for the next three shipments.

'It's good, Patrick,' said Abdul, relaxed and happy now that business had been concluded. 'It's good for you and it's good for me. God is smiling on us.'

There was no need to talk about how the money and drugs would be exchanged. At this level of the underworld, no one trusts anyone so it's always done exactly the same way. You don't just turn up at someone's house with £200,000 in a briefcase and hand it over, not unless you want to get ripped off and have your throat cut. Instead, a member of the buying gang will hold the money and a member of the selling gang will hold the drugs. The buyers show the sellers the money at a safe house, let them count it if they want to, and then take it away. After that, the sellers bring the drugs to the safe house and let the buyers test them. Once everyone's happy, the money is brought back and the exchange is made.

Even though we're not really drug dealers, just police playing at it, we still have to stick to the rules. If the price is over the odds, we have to argue it down or walk away. If the quality's not what we expect, we have to complain about it. If you just take whatever old shit they want to give you for whatever price they fix, it makes you look desperate, and as soon as you start looking desperate, you start looking like Old Bill.

But of course, we were Old Bill. And things weren't quite going to follow Abdul's expectations, because when I got to the safe house, I would contact another SO10 officer who would be playing the part of the money man. Once he arrived, I would go out to his car to watch over the money and leave him to check the gear. He would then come out of the house – on the pretext of getting the money – and give the signal for the arrest team to move in and take everybody out, drugs and all. Simple.

I couldn't sleep that night. I kept running through the meeting in my mind and trying to work out how to play things the next day. The prospect of going back on my own absolutely terrified me. It all seemed so easy and straightforward when Patrick was there but now it was all up to me. And I couldn't help feeling unnerved about the way Abdul kept staring at me. What was on his mind? Did he recognize me? Did he see through my cover? I told myself over and over that it was just first-time nerves. But at night your mind plays tricks on you taking you deep into your worst fears. I worried that the gang might have found out about us. If they had, I'd be walking into a death trap. I'd have to be on my guard the whole time.

The top brass at SO10 weren't taking any chances either. There would be a surveillance team from SO11, the Criminal Intelligence Branch, following me from the moment I left the Bayswater flat so they'd know in advance where the deal was going to take place. According to the informant, the gang had access to a couple of properties in Harlesden and it was 99 per cent certain that one of those would be the venue, but they didn't know which one.

At a short briefing at Kensington police station early the following morning, I met up with the bloke playing the money man and some of the back-up squad. Because of the amount of money involved and the reputation of the dealers there was always a chance that they might try to rip us off, taking the cash and running without giving us any drugs. To counter that threat a team from SO19 – the tactical firearms unit – would be joining in the final raid. I made sure they all had a good look at me and knew which side I was on – if it all came on top, I didn't want to end up getting shot by accident.

We ran through the signals we would use: if the money man came out of the house and put on his coat, that would mean the drugs were there and the arrest team should move in; if I came out and took off my cap, it would mean the drugs were somewhere else and I was being taken to them; if anyone on the team put their hands straight up in the air, it meant we needed urgent assistance. We practised the moves a few times and then it was time to go. I was on my own.

There's a certain feeling people get when they know they're being watched, something tickling the hairs on the back of their neck or a sixth sense nagging in the far recesses of their mind. One of the hardest things about working undercover is learning to ignore this feeling so as not to react to it, even involuntarily. As I stood in the street outside the flat and hit the buzzer, I knew the SO11 team were out there somewhere but I had to stop myself from looking out for them. Nothing would make a target suspicious faster than someone who is constantly looking over their shoulder or jumps at every little noise. You have to put it out of your mind completely and concentrate on the job in hand.

I stepped inside and was greeted by Abdul who seemed pleased to see me, very excited and making a fuss of me. He rushed over and gave me a big hug. 'Martin. Martin my good, good friend. It is wonderful to see you again,' he said. The hug sent an icy shiver down my spine. Many of the bigger, more sophisticated drugs gangs make a habit of hugging every new person they meet because it's a chance to grab hold and check if they're wearing a wire. I wanted to push him away in disgust but that would have looked bad. I just had to let him get on with it.

'Today is a good day to do business,' Abdul continued, his strong Middle Eastern accent making him sound to me like the villain in a James Bond movie. 'And you Martin, you are a good man to do business with.'

I sat in the lounge while Abdul gathered his things. I couldn't help noticing that he was still staring at me when he thought I wasn't looking. The fears I had managed to push aside during the night now rushed back with a vengeance. His dark eyes seemed to be looking right through me. I could feel a knot of fear growing inside my stomach and had to fight to stay calm and relaxed.

A few minutes later we climbed into the back of his big S-class Mercedes and his driver, a thick-set Arab guy with no neck, set off for the safe house. There's only one rule to remember when you're in a car that a surveillance team is trying to follow: keep talking. You have to do your best to focus everyone's attention on you so they don't spend too much time looking in the mirrors to see who or what is behind them.

The driver didn't seem the chatty type but I wasn't so worried about him. Abdul was the brains of the operation and I didn't want him getting jumpy. Luckily he was up for talking about pretty much anything. 'Nice car,' I said as we moved off.

'Mercedes kick arse,' he replied enthusiastically. 'Engineered like no other car in the world, that's what they say in the adverts and they are right, 100 per cent right my friend. Every other car is like a toy compared to one of these. Tell me, what do you drive?'

I actually had a very unspectacular Ford Escort but somehow I didn't think it would fit in with the image I was trying to portray. 'Well, I have a lot of cars really. I like to change my car regularly, stay one step ahead and all that. I like BMWs.'

'Ah yes,' said Abdul. 'Also very fine cars. Anything German. They make the best cars in the world.'

Getting to Harlesden from Paddington is so straightforward a child could do it – the Harrow Road takes you all the way there. But the driver set off in the completely wrong direction, taking us down towards the River Thames and out towards Liverpool Street. From there he took a few back streets and ended up at King's Cross. And then it got even crazier. He started turning down roads that were obvious dead ends and would have to do three-point turns to get out, he'd indicate left and swing right at the very last minute. Every now and then he'd pull over and let a few cars pass, then set off again. And every time he came to a roundabout, he went round at least four times.

There was method in his madness though. It was classic anti-surveillance stuff, designed to make it much harder for someone to follow. I had no way of knowing if he'd managed to throw off the team or not. On any kind of undercover job, you never know where the back-up are going to be, what cars they are driving or anything. It's for your own protection. If you meet someone in a car park and you know that there is a sniper up on the roof of a certain building, you won't be able to help yourself, you'll want to look over to see if you can spot him. And if you know the back-up team are in a dark blue Transit van, then every time one pops up in the road, you'll double take. You could easily give it all away and blow an entire operation so you're better off not knowing anything.

I didn't let it faze me right away. All the top crooks practise anti-surveillance as a matter of course. They work on the principle that they are always being watched, always being followed and that their phones are always bugged. That way they never get careless. So the fact that the driver was giving the back-up team a bit of a run-around was no cause for alarm. But then Abdul suddenly turned to me, his voice sounding more serious than before.

'I like you, Martin. I like you a lot, but you have a great deal to learn about this game.'

'Oh yeah?' I said, prompting him to continue.

'A great deal. Oh yes, my friend. Much to learn. But I could teach you a good lesson. You may not believe it to look at me now, but once upon a time, I had it all. You see, I used to work with another man, a very clever man. And together we would bring in shipments of cannabis from Morocco. Containers. Tons. We were so successful. Together we made millions. Everything a man could ever want, I had it. Fast cars, a string of hotels, yachts, more money than I could ever spend, villas and mansions all over the world. And then. It went. I lost everything. Do you want to know how?'

'Tell me.'

'Martin . . . I lost it all because of a fucking undercover policeman.'

My heart leapt up to my mouth. His words sent a bolt of adrenalin shooting through me and I fought to retain my composure. I was trapped in the back of a car with a thug of a driver, who had been doing his level best to lose the surveillance team and for all I knew had probably succeeded, and a major villain, with no idea where I was going, no back-up to hand and no way to contact the outside world and he knew, he fucking knew. I swallowed hard. 'Really?' I said as casually as I could manage.

'Yes, Martin,' Abdul's voice had changed. There was a streak of anger running through it, I could see him clenching his fists as he spoke, winding himself up with each new sentence. 'I'll tell you what happened. My partner made a stupid mistake. The fucker. He brought a fucking undercover policeman in on the deal. We all got arrested. They had us on tape and everything.'

By now Abdul was spitting with rage. 'My friend got sent to prison for eighteen years. Eighteen fucking years! I managed to get away with it in court, convinced the jury that I was not involved. They gave me my freedom but they took everything. They cleaned me out, Martin. So now I'm reduced to these small deals. No disrespect to you my friend, but this business we are doing today, this is nothing compared to what I used to do. I just want to get back on my feet, to get back to where I was.'

I couldn't let myself believe that he knew, that my worst nightmares had come true and I'd been found out. It had to be a coincidence. It just had to. For Christ's sake, where were they taking me? And why did he keep saying how much he liked me? Was it some kind of warning to get out now, to drop the operation? Surely not. And what did he mean 'teach me a lesson'? He couldn't be that clever. Could he?

I had to steady my nerves. The truth was it didn't matter whether they knew or not. One thing that echoed in my mind from the undercover training course was that, no matter what happens, you never, ever break cover. If the police pull you over for speeding while you're on a job, you don't say anything. If you get arrested and slung in the cells, you still don't say anything. And if someone makes out they know you're a copper, you never admit it.

I calmed myself down enough to look across at Abdul who was staring at me again. But this time he held my gaze. It was as if he was trying to stare me out, waiting for me to crack. I stared back, too scared to look away. 'Martin,' he said at last. 'I have something that I want to say to you. We are nearing the end. Our business will soon be completed. But I like you Martin, and when this is all over, I want you to come on holiday with me. I want you to come to Morocco with me. Just the two of us. You will love it there. We will have a little trip and spend a happy time together.'

'Er. OK. That sounds . . . nice.'

Abdul shuffled across the seat and pushed his face a little closer to mine, peering under the brim of my baseball cap. 'You look like you've got some Arab in you. Are you part Moroccan perhaps?' he asked.

'Nah, no mate, I'm not.'

'Are you sure, Martin? I can see it in your eyes, in the shape of your face, the lines around your mouth and nose. I would swear you have a bit of Arab in you.'

And suddenly it all clicked, everything fell into place. Now I knew why Abdul had kept staring at me, why he'd hugged me for that little bit too long and kept telling me how much he liked me and why he wanted to take me under his wing. It was obvious. He wanted to shag me. The man fancied me like crazy and wanted to shag me. He wanted to grab hold with both hands and screw the arse off me. It was all I could do to stop myself from laughing out loud.

'So will you come to Morocco with me? Will you, Martin?'

I looked across at him. He thought I was just like some young Arab boy he could have his wicked way with. The truth was that if everything went to plan the only screw he was going to get was the one locking his cell door. 'We'll see, Abdul,' I said softly. 'We'll see.'

I was feeling a little more relaxed as we finally reached Harlesden. I tried not to dwell too long on what was to come. The driver turned into Fortunegate Road and slowed down as if looking for a parking space. It was plain to see that we weren't in Bayswater any more but it was still a nice, well-kept street full of brightly coloured terraced houses each with a neatly trimmed hedge at the front. As we moved further down the road, though, so it began to look increasingly rough and squalid.

At the bottom end, on a triangular plot of land opposite a parade of shops, sat a monstrous brown brick house surrounded by a decrepit wooden fence. It was a real mess. The window frames were cracked or missing, broken roof tiles lay scattered about the front garden, rusted drainpipes clung desperately to the outside walls like varicose veins and makeshift washing lines supported rows of threadbare clothes all around the outside.

The front door, in dire need of a fresh coat of paint, was opened by a sad and dowdy-looking woman I assumed was Abdul's wife, and in the hallway behind her a bunch of kids were running about. I couldn't see Abdul trying anything dodgy while they were around – and with a bit of luck, it might save me from being pounced on.

As we walked in, I could smell damp in the air. I couldn't say anything but I wanted to ask Abdul why the hell he left his wife and kids in such a hovel when he had a fantastic flat in Bayswater at his disposal.

We sat in the living room and waited for Mohammed to turn up with the drugs. He called a couple of times to say he'd got stuck in traffic and would be longer than expected which meant I had to keep finding new things to talk about. It wasn't easy. We exhausted African music, the history of Morocco, detailed descriptions of beaches he had been to, tales of his life as a multi-millionaire. It was really starting to piss me off.

At one point I got so bored with talking nonsense that I just had to get away from him, even for a few minutes. I asked if I could use his bathroom and he got up to show me where it was. As we passed the hallway, I caught a glimpse of a familiar figure through the glass panels of the front door. It was the wild-haired guy from the flat, keeping a look-out on the other side of the road. He had probably been there when I arrived, checking that we weren't followed. As Patrick had told me the night before, these geezers were very clever and very careful.

Abdul led me down the hall and threw open a door at the far end. His wife, who was standing in the bath stark naked having a shower, let out a blood-curdling scream and tried in vain to cover herself up with the nozzle. 'Pah. Don't worry about her,' said Abdul as if this sort of thing happened all the time. 'You just carry on. Ignore her. She doesn't matter.'

He treated her so badly I had to bite my lip to stop myself saying something. Apart from the scream, she never uttered a single sound the whole time I was there. He just barked orders at her – 'fetch drinks, quickly', 'tell the children to be quiet', 'get me a cigarette' – and she did exactly what she was told. I don't think her eyes ever left the floor. It was hard to stomach but I had to pretend it was all OK – I had to keep Abdul happy, no matter how hard it was. But using the toilet while his wife was having a shower was going too far. I told him I'd wait outside until she finished. He seemed genuinely confused, shrugged his shoulders and walked off. Abdul was pond life but I knew I had to put up with him only a short while longer before he got what was coming to him.

By the time I returned to the living room, even he was struggling to find new topics of conversation. 'So Martin, tell me more about Patrick. He seems a nice guy. What kind of work have you two done together?'

It was a legitimate question but one that I couldn't even begin to answer. Patrick and I hadn't had time to sit down and work out a fake scenario for how we'd met or what we'd done. I didn't know what else Patrick had said about me before I was introduced and I didn't want to mess things up when we were so close to nailing the gang. I had to find a way out, and fast. 'Look Abdul,' I said firmly. 'Patrick's my boss right, and he wouldn't like it if I started telling people his business any more than you'd want your driver talking to me about yours. If you want to know about Patrick, you ask Patrick.' Abdul smiled warmly. 'You're a good man, Martin. You are loyal and you are honest. I like that a lot.'

After the waiting, when the doorbell finally rang the relief was so immense that I wanted to jump up and clap. A nervous-looking Mohammed came in with the Oriental man from the flat following close behind. I hadn't got to know Mohammed anything like as well as Abdul but I could tell he was a wide boy and probably thought of himself as a bit flash. He looked like a younger, slimmer version of his boss but he dressed and sounded like a used car salesman. His dark wavy hair had been slicked back and he was wearing a pair of dazzling white shoes without socks. He'd taken a back seat in the proceedings so far, but now wanted to assert himself. 'The merchandise is close by,' he said. 'But I want to see the money first. I want to make sure it's all there and that everything is in place before we go any further.'

'No problem,' I said. 'I just need to make a phone call.'

Twenty minutes later, Robin and Steve, the two final members of the undercover team, turned up. Robin was playing the part of the money man while Steve, who stayed in the car, was acting as our driver. Robin, tall and sandy-haired, came into the house and introduced himself to everyone. 'Everything all right, Martin?' he asked me, checking the deal was on and that I was comfortable in my undercover role.

'Yeah, everything's sweet. Let's show them the money.'

Robin and I escorted Mohammed out to our car, another brand-new 5-series BMW from the SO10 pool, and sat him between us in the back. Steve set off around the block and, as we passed McDonald's on Harlesden High Street, we flashed Mohammed the money. There was £200,000 of it, all in used tens and twenties, folded into bundles of £100 and stuffed in a Tesco's carrier bag. It was an amazing sight. And it totally blew Mohammed's mind. It was obvious he'd never seen anything like it before.

'Wow,' he gasped. 'Look at that. Look at all the money. Fuck.'

'Do you want to count it?' I asked him.

'Nah, it's OK,' he said. 'I'm sure it's all there.' I looked at him closely. His eyes had lit up. He was really excited about the deal now, thinking about how he was going to spend his new-found wealth. His mind was no longer on the job.

'Are you sure? Don't you even want to check some of it?'

'Nah man, put it away, put it away before someone sees. Come on, stop fucking about.'

'Go on, Mohammed. Touch it, feel it, smell it. It's good. You know you want to.'

We got back to the house and Mohammed left immediately to go and get the drugs. He was trying to be cool again but there was a spring in his step that gave it all away. He bounced back ten minutes later with a big canvas holdall which he dumped heavily on the dining-room table. As he started to unzip it, I could see the neatly stacked polythene bags of white powder inside. That was my cue to leave. 'OK guys, while Robin runs a few tests, I'm going to go and sit in the car, keep an eye on the money,' I said, then headed for the door.

Steve had parked on the other side of the road from Abdul's house outside a boarded-up, disused shop. I sat in the back and a few seconds later watched as Robin came out with his coat over one shoulder. He reached the pavement, swung his coat off and put it on. That was the signal and at that moment all hell broke loose.

I didn't know where to look. To my right, the doors of the disused shop burst open. That turned out to be the main SO19 observation point. To cries of 'Attack, attack, attack!' eight men in black combat trousers came running out, weaving their way past the front and back of the car, to take up positions outside Abdul's front door. They wore bullet-proof Kevlar body armour and open-faced helmets with built-in microphones. Each member of the team carried a Heckler and Koch MP5 carbine, a powerful rifle but short and manoeuvrable enough to be used in confined spaces. It was the gun made famous by the SAS during their raid on the Lybian embassy. On their hips they carried Glock 9mm pistols, more than a match for anything on the street. Both weapons fire identical soft-pointed 9mm ammunition specially designed to expend all their energy within the selected target, creating maximum knock down. It also reduces the risk of over-penetration: the bullets slow down so much within a human body that they are unlikely to pass out the other side and strike anyone else.

Three members of SO19 vanished through an alleyway to cover the back entrance. Four of the remainder lined up on the left, weapons pointed dead ahead, while the last man produced an enforcer battering ram and swung it at the front door, reducing it to splinters.

The firearms team were moving with military precision, using procedures they had practised thousands of times. SO19 officers spend weeks training at a centre in Lippetts Hill, practising every possible form of armed confrontation from sieges to ambushing armed robbers. Their expertise shone through as I watched them work. With the door gone, one female officer flung herself on her knees directly in front of the gap and raised the sight of her gun to her eye. 'Clear!' she yelled, signalling to the other members of the team to move in. I could hear that a similar action was taking place at the back door. I almost felt sorry for Abdul and the others, especially his kids. They must have been absolutely terrified.

At the same time a seemingly empty Transit van parked with two wheels on the pavement 200 yards up the road suddenly burst into life. With a screech of burning rubber it tore down the road towards us and skidded to a halt directly outside the Chinese takeaway next to the target house. The back doors sprang open and out poured one of the back-up teams, all wearing jeans, trainers and chequered police baseball caps.

This was followed immediately by two unmarked Vauxhall Vectras screeching to a halt just beside our BMW from opposite ends of the street. Six blokes in plain clothes but also wearing police-issue baseball caps and stab-proof vests piled out of them and joined the others in running towards the front door of Abdul's house. I wound down the window, letting in the muffled shouts of 'Armed police, put your hands up!' and 'Get on the floor and freeze!' mixed with the sound of screaming, breaking glass and splintering wood. I could hear the surveillance helicopter beating the air as it hovered overhead.

Finally, a Panda car, two marked Transit vans and an ambulance turned up, ready to take the arrested members of the gang into custody.

The whole time this was going on, Robin kept on walking coolly through the mayhem towards the car. The arrest team was whizzing past him in their rush to get inside but all he could do was smile and then giggle. By the time he sat down beside me, he was chuckling away. 'That was beautiful,' he said, sitting back and closing his eyes. 'Just like clockwork. We got the drugs and we got them. Couldn't have been better.' He turned and looked straight at me, 'Nice one, Martin. You're not bad, for a beginner.'

It didn't take the gang long to realize that they had no defence. They had been caught red-handed and, if necessary, there were about half a dozen undercover police officers ready to testify against them. Everyone pleaded guilty and went away for up to twenty years. Abdul's wife was the only one who didn't go down, and I can't help hoping she was able to leave him and her old life behind for good.

I looked through the local paper the following week and couldn't see any mention of the bust but tucked away in the crime report section there was a small paragraph simply stating that a large quantity of drugs had been recovered from a house in Harlesden following an undercover police operation. They didn't know the half of it.

4

Philip: Skank, a notorious Yardie gangster, was cheerfully puffing away on a giant roll-up as I drove him through the streets of Soho in a smart black Golf GTi. We weren't going anywhere in particular, just looking sharp in our matching Ray-Bans, cruising around with the windows down and listening to the radio blasting out Kiss FM.

We turned up a narrow side street to get to Camden and I slowed down to weave through the lines of double-parked cars. Up ahead a Suzuki Jeep appeared from round a corner and started coming towards us. There wasn't enough room for them to get by and nowhere for us to pull over. We had right of way but it was no big deal so I got ready to reverse and let the Jeep squeeze past. As I reached for the gearstick, Skank knocked my hand away.

'Don't move the fucking car,' he said in his rough Jamaican accent.

'Eh? What?'

'Don't move the fucking car man. We were in the road first. They should move. Let them go back.'

'Come on Skank, it's no big deal, I'll just . . .'

'Fuck them. I tell you now one time – don't move the car. Ya hear me?' I could tell he was deadly serious. Normally I'd just reverse anyway but my undercover role was to keep Skank happy. He was the boss, I was just the footsoldier – I had to do whatever he said – so we stayed put.

The Jeep stopped ten feet in front of us and flashed its lights. And again. And again. The driver, a nice-looking twenty-something black woman with a fancy hairstyle, started gesticulating for us to back up. As the seconds ticked by she got more and more animated and her passengers, two tough-looking black guys, joined in as well. I looked across at Skank. He was just staring straight ahead, totally motionless, as if he couldn't care less. The woman began using her horn. First a few short blasts then a continuous one. Skank flicked the remains of his butt away, turned to me and said wearily: 'Switch the engine off, we ain't going nowhere.'

I started to protest but Skank wouldn't let me get a word in. 'No,' he said as I reached for the gearstick again. 'No, don't. Hey man, *no*! Just switch the fucking car off then sit there with your hands on your knees and don't fucking touch nothing.' There was real venom in his voice so I decided to go along with it, just to shut him up.

By now there were cars queuing up behind us and the Jeep. Horns were going off all over the place, people were shouting and screaming obscenities and groups of shopkeepers and tourists were gathering to watch the show. They didn't have long to wait: the door of the Jeep opened, the woman stepped out and stomped over to our car. She was quite pretty if a little on the heavy side, smartly dressed in flower-patterned hipsters and a bright orange halter top with a sleeveless puffa jacket over the top – and totally pissed off. She made straight for Skank's window: he was clearly the one in charge.

'What the fuck you playing at?' she said wagging her finger. She had one of those really grating, high-pitched London accents, straight off a market stall in *EastEnders*. 'Move the fucking car, will you? Are you stupid or what? Shit, man. We was here first you know.'

Skank slowly turned his head and looked the woman up and down, then let rip with a fury that was straight out of the Kingston ghetto. 'You want me to move? You want *me* to move? You come over here with your piece of shit body and that cheap weave in your hair, wearing some hand-me-down outfit and you think you can tell me who was in the street first. No. You, your fat arse and your shit Japanese car can't tell me nothing. Look at you with that big piece of bottom sticking out like a ledge. Man, I thought you was ugly when you was in the car but now, close up, shit. Girl, you look bad! W'happen? Dress in the dark today? Hallowe'en already? If that's your idea of looking good then I wouldn't trust you to tell me which way is up.'

The woman's mouth fell open in disbelief. She was so stunned she could hardly speak. 'Who the fuck do you think you are?' she gasped.

'I *know* who I am,' Skank hit back. 'I am the man who is not going to let you and your car get past until you learn to show some respect. Now listen up and listen good. 'Cos if you want to get on with your journey you're going to have to move your car back, 'cos we were here first and we are going nowhere until you back up. This ain't no game, girl. We ain't playing at this. Some people got better things to do than look at you making a fool of yourself. So just shut up and back up. Right now!'

She just stood there, shaking with rage. I could tell she was thinking hard, desperately trying to come up with some really clever, cutting remark to win the argument. It wasn't to be. In the end she gave up, screamed 'Fuck off!', then turned on her heels and marched back to her car.

Skank and I watched as she talked to the two guys inside, telling them what had happened. They threw a series of increasingly angry glances in our direction, then got out and started coming towards us. It was getting serious: they were both well over six foot and powerfully built. The man nearest me had a Krooklock in his hand. 'For fuck's sake,' he said as the two of them advanced, 'what is your problem? Move yourself, man.' I jumped out of the car and got ready for the inevitable fight.

It was a tricky situation. I was on duty, playing the part of a hardcore gangster and I had to stick with it. There were eyes and ears all around us. I had no idea who might be about, who might be watching. The whole thing could have been a set-up to see how I'd react, just to test me out. I could put a stop to it there and then by telling them I was Old Bill and calling in back-up, but blowing my cover would undo months of painstaking work. It just wasn't an option. Either Skank and I were going to take a beating and swallow it or we'd dish one out and hope things didn't get too out of hand.

Then Skank did something that took everyone by surprise: he went for his gun.

He sprang out of the car like a jack-in-the-box, took a few steps forward and thrust his right hand deep inside his baggy leather jacket, right down to the waistband of his jeans. Then in the roughest, nastiest yard-man accent you ever heard, he started screaming at the two guys. 'Move the car? Move the fucking car? You want me to go for it? You want me to pull it? You want me to pull my piece and shoot ya?'

Pedestrians screamed and scattered and the two tough guys instantly turned to jelly. 'Whoa there. It's OK, brother,' stuttered one. 'Just hang on, hang on now, we can sort this out, peace bro, no need for that,' bleated the other.

But Skank was in full flow. His eyes were wild and he looked mad enough to do it, right there in the middle of the street in the middle of the afternoon. 'You want me to give it to ya? Ya pussy. Ya wanna see what it is you're messing with? You want me to do it right here? Me put shot in ya face *now*!'

The guys were backing off at the double, hands up in the air. 'Easy, bredren. Just stay calm and relax. Everything's cool. Just take it easy.' They got back in the Jeep and started arguing with the woman who was now back in the driver's seat. The men were clearly terrified, yelling at her to 'Move the fucking car!' but she was having none of it, trying to salvage a sliver of self-respect from her humiliation at Skank's tongue-lashing.

Eventually the guy in the front passenger seat reached across, opened the driver's door and shoved her out. She stumbled into the road, flicked Skank an evil look, then climbed into the back. The guy in front scrambled across to the driver's seat and started the engine. The woman only barely had time to close the back door before the Jeep shot back fifty yards at what seemed like warp ten.

Skank walked arrogantly back to the Golf, his hands resting calmly by his side. 'Now you can start the car,' he said. We drove up the street until we were parallel to where they had pulled over. 'Stop the car,' yelled Skank. 'Stop the fucking car right now.' I stamped on the brakes and we skidded to a halt dead level with the Jeep. Skank hauled his entire upper body out of the open window and made the fingers of his right hand into the shape of a gun. 'If me see any of you again,' he hissed, 'ya dead. Me gonna pull me piece and shoot ya.' Then he pointed at each of the three in turn. 'Ya dead, ya dead, ya dead. All a ya dead. Me shoot the lot a ya.' He settled back in his seat and we drove off.

We managed to get only a few yards down the road before Skank exploded in a fit of hysterical laughter. He was laughing so hard that he was holding on to his sides and thrashing about in the seat. It was nearly ten minutes before he'd calmed down enough to be able to speak.

'Er . . . Skank . . .'

'Yes, bredren?' he replied, in between giggles.

'Er . . . You don't really have a gun on you, do you?'

Skank smiled big and wide, then gave me a little wink and patted his waist. 'I tell you man, if this was Jamaica, we'd still be there, we'd be trading gunshots. I've seen plenty man die for less.'

Working with Skank in a bid to penetrate the heart of Britain's Yardie underworld turned out to be one of the longest, most stressful, difficult and dangerous undercover jobs I was ever involved in. It also formed a major part of what was to become the most expensive, ill-conceived and disastrous infiltration that the Metropolitan Police has ever attempted.

The operation was born out of desperation, an urgent need to somehow tackle the increasing problem of crack-related violence which first exploded on to Britain's streets in the early nineties. It began with reports of guns being fired in the air as a 'salute' at certain nightclubs, grew to stories of street dealers having the barrels of mini machine guns thrust up their noses as they were robbed of their takings and ended with what can only be described as all-out turf war.

The murder of Christopher 'Tuffy' Bourne was typical. He specialized in robbing other dealers, often making them plead for their life on their knees while stripping them of cash, jewellery and merchandise. One particularly successful raid involved a crack house in Brixton and left him with £10,000 in cash and two kilos of cocaine. A month or so after the first raid, he was told by the members of his gang that the owners had re-stocked. They encouraged him to rob it again but it was a set-up.

The second he opened the steel-reinforced front door of 54 Vassal Road, he was met by a blaze of gunshots. He had taken his own gun out but never managed to fire a single shot. When it was all over, a split second after it had begun, three bullets were embedded in his chest, four more had passed straight through him and a further ten were dug out of the wall behind him.

There was another wake-up call when Patrick Dunne, a bicycle-riding community policeman in the *Dixon of Dock Green* mould, was gunned down near Brixton by three men who were heard laughing as they blasted him to death. They then fired a victory salute into the air and ran off into the night. Seconds earlier, the same men had shot small-time Ghanaian drugs dealer William Danso, chasing him around his front room and firing repeatedly. He was hit five times with twelve more bullets, later found in the walls and furniture.

In the years that followed, there was a sevenfold increase in the number of gun incidents in London alone, virtually all of it down to the Yardies. Their willingness to brandish and use guns forced other criminals – black and white – to do the same or risk being ripped off or killed. The introduction of armed response vehicles, the issuing of bullet-proof jackets for officers on standard beat patrol – all of that was because of the Yardies too.

As the months went by, the situation got more and more out of control. Drive-by shootings and cold-blooded executions in broad daylight became so commonplace they no longer made the front pages of the newspapers. Sometimes they were hardly reported at all.

The police formed special squads to try to tackle the gangs and had some success but also discovered just how massive the problem had become. When one single faction, the Spanish Town Posse, was targeted for just two months, the squad ended up arresting 175 people, including twenty-two for firearms possession, sixteen for attempted murder and ten for armed robbery.

The killings were sometimes over disputes of territory, sometimes out of a desire to gain respect and sometimes just purely personal. But in every case, the violence was extreme and the witnesses were nowhere to be seen. Even when a murder took place on someone's doorstep and was committed by someone they saw every day, no one would come forward. They were simply too terrified of reprisals.

The presence of the Jamaican gangsters was also having an effect on our home-grown black youth. Kids in Brixton, Hackney and Harlesden were growing up thinking the best way to get rich quick was to buy a gun and go sell some crack. Gangs were everywhere. London seemed to be on the verge of turning into Los Angeles. Something had to be done.

A joint initiative involving the police, customs and immigration service was set up with the brief to tackle the Yardies from all angles. At first they wanted to call it the Jamaican Crime Unit but the government was worried that such a name would prove highly offensive to the law-abiding Jamaicans who form the majority of their community. They tried out the Caribbean Crime Unit but when a visiting Foreign Office official saw the name on the door, that too was declared too inflammatory. Out of desperation, they became the National Drugs Related Violence Intelligence Unit.

Once the NDRVIU was up and running, they concluded that the best way to deal with the Yardies would be to launch a major SO10 operation against them. But that idea was a complete non-starter. Even the most experienced undercover officers couldn't get inside the gangs because they were all based on friendships that went right back to school playgrounds in Jamaica. The Yardies worked in small groups of four or five at the most and absolutely everybody knew everybody else, even if they were in a rival gang. The rare times they met someone they didn't know directly, there was always a friend or cousin back in Jamaica who could provide a reference.

Then we got our first break. A man called Aldridge Clarke, wanted for a series of brutal shootings and stabbings back in Jamaica, was arrested on a minor traffic offence in Brixton and found to be carrying an offensive weapon. Desperate to avoid being deported,

Clarke agreed to become a registered police informant, the first true Yardie ever to do so.

The information that came from Clarke was first class. There were hundreds of names, details of movements, drug purchases, gun exchanges, arrivals, departures, kidnappings, beatings, robberies and murders across the whole country. Like all informants, Clarke was entitled to payments in return for his information and such was the quality of his intelligence, he regularly received fees of £1,000 a time. No one minded: he was our secret weapon in the war against Jamaican organized crime and opened up the possibility of a new way of tackling the gangs.

A few other minor informants followed but it soon became clear that what was really needed was a high-ranking Yardie who would be willing to introduce undercover officers posing as the London end of his operation to members of the Jamaican underworld.

What happened next was little short of sheer lunacy and, until now, has never been made public. A team of senior officers from Scotland Yard travelled to Kingston, Jamaica, with the express intention of recruiting active Yardie gangsters to work as informants in London. Unlike British undercover officers, they would be able to reference themselves back to Jamaica, people would know them and they would be able to move among their fellow gangsters without arousing suspicion. Some of those targeted had previously worked as informers for the Jamaican police, others had been deported from Britain on drugs or firearms charges and were seen as 'good bets'. Some were approached simply because they had been recommended by Clarke or other informants. The incentives on offer were many and the restrictions that would be placed on them were relatively few.

The informants would receive 'lifestyle' payments to cover the cost of day-to-day living as well as a weekly salary. On top of that they would be able to claim any out-of-pocket expenses, from eating and drinking to clothes and toiletries. In return, they would be encouraged to indulge in all the usual activities – setting up drug deals, buying guns, organizing prostitutes and so on – but supposedly participate only to a minor degree themselves.

They would agree not to handle any drugs personally and not to act as *agents provocateurs*. They would have to report anything that seemed important and relay details of any crimes that they came across. Using their contacts and reputation, they would gather as much information about top gang leaders as they possibly could. No one was particularly concerned about mules and foot soldiers. The only thing that would look good in the eyes of the tax-paying public would be a few of the big players being brought to book.

A month before Skank arrived in the country, I'd received a call from SO10 saying they wanted to do a job for the NDRVIU. 'We want to bring in someone from Jamaica to work as an informant and we want you to be their chaperon. It's a very long-term operation, you'll be under for at least four months, maybe longer. Are you up for it?'

'It sounds fine to me,' I replied, 'but you'll have to clear it with my guvnor.'

In the UK there's no such thing as a full-time undercover officer. First and foremost, you're a policeman and you have your day-to-day duties to deal with. If an undercover job comes up, you can be released to work on that but you always have to get permission first so that everyone knows what's going on.

I was working in the CID office at Wood Green at the time and if I went away for four months, it meant that all the cases I was on would grind to a halt. It's always the same. If you're working on a GBH case and you need to go and interview some witnesses, take statements, that sort of thing, it's down to you. No one takes over anyone else's job unless they absolutely have to, for instance if the case is going to court. I had at least a dozen cases in my file and such a long absence would be a real pain in the arse.

My guvnor was a true classic, like something out of *The Sweeney*. A big ox of a man with thinning red hair and a booming Scottish accent, he was one of those blokes who believed that great leadership was all about shouting. And swearing, always as loud as possible. Soon after I'd spoken to SO10, I heard the phone ring in his office followed by the muffled sound of his furious ranting. I waited for things to quieten down and then casually strolled in.

'I think you'll be getting a phone call about me some time today guv.'

He was still fuming. 'Yeah, too right, I just fucking did. They want you released for four months. Four fucking months! I told them no way. I'm just not having it. I can't afford to lose you for that long. The office would grind to a halt. It's not on. Those arseholes at SO10, they think they're fucking God or something. Well, they're not God. I am. And what I say goes. They can go fuck themselves.'

At that point his phone rang again. I made to leave but he signalled for me to stay. He started off his usual aggressive self but this time it quickly faded. Soon there was no shouting or swearing at all. Quite the opposite. As he listened to what was being said, a huge smile began to spread across his face. 'Yeah? . . . oh yeah . . . yeah. That's more like it. I'm glad you've seen sense. OK, you're welcome. Thanks. Bye.' By the time he put down the receiver, he was grinning like a Cheshire cat.

'Well, apparently they've had a change of heart,' he said smugly. 'They only need you for six weeks now. That might not be so bad. They're finally starting to understand that they can't just fuck around with CID whenever they want, just because they think that what they're doing is more important. They're showing a bit of respect, and not before time. I'm gonna let you go, Philip. Go on then, fuck off before I change my mind. I'll see you in six weeks then.' He was on cloud nine as he waved me out of his office, proud of himself for having got one over the boys down at the Yard.

I went back to my desk and called up the SO10 office. 'So, my guvnor says it's only six weeks now, then?' The bloke on the other end of the phone tried to stifle a chuckle but failed. 'No, it's still four months but fuck him, we've told him just six weeks. When it gets to five and a half, we'll tell him it's being extended and it'll be too late for him to do anything about it.'

The following day I went to Scotland Yard to meet the team

from the NDRVIU. The name may have been watered down but once you got through the door of their office on the seventh floor, you could have no doubt exactly who they were after. The moment you entered, you were confronted by a huge map of Jamaica on the wall opposite. No other island, no other country. Just Jamaica. There were Polaroids of ghettos in the capital, Kingston, and hundreds of mug shots of suspects and their contacts. And every single one of them was black. There was even a Jamaican flag in the corner.

I was led to a small white-walled side office filled with a haze of cigarette smoke where Malcolm Stone, the head of SO11, the Criminal Intelligence Branch, his deputy, Detective Superintendent Roy Gunn, DS Chris Taylor from SO10 and DS Donald Matthews, the man who would be Skank's 'handler', were waiting for me. It was an impressive line-up and for the first time the size of the operation began to dawn on me.

DS Matthews, a softly spoken Geordie who had shaved his head to hide his growing bald patch, did most of the talking and most of the smoking. He and Roy Gunn were the ones who had travelled over to Jamaica and hand-picked a selection of 'tame' gangsters who would be travelling to London over the coming months. 'We are expecting a significant amount of Yardie activity across our patch this summer,' he said. 'What we learned on our research trip was that these guys are attracted to London as they see the police as less of a threat than elsewhere. With the US market for cocaine somewhat saturated and the price over there falling, the profit available from drugs is much higher in the UK and the sentences imposed by the courts for those captured are far more lenient. Finally, despite all the shootings we've had, the Yardies say there is less danger from rival gangs here than anywhere else in the world. In a nutshell, they think we're a soft touch. What we're going to do now is shatter that illusion.'

There would be a number of separate operations running at the same time, all with different goals. In Skank's case, the idea was that he would infiltrate one or two of the larger Yardie gangs operating in the capital and, once he was comfortably inside, begin introducing undercover officers. 'This is going to be brilliant,

76

Philip,' said Chris Taylor. 'We should have done this years ago. This guy is the real McCoy so he'll be accepted right away. It's a whole new way of working.'

Unlike Aldridge Clarke and some of the others who were set to arrive, Skank had previous experience of working as an informant, having carried out similar operations for both the Jamaican Police and the US Drug Enforcement Administration. It meant he would cost considerably more but he should be more reliable and his intelligence reports of higher quality.

During the meeting we discussed my own role. Skank had never been to London before and didn't know his way around. One of my priorities would be to show him all the right places – the nightclubs, pubs, bars and restaurants where top Yardies liked to hang out. I would also be his chauffeur and his right-hand man.

As soon as the meeting ended Chris handed me a requisition slip to go up to the seventh floor to withdraw some money to buy Skank a car. 'Get something a bit flash but not too over the top. Twelve grand should do it,' he said. 'There are a couple of garages in South London that are worth trying. I'll scribble down the addresses for you.'

Back in Jamaica, all Skank's associates believed he was coming to London of his own accord. To ensure there could be no leak of information which proved otherwise, I arranged his flights personally, putting them on my 'company' credit card. Almost every SO10 operative is given a set of credit cards in the name of companies set up and run by SO10 itself. They're not ideal – most criminals prefer to pay for everything in cash and those that are successful enough to have cards tend to have personal rather than company accounts – but with at least 100 undercover officers out in the field at any one time and hundreds more in reserve, it would be an administrative nightmare if SO10 had to track the spending on an individual by individual basis. Having company cards means all the payments end up in the same place. I rarely used my credit cards in undercover work but every now and then, as was the case with Skank's airline ticket, they did come in useful.

I phoned him a couple of times in Jamaica to make sure he was happy with the travel dates and to gauge whether we'd be able to work together or not. At first I found his heavy accent hard work, especially as he spoke quickly, as if there was no time to waste on idle chat. But as I got accustomed to the rhythms of his speech, I realized he was surprisingly good company.

'So when you get here, I'll be the one showing you around, making sure you've got everything you need and giving you the big tour of all the places you need to know. You've got your own car, a Golf GTi, but it's probably better if I do the driving first until you get to know the layout of the streets. Otherwise you'll just end up getting lost all the time.'

Skank thought this was absolutely hysterical and his laughter echoed through a poor line. 'You mean I'm going to have my own personal policeman with me the whole time? Shit, man. I better not get up to no mischief. Better not be no bad bwoy.'

Ten days later I met him at Heathrow airport. It was September and just starting to get a little chilly but Skank came sauntering through the arrivals gate dressed for the height of the Jamaican summer. My first impression was that he seemed very clean cut for a gangster. Most Yardies dress to a stereotype – baggy pants, Timberland boots, big puffa jackets. But Skank, in his neatly pressed chinos, brown leather shoes and short-sleeved blue denim shirt and with his short hair and neatly trimmed moustache and beard, was obviously a class apart.

We went straight to Scotland Yard for a coffee with Chris Taylor who wanted the earliest opportunity to ensure Skank knew all the limitations on his behaviour so that the operation would not end with him being accused of acting as an *agent provocateur*. The Jamaican's patience ran out almost immediately. 'I've been through all this already when them two guys came over. They've told me what to do and what not to do. How to act and how not to act. It's all bullshit anyway. I ain't no cop. What I want to know is where I is gonna be sleeping tonight. You see me, I just come off a seven-hour flight. Last thing I need is a lesson in law.'

Chris looked over at me and I shrugged my shoulders. 'Book

him into a hotel, somewhere that's handy for all the places you're going to be going,' he said with a sigh.

'And another thing,' said Skank, getting more assertive by the second. 'No one has yet told me how much I am being paid. I think that's something we should sort out here and now, less you want to see me leave here next flight home.'

'Well,' said Chris, 'obviously we'll pay all your expenses . . .'

'That goes without saying,' Skank cut in. 'I want to know how much I'm going to be paid on top of that. Or do you want me to get a little job maybe? You know if you want me to pose as some big don, then I've got to have money to throw around. And it ain't gonna be my money.'

Chris looked at me again and I looked at the floor. This was one he was going to have to sort out on his own. A few phone calls later and Skank's total package had been worked out. He would receive a 'lifestyle' payment of £500 per week, plus all his expenses would be settled in cash on a weekly basis. If Skank bought a new pair of socks, the Met would give him the money back. If he filled the car up with petrol, he would be refunded. Every time he went out, ate a meal, had a drink or bought pretty much anything, he would get the money back. On top of that he would be given a mobile phone whose bill would be paid as would his hotel bills. From the off, I could see the operation was going to cost a fortune.

'These people are completely fucking mad,' said Skank, shaking his head in disbelief as I drove him away from Scotland Yard after the meeting. 'They think I'm fucking Superman or something, like I'm gonna sweep all the shit off the streets in just a couple of months. Crazy.'

That night I booked Skank into the Cleveland Hotel off Marble Arch, paid with the company credit card, and helped take his luggage up to his room. I was lingering by the door when Skank spoke to me. 'OK,' he said, flopping down on the bed and fixing me with a hard stare while lighting a roll-up. 'What do I do now?'

I'd planned to spend some quality time with Joanne that evening but I realized that I couldn't just dump Skank in a strange town where he didn't know his way around. Instead we had a couple of hamburgers at the hotel, sitting at a circular table draped with a pink tablecloth in the centre of a half-full restaurant. While a pianist played softly in the background, Skank told me about life in Jamaica.

'You grow up in a place like that, you gonna burn to be someone from day one. When a man grow up with nothing and then he get something, he don't know how long it will last so he use it there and then. When a man migrates, especially when he comes from a certain section of Jamaica, the life he sees, it's like heaven. I have bredren who never even know a toilet until they come to England or America. One man visit me one day and say: "Boy, that toilet is nice for when it take away ya doings, it does bring back nice clean water with which to wash your hands."

'I tell you Philip, compared to Jamaica, life here is sweet. You know how many men die in Kingston last week? Eight. In one week eight men dead. And that's lower than normal. Last year there was more than 600 murders. Everyone knows someone who got killed. There's only 100,000 people living in the whole city.'

'Why?' I asked. 'What's it all about?'

'Used to be politics,' Skank replied, settling back in his seat. 'The leaders of the two main parties would give kids in the ghetto guns and tell them to scare people into voting one way or the other. But after the elections, the kids kept the guns because that gave them power. Then they discovered drugs. Ganja was OK, just something people sold to get by. But then came crack and the chance to make big, big money.

'Crack is the killer,' continued Skank. 'Drugs has always been a part of life in Jamaica, but not like this. Before crack, there was no violence. No man ever got dead of the weed.'

We'd finished eating so Skank rolled another cigarette and belched loudly, causing the other, better behaved diners to look over disapprovingly. It was almost as if he wanted an audience for his story.

'In Jamaica I have to have a gun with me all the time you know. I got myself a whole set. I have a Glock and an old Luger 'cos I used to see it in all them old war films, it was the same gun those bad ass SS officers used to carry, and I thought it looked cool so I got me one. I used to have a .44 Magnum too, all because of Clint fucking Eastwood and them wicked *Dirty Harry* films. But I had to get rid of it. Most powerful handgun in the world. Yeah, right. Too powerful. You couldn't hit shit. You fire one time and you can't stop your arm from flying up in the air with the recoil.'

Skank made his fingers into the shape of a gun and took aim at a passing waiter to demonstrate, complete with authentic gunshot noises. Then he leaned forward and spoke softly, suddenly recalling another anecdote he wanted to share. 'There was one time I saw two guys having a gunfight across a field. Both men had Magnums, one at one end of the field, the other at the other. *Boom!*' Everyone in the restaurant looked round again. Skank ignored their stern glances and carried on, ramping up the ghetto speak even more. 'The noise was like cannon fire. *Boom!* But neither man could hit the other. There was a big crowd of people sitting around watching. We just laughed.'

By now every other diner in the restaurant was looking at us, wondering what on earth was going on, and I was feeling distinctly self-conscious. Skank, however, was in his element and sat back with a big grin on his face. He was the centre of attention in the centre of London and he hadn't even been there a day. I made sure we never ate in the hotel restaurant again.

We met up the next morning and got straight to work. Skank had made some calls in advance to friends who were in London and we visited a couple of houses in Stoke Newington and Brixton so he could say hello. Everywhere we went, people welcomed Skank with hearty handshakes and big bearhugs. It was clear that he was not only well known but also highly respected. I would be introduced as his 'friend from London' or his 'driver' or 'minder' depending on who we were meeting.

These early conversations were primarily about gathering information that would help Skank to fit in and make more contacts – where to go for authentic Caribbean food, where to shop for stylish, warmer clothes, where to find the shebeens and gambling dens.

At the end of our first week together, Skank took me to a crack house on the Milton Court estate in Deptford which was being run by a guy called Claudie, another friend of his from Jamaica.

The estate consisted of a handful of high-rise buildings, each looking as if it had been carved out of a single breeze-block, interspersed with rows of two-storey terraced houses with tiny gardens. It might have been nice when it was built but it had rapidly turned into a litter-strewn, graffiti-riddled, piss-soaked squalid mess. Just walking through the place made me tense up. I expected the crack den to be just the same but once we got into the heavily fortified flat, past the guard on the door and went through to Claudie's living room I found myself in an oasis of calm. The walls were painted pastel blue and hung with beautiful scenes of Caribbean landscapes enhanced by the soft lighting. But despite the tasteful décor, it was still a crack house and a regular stream of customers knocked at the metal door to receive their wraps of rock through a small flap.

The crack itself was being prepared in the kitchen in several large frying pans, which were being monitored by Claudie, a thin, tall man with a baseball cap covering his shaved head. Crack isn't a new drug, it's simply a new way of taking a very old one. It is made by dissolving cocaine in water, mixing it with baking powder and heating the result. Once the water has boiled away, the magnolia-coloured substance left behind is crack.

The reason for the drug's infamy is its high potency. Cocaine bought on the street is generally 30 per cent pure at most, mixed with anything from washing powder to salt to boost a dealer's profits. The process of manufacturing crack removes many of these impurities, leaving a product that is somewhere between 80 and 100 per cent pure. That, combined with the fact that the drug is smoked rather than snorted, allowing it to get into the bloodstream faster which gives users a more intense high, means the end result is almost literally mind blowing. The intense euphoria is accompanied by an exaggerated sense of well-being but can wear off in as little as twelve minutes to be replaced by feelings of depression and anxiety. The only way to get rid of these is to take more crack, hence the drug's reputation for being instantly addictive. Side effects include sleeplessness, hallucinations, tremors and convulsions; most commonly, paranoid delusions can lead to violent behaviour.

Although I'd seen people smoke cannabis and I'd arrested dozens of people who were off their heads on anything from heroin to ecstasy, it was only in the crack house that I first saw someone take the drug. It wasn't an experience I relished.

Claudie and Skank were busy chatting in the kitchen so I sat on a sofa in the living room and, with a television flickering away quietly in the corner, watched one of Claudie's regulars, a guy called Bucky, take his first fix of the evening. Bucky was so skinny his chest seemed to cave inwards. His skin was extremely dark and shiny, his cheap clothes way too big for him and his hair shockingly unkempt. He had handed over his money – £20 – and in return was given a lump of crack the size of a large garden pea. He squatted in a corner opposite where I was sitting and shaved off a few fragments of his rock with a Stanley knife. The knife itself had two blades taped together, an ideal ghetto 'revenge' weapon because it causes wounds that are almost impossible to stitch back together.

He saw me looking at him. 'You can't have none, not unless you gonna buy more,' he said firmly.

I shook my head. 'Don't worry, I'm here on business, not pleasure.'

'You ever take crack before?'

I shook my head.

'Didn't think so,' said Bucky. 'From the look of you, I don't think you could handle it. If you'd never touched drugs before in your life, then taking crack would do to your mind what lying in bed for a year then running a marathon would do to your body. It would be too much. With coke, it's a subtle sensation, you know what I mean, not so much a high but a feeling of super-awareness. Some people can take coke and miss the buzz. But with crack there's never any mistake. If coke is, say, 5 per cent, crack takes you all the way. It's a heavy-duty rush.'

Out of his pocket Bucky dug a miniature vodka bottle which had the bottom knocked out and a piece of metal gauze tightly stuffed into the neck. He pushed the shavings of crack into the gauze, put the bottom of the bottle to his lips and then, using a lighter, lit the other end and inhaled a big lungful of the swirling mist that formed inside the bottle. He held it for a moment or two and then blew out, sending clouds of smoke spinning around his body.

As the rush hit him, he looked over and smiled at me again, but this time his eyes were completely unfocused. Elsewhere in the room, two other users were smoking their own makeshift crack pipes and one young white girl was getting ready to inject herself, mixing small amounts of crack with warm water and drops of lemon juice to make it soluble.

Claudie finished cooking up the day's batch and came into the living room, followed closely by Skank. Claudie loaded up a pipe and began to smoke but Skank declined. 'When I was addicted to crack, I was addicted big time. Whatever money I had, ten dollar, twenty dollar, thousand dollar, I would use it all up. All you can do is binge. It's like an orgasm only stronger, much stronger. Sex doesn't come into it. You don't want sex. You don't want nothing. Just more crack. You do anything. Carve up a woman, kill a man, anything to get the money. Now I know to leave it alone.'

Over the next hour, Skank and I watched Claudie, Bucky and the others swing between narcotic bliss and coke-induced paranoia as their short-lived crack highs ended and they were left lingering in the real world before they could prepare their next hit. During those times, they'd all look at me accusingly and ask me who I was. A few minutes after I had told them, they would ask me again, and then again. The aura of violence that goes hand in hand with crack use hung over the room.

The same sense of menace was with us everywhere we went, often emanating from Skank himself. The most amazing thing about genuine Yardies, when you get up close to them, is that they are often not physically big men. What they do have, though, is real charisma and an ability to switch on the side of their personality that causes terror in their fellow men.

Skank and I always got on well but the dark side of his character was never too far from the surface. One time we were in a club in Dalston at two in the morning, standing by the bar chatting, when a man cut between us, trying to get a drink.

He was a big bloke, taller and wider than both of us. 'Excuse me,' I said. 'We're trying to have a chat here. Do you mind?'

The guy just looked at me, then turned back to the bar.

Skank gently tapped him on the shoulder and stared at him. There was something in Skank's eyes that was just plain scary, especially when he talked with that accent.

'In Jamaica you'd be dead now, cutting across people like that.'

There was a pause. The guy looked at Skank and saw his eyes were dead. No fear.

'Yeah,' Skank continued. 'You know you'd be dead now, don't you?'

'I don't want no trouble, brother,' said the man sensing Skank's violent tendencies. 'I'm just trying to get a drink. I'm sorry. I'll get out of your way.' And he did, knowing it wasn't worth his while to argue.

Because all his best contacts never seemed to be available until the early hours of the morning – they were either sleeping or out selling drugs during other times – being with Skank was turning into a full-time job and then some. It wasn't quite twenty-four hours a day but most days it felt like it. He didn't seem to like spending time on his own. I could understand it at first when he didn't really know his way around London but even as he became more familiar with the city, he still preferred to have me there to ferry him around. I think he liked the idea of having his own driver and someone on hand to sort out his daily routine.

It might have been good for him but it was hell for me. My family life really suffered during the operation with Skank. Although for security reasons he never knew where I lived, Skank had two ways of contacting me. There was the number of my covert mobile phone and also a second land line, known as a Cascade phone, that I'd had installed at home. While a mobile number is fine for most occasions, there are times when villains need to be reassured that the undercover officer has a house in a certain area. The covert land lines fitted by SO10 can have an area code from any part of London, regardless of where the officer lives. Like the mobiles, they are registered to false names and addresses. I had to keep the Cascade phone hidden away so that my son couldn't answer it and give the game away.

Skank would ring at all times, day or night, and I'd usually have to rush out of the house minutes after he called to go and join him somewhere. My son was just coming up to two years old and I really felt I was missing seeing him growing up. On a number of occasions my wife, Joanne, accused me of caring more about my job than I did about her and the phrase 'It's that sodding Jamaican again' became her mantra every time the covert phone rang at some ungodly hour.

More than once I had to leave the house in the middle of the night because Skank had received a call from a contact, had to go to a 4 a.m. meeting and didn't know how to get there.

'Get a cab,' I'd say.

'Philip, man like me don't take no cab. I need my driver. Get over here.'

From SO10's point of view, however, the job was going well. Skank and I had weekly briefings with Chris Taylor or Donald Matthews and others during which he would pass on the intelligence he had gathered and talk about who he was planning to target in the coming week.

There was usually little I could add. Because I was posing as only a low-ranking member of Skank's gang, it was difficult for me to hang around and listen in whenever he started discussing 'business'. Although Skank would reference me as a stand-up guy, a top member of his team, at the end of the day he was the one who was known in the underworld circles in which we were trying to mix.

'These boys are headstrong,' he would tell me, explaining why I had to wait in the car or sit at the other end of the room while he discussed business with one of his contacts. 'They don't come here for to mix an' mingle. No time for rap, no time for laughing, no time for socializing. The only thing they come here for is to earn plenty dollars and to get themselves bigged up.'

Sometimes I'd hear snippets of conversation, though. There was a deal to buy twenty kilos of cocaine being shipped over from

Colombia; another involving a batch of handguns that had been stolen from a shooting club, complete with ammunition. One time I watched from across a bar as Skank flicked through a sample of counterfeit American Express travellers' cheques.

I mentioned my concerns to Chris Taylor a couple of times but there wasn't really much I could say. After all, Skank appeared to be doing exactly what we had brought him over to do – make contacts, work up a little gang of his own and get into a position where he'd be able to make buys from other Yardies.

Even so, I couldn't help the suspicion that not all the deals that were being set up were then being cancelled at the last moment, as per his instructions from SO10, and that not every contact that he made or every new fact he uncovered was being reported back to his handler. Skank may have been on our side, but I suspected he was still very much working for himself.

I had not set foot in my CID office for almost two months when my guvnor paged me out of the blue.

'Where the fuck are you?' he screamed when I called him back. 'Why the fuck aren't you at your desk?'

'Come on, guv, you know I can't tell you.'

His voice grew even louder. 'What the fuck are you talking about? I'm a fucking detective just like you. Why can't you tell me what you're doing? Are you saying I'm untrustworthy? You're the one who can't be trusted, not when it comes to coming into the office and doing your work. You might think you're some hot shit undercover bod but I want to see you in the office tomorrow morning.'

I arrived at the office the following morning and the shouting began almost immediately. 'Three months! You've been away for three fucking months. I can't believe it. What about all your work? It won't get done on its own, will it? How the fuck am I supposed to run this office if there's no one in it?'

I just let it wash over me. 'I hear you, guv,' I said calmly. 'And I know you're angry, but your argument's not really with me, is it? It's just because you can't tell the SO10 superintendent to fuck off so you're taking it out on me instead. That's basically it, isn't it?'

He paused for a second, considering what I'd said. 'That's not the fucking point. When are you coming back?'

'I'll tell you what, guv. If you let me use your phone, I'll try and find out.' I called up Chris Taylor and explained my guvnor's concerns.

'Tell him to fuck off,' said Chris. 'You're a police resource. We need you.'

I could see myself being drawn into the middle of a massive argument and I decided to do the decent thing: to step aside and let the two of them get on with it. 'Actually, Chris, you can tell him yourself, he's sitting right here.'

Chris jumped at the challenge. 'Yeah. Fucking put him on the phone.'

For the next ten minutes I sat and stared out of the window. I could hear a succession of increasingly angry exchanges being traded down the phone: 'No, *you* fucking listen', 'No, *you* fuck off'. Finally my guvnor slammed the phone down. I turned to see him looking sad and dejected.

'You've got two more weeks,' he said softly, running his fingers through the remains of his red thatch. Then his old voice returned. 'But for fuck's sake, pop in every now and then. Do some work. Otherwise the whole fucking office is going to go undercover and I'll be here on my own. It's a fucking nightmare. Now get out of my office.'

Later that same day Skank called me up. 'Philip, I'm fed up with living in a hotel. I mean, it's all very nice and everything, but I am supposed to be a man of stature. I need my own flat.'

I put it to Chris Taylor who agreed that he had probably stayed at the hotel as long as he could and that, in theory, it would be cheaper to move him into a flat.

Again, for the sake of security, there had to be nothing to show any police involvement in the property. As part of my fake background for SO 10, I had a CV made up saying that I had a job as a TV researcher with a fictitious company. The telephone numbers both for my supposed current employer and for the referees all went back to the SO 10 call centre at Scotland Yard.

When a call came through I would get paged and then phone the estate agents back. 'I'm just out of the office at the moment,' I would say, 'How can I help?'

After two days of searching, I found a brand-new fourth-floor, two-bedroom flat at Phoenix Court in Docklands. It was beautiful. Stripped-wood floors with ceiling-height windows all along one wall providing a fantastic view of the Thames. The living room was bigger than my entire house and had a metal spiral staircase beside the state-of-the-art kitchen which led up to a balcony with two bedrooms on either side. The furnishings were a mixture of black ash and soft leather. The cost – £550 per week – was immediately approved and Skank moved in the following day.

After two and a half months, Skank had found his feet and we saw a lot less of each other, much to my wife's relief. He got picked up by the police a couple of times for minor traffic offences and I had to be on hand to make sure he produced his documents and sorted it all out but other than that, I was starting to move on to other jobs.

He called me one day. 'Listen, bredren. I'm supposed to be setting up my own little gang, putting together deals and mixing with all these bad guys, right?'

'Yes, that's right.'

'OK. Good. Well, if I'm going to do that properly, I need to have myself a bodyguard. Every man in my position would have one. Someone who looks the part, you know what I mean?'

'Sounds like you've already got someone in mind.'

'Name is Junior. I know him from Kingston, worked for me out there. He's a real bad man, has been in lots of fights. He has the machete scars to prove it.'

'Ever killed anybody?'

'No one . . .' he paused, 'that I know.' And again. 'Well, no one that I know all that well.'

After getting clearance from SO10, I used my 'company' credit card to book Junior a flight to London. Skank met him at the airport alone. The following day I called the Docklands flat to make sure everything was OK. The man who answered had a voice I didn't recognize, a voice so low that it sounded as though he was growling rather than speaking and laced with thick Jamaican tones.

'Is that 5687?'

'Yeah.'

'Is Skank there?'

'Yeah.'

'You must be Junior. I'm Philip. How you doing?'

Silence.

'Hello, you still there?'

'Yeah.'

Then Skank came on the line.

'He doesn't say much, does he?'

'Nah. He's a man who prefers action to words. I can't talk now. I'll call you later. Bye.'

By May I had not spoken to Skank for almost three months. But I'd completed my part in the operation, familiarizing him with London, and he and Junior had been left to their own devices to build up contacts with gangs. Apart from a weekly debriefing session at Scotland Yard with his handler, DS Donald Matthews, where Skank would give the who, what and when of Yardie activity in the capital, the police had no contact with him at all. He was still in his flat, still on £500 a week and still claiming expenses.

On the last day of the month, a ragga pay party was taking place at a disused warehouse in Nottingham. A dozen gun salutes had been fired into the ceiling during the course of the evening so no one was too concerned when shots were heard once more just before 3.30 a.m. The song playing was 'Deportee' by rapper Buju Banton, a vicious snipe at Yardies who go to England or America to make their fortune but end up deported back to Jamaica with nothing more than the clothes they stand up in to live 'like dogs', and always provoked a strong reaction. Banton, who had earlier caused controversy with his big club hit 'Boom Bye Bye' which called for gay men to be executed, even received death threats.

But as the sound of gunshots echoed throughout the club, the music was suddenly switched off and a man climbed on the stage and snatched the microphone away from the DJ. 'We are the Seek and Destroy Posse,' he said in his Kingston accent while holding a Uzi sub-machine gun high in the air. 'We are here to seek and destroy.' He was quickly joined by four other men carrying handguns and every one of the 150 party guests was then robbed of credit cards, cash, mobile phones and jewellery, right down to the rings on their fingers.

The women were targeted first and offered little resistance other than the odd complaint and curse. When it came to the turn of the men, one was foolish enough to try to make a stand. The villain with the Uzi didn't miss a beat. He shot him in the leg. 'Bleed, pussy, bleed,' he jeered as his victim writhed in agony on the floor. Two other men were viciously pistol whipped until the message finally got through – give graciously and walk away unhurt.

It took a week before detectives in Nottingham discovered the identity of the gunman. It was Aldridge Clarke, the first Yardie informant, and at the time of the robbery he was still on the Met's payroll.

It soon emerged that the robbery was not his only crime. Clarke was also running a number of protection rackets, extorting money from black businesses across south London, selling crack on a regular basis and running a string of prostitutes. The only time he would ever go unarmed was when he was meeting his police handlers.

Clarke wasn't the only one. A short time later Jamaican-born Delroy Denton, otherwise known as 'Epsi', was sentenced to life imprisonment for murder. His victim, twenty-four-year-old Marcia Lawes, had been raped then stabbed seventeen times in the neck and once in the heart. At the trial, where Denton was described as a 'sex-fuelled psychopath', it also emerged that at the time of the offence, he too was a registered police informer. Like Aldridge Clarke, Denton had been 'turned' by the police after being caught in a raid at the Atlantic pub in Brixton carrying a knife and some cocaine. Back in Kingston he had served jail sentences of up to eight years for shootings and robberies.

Clarke's record was even worse. When his informer file was eventually released, whole sections had been removed, supposedly accidentally shredded. One report revealed that when Scotland Yard had sent him to Holland on an intelligence-gathering mission he had used a Uzi sub-machine gun to rob other dealers. After he was convicted of the Nottingham robbery, Clarke confessed to eleven execution-style killings back in Jamaica, one of them supposedly on the orders of a senior Jamaican politician.

It was soon after the story of Aldridge Clarke broke in the newspapers that I got a call from the property company. Skank and Junior had moved out leaving hundreds of pounds in unpaid bills. I tried the numbers for their mobile phones but they had both been disconnected.

To this day, their whereabouts are unknown.

5

Martin: I was wearing an £800 Hugo Boss suit, handmade Italian shoes, a Paul Smith shirt and a Jasper Conran tie. It was one of those jobs where having the right look was essential and the second I stepped into the lobby of the Kensington Hilton, I knew that my efforts had been worthwhile. You could almost smell the wealth hanging in the air and I blended in perfectly.

I'd been assigned to infiltrate a gang of high-class fraudsters who were blitzing their way across the South East, conning banks and building societies out of tens of thousands of pounds. They would set up accounts using fake names and references and make regular payments in and out for a few months until they had built up a credit rating. They would then apply for a large loan, withdraw all the money and vanish. They'd become so successful that they were now urgently looking for someone to launder their profits and I was posing as a businessman with dodgy connections who, for a slice of the action, would be willing to help them out.

I knew nothing about fraud and even less about money laundering but that didn't matter – I was just kicking the job off as the first undercover officer the gang would meet. All I had to do was gain their trust, find out exactly what they were after and then introduce them to the next man in the chain. That was Max, an SO10 officer who had joined the police after a career in the City. He understood the financial world inside out and was going to play the role of a bent bank manager. He'd be the one to draw the gang right in and line them up for the final bust. In the meantime, if they asked me any awkward questions, I'd just tell them to wait to talk to my 'boss'.

It should have been a fairly straightforward job but things hadn't started well. During my first phone call with the two main targets, Steve and Mo, it became clear that they would be calling all the shots. 'We're based in Kensington,' Steve told me firmly. 'If you want to do business with us, you come to Kensington. If you don't come to Kensington, there's not going to be a deal. We won't be interested. Period. When it comes to business, we're like a couple of little kids me and Mo – we don't talk to strangers. The truth is, if Leo hadn't recommended you, we wouldn't be talking to you at all. We wouldn't be wasting our time.'

Leo was a close associate of the gang, a man who specialized in producing fake IDs and ripping off credit cards. He had worked on and off with Steve and Mo for several years but I got the distinct impression that, while they tolerated him, they didn't really consider him much of a friend, not someone they could rely on 100 per cent.

Their suspicions were well founded. A few weeks earlier Leo had been arrested while trying to pass a stolen cheque for £15,000 through a bank account he'd set up with fake references. When police searched his house they found hundreds of cheque books, credit cards, passports and driving licences, all of them in different names. The truth was that none of them belonged to him – he was simply holding them for Steve and Mo – but with a string of previous convictions as long as both his arms, no jury in the land was ever going to believe that. Leo was in deep shit and he knew it.

Prison was inevitable, but if he turned stool pigeon and ratted out some of the people he worked with there was a good chance he would end up serving only a couple of months rather than a good few years. He spilled his guts to the detectives who made the initial arrest and, once it was established that his information was genuine, SO10 were brought in to bust the gang from the inside by catching them red-handed.

Normally Leo would have been there with me at the first meeting to make the introductions in person, but he was banged up in Wormwood Scrubs and no one wanted to risk giving him bail. Instead, we devised a plan whereby he would call up the targets, apologize for having lost their merchandise in the raid and offer to set them up with a team of money launderers as a way of making amends. It's pretty standard practice in criminal circles. If you're holding items on someone else's behalf or you're a courier transporting someone else's drugs and you get arrested you have to offer something to make up for it, even if you're in prison at the time, especially if you ever want to work for the same gang again.

In order to pose as one of Leo's associates, I needed a convincing background story to explain how the two of us knew one another and that meant sitting down with him for a couple of hours to find some common reference points. I didn't really fancy showing my face in the visiting room of the Scrubs so I arranged for him to be smuggled out to Brixton police station and went to see him there.

Set back from the main road on a small triangular plot off Canterbury Crescent, Brixton nick looks like an ageing secondary school block, its once-pristine fascia crumbling under the onslaught of traffic fumes from the permanent gridlock outside. I went in through the double glass doors, flashed my warrant card at the front desk and was buzzed through the security door. I made my way straight up to the CID office where the informant and his handler were waiting for me in an interview room.

I don't usually make snap character judgements, but the instant I met Leo I disliked him intensely. He was a real weasel of a man, skinny with long, bony fingers and an annoyingly wispy goatee beard that made me want to grab the nearest razor and get rid of it. On top of that there was his whining nasal voice – he couldn't have been more of a spiv.

'Great to meet you, Martin. This is going to be cool. This is going to be so fucking cool,' he told me as we shook hands. 'You won't have any problems. I'm going to make the call right now. I'm going to tell them that you're a good friend of mine and that I've known you for a couple of years, that we've done a bit of work together every now and then, that I've sold you a couple of cars, shit like that. I'll tell them that I vouch for you 100 per cent.'

'OK. That all sounds fine. But don't make it seem like I'm the one with all the expertise. Say I'm a go-between, that I've got connections, that I'm a representative of someone else but that all the work has to go through me.'

'Sure, sure thing, Martin. I can do that. I'll tell them we've done some ducking and diving, a bit of bobbing and weaving, that sort of thing, that you do a lot of business in town, you're a stand-up guy. Yeah man, trust me, it will be really cool.'

I wanted to tell him that in my experience, the words 'trust' and 'informant' didn't belong in the same sentence, but I thought better of it.

'So,' Leo continued, wiping his nose noisily on the sleeve of his prison issue shirt. 'Let me give you the full SP on our mutual friends. You won't believe some of the stuff they've got up to in the past. Steve's all right but Mo's a right fucking psycho. There was one time when . . .'

I held up my hand to signal him to stop talking. 'Listen, Leo. I don't want to know about it. I'm not interested. I don't care how tasty they are, how many people they've cut up or killed. I don't give a shit about what they do or what they've done. It's just not important.' Leo looked almost hurt. There was clearly some horrendous story of gangland brutality that he was dying to relate and holding it in was killing him.

It's standard SO 10 procedure that officers going undercover learn as little as possible about the people they are targeting. The reason is clear: the more you know about someone, the more you'll end up thinking about it, even if it's only at the back of your mind. If an undercover officer sitting with a guy, pretending to be relaxed and talking business, has been told that the target always keeps a gun down the side of his boot, he will find it nearly impossible not to flinch if the guy suddenly gets an itch on his leg and reaches down to scratch it. And then the guy's going to ask, 'What are you so jumpy about?' That kind of instinctive reaction could jeopardize an entire operation so it's better that you don't know in the first place.

There's a similar problem when it comes to identifying the targets. Often undercover officers will be given pictures of them beforehand so that they can ensure they're dealing with the right people. But, obviously, they are not supposed to know what their targets look like and have to remember to ask how they will recognize them at the first meeting.

'The only thing I need to know is what they are into now and how to pitch things to get them to take me on.'

Leo shrugged. 'The main thing with Steve and Mo is that they're very, very cagey. You don't want to do anything to ruffle their feathers. And you don't want to go in too big.'

'What do you mean by too big? What sort of amount are we talking about?' I asked.

Leo scratched his chin for a moment. I was comforted to see that he was putting some genuine thought into his advice. 'They are going to have all these dodgy bank accounts full of dirty money. What they want to do is to give you a cheque for some of it and for you to give them back clean cash, minus your commission of course. If it was me dealing with them for the first time, I wouldn't go any bigger than three and a half grand for the first cheque. Tell them that you'll do that as a test and if it goes OK, then you'll put the amount up.'

'Right. Three and a half grand it is. If you're sure.'

'Yeah, definitely. I know these guys, Martin. If you go in too big, they'll just get suspicious. They'll freeze up. You can't overstep the mark. They just won't deal with you at all. It's not like they're heavy or anything, they are just very, very careful. They spook easily. You have to pitch things to them just right.'

All that was foremost in my mind as I walked through the revolving doors into the hotel's lobby. It was pretty warm outside, T-shirt weather, but I had decided to keep my jacket on because it made me look more professional. Once inside, I knew there would be air conditioning and I'd need it anyway. I walked past the hotel's reception desk and turned right past the lifts out into the café area. Against the backdrop of ceiling-high windows and a small circular bar were dozens of sets of wooden tables and cloth-covered arm-chairs. The place was almost empty so I spotted the targets immediately. Steve, the bigger of the two, was in his late thirties with a pencil-thin moustache. He was a wearing a dark suit with a crisp white shirt and his hair was so short you could see his scalp. As he sat there, casually eating olives from a bowl on the table, I noticed there was a gold ring on every one of his fingers and a thick silver bracelet hanging from his wrist.

Sitting alongside was Mo. He looked like a wannabe Steve, dressed almost identically but with slightly less jewellery and considerably more hair. Mo looked Mediterranean and I later found out that he was a Cuban with connections to some of the big drug smuggling gangs operating out of Florida. They were deep in conversation but as I got closer, Steve caught my eye and gave me a small nod. Then he got up from his seat and moved to one right alongside it.

And at that moment I started to panic. I knew that the job was going to be a disaster, that I would be lucky to get away without getting my cover blown or having my head kicked in. If they hadn't already seen me, I would have turned and walked away. I considered carrying on straight past them, pretending I was meeting someone else but there was no one around. I was stuck. I had to go through with it.

It wasn't the prospect of talking to Steve and Mo, it wasn't the fear of failure or what they might have got up to in the past. It was the way they were sitting. Steve was on my right, Mo was on my left and bang in the middle was an empty chair. The chair they wanted me to sit in. I remember walking towards it, staring at it, trying to move it with my eyes. I didn't want to sit there, I just couldn't let myself sit there. But there was nowhere else to go. And as I got closer and closer, all I could think of was something that had happened while I was on the undercover course a year or so earlier. An experience that had come back to haunt me.

We were just three days into training when I got picked to take part in a big role-playing exercise. The scenario was that a bunch of hardcore animal rights activists had launched a letter bomb campaign against various scientists involved in vivisection. The regional crime squad had arrested someone on the periphery of the campaign and they had turned informer, offering an introduction to some of the more senior activists. SO10's job was to meet with the heads of the gang and gain their trust with a view to sabotaging the bombing operation.

There was a quick class discussion about the most effective way to go about such a task and we agreed it would be best to pose as a couple rather than have one person going in alone. A female officer on the course, Helen, was picked to play my girlfriend and the two of us trooped down to the main car park in the Hendon police training school where the exercise was to take place.

Although you know it's only make-believe, the role-playing exercises are taken deadly seriously. The bad guys are always played by experienced undercover officers who have been out in the field and know the mistakes you're likely to make and the problems you're most likely to come up against. They play their parts with total conviction and you have to do the same otherwise you learn nothing. And at the end of the day, that's what the job's all about. If you can't stay in character in the safety of a police car park, you won't last five minutes out on the street.

Helen and I started walking towards a big white Transit van parked opposite the main building alongside the fence. We'd been told beforehand that the vehicle had been fitted with an open mike, a tiny radio transmitter, linked back to the classroom so that the instructor and our ten remaining fellow students could hear everything that went on. It was my first big test and I relished the challenge.

As we got closer to the van, the driver, a young white guy with straggly blond hair down to his shoulders and a tatty green army jacket, wound down the window and poked his head out. 'Who the fuck is that?' he said, pointing at Helen.

It totally threw me. 'She's . . . she's just my girlfriend,' I stuttered.

'Well, get rid of her. I don't like the look of her.'

'What?'

'Get rid of her or piss off.'

'Ah, come on mate,' I said, getting into character. 'We've come a long way. We do everything together. We always have. She's all right. She's just as much a part of the movement as I am.'

Helen joined in. 'I'm not going anywhere. You can't just keep me out of this. He'll only tell me about it later anyway.'

The driver completely ignored Helen and carried on talking to me. 'Are you deaf or something, mate?' he asked. 'Either she fucks off or I do.'

It was a delicate situation. Helen was there as my back-up and to corroborate the meeting. If he wasn't prepared to deal with her I had to push as hard as I could to get her to stay but not risk losing the job altogether. As I stood there thinking what to do, the driver started up his engine. 'Well you've obviously made up your mind. I'm off. See ya.'

I'd backed myself into a corner. If I was going to keep the job going, I had no choice but to do what he asked. 'Whoa. Wait up. OK, OK.' I turned to Helen. 'You'd better go, love. I'll catch you later.' Helen stamped her feet in frustration, turned round and set off back to the classroom, leaving me alone. Once she was out of earshot, the driver switched off and waved me round to the passenger door. 'Get in, I ain't saying shit in the middle of the street.'

The second my fingers touched the handle, the sliding door towards the back of the van flew open and out jumped this enormous black guy wearing a full-length leather trench coat. It was as it he'd appeared from nowhere and he scared the shit out of me. 'Yeah, get in the van!' he screamed. 'Get in the fucking van right now!'

That was twice they'd got the jump on me but the worst was still to come. I numbly climbed in, still shaking with surprise, and the black man got in beside me and shut the door. And that's when it hit me. I'd walked right into their trap. There I was, sitting in the cab of this van with both exits blocked, in between two massive blokes. I felt a complete idiot. I couldn't believe I'd let myself get into such a vulnerable position. But there was nothing I could do, I just had to stick it out.

And then the questions started.

'Who are you?' said one.

'I'm Martin, I . . .'

'Where do you come from? Where do you live?' said the other.

'Well, I don't see how that's got anything to do with what we're doing here, I . . .'

'What are you doing here? What do you want?'

They weren't even giving me time to answer. It had been only a few seconds but I was already starting to panic. I had to fight to concentrate and stay in control. 'I was told you guys were doing some business and . . .'

'Who told you that? Who told you about us?' asked the black guy.

'What the fuck do you know about our business?' asked the driver. 'Who put you in touch with us?'

'Well Pete Duncan said . . .'

'Pete Duncan?' The black guy shook his head. 'Never heard of him.'

'That's a new one on me. I think you just made it up,' agreed the driver. 'Who are you again?'

I tried to say something but the black guy cut in straight away. 'I don't like this. I don't feel comfortable with you. You could be anyone. I don't know you from Adam. You come here talking about our business, giving names of people we don't know. I want to know more about you. What does your wife do?'

'I'm not married.'

The black guy grabbed my left hand in an iron grip and held it up to the windscreen. 'Not married. Then what you got a fucking wedding ring on for?'

I'd stupidly forgotten to take my ring off before the exercise. 'I . . . I . . .'

'You're lying, you're fucking lying to me, ain't ya? Don't you tell me no lies, son.'

For the next twenty minutes the questions just kept coming and kept coming. There was barely time to draw breath. They were playing it as bad cop and badder cop. I felt like a kebab: I'd been grilled, now they were just slicing away.

'What have you ever done for the campaign?' said the black guy. 'Tell me one thing you've done, tell me one person you've worked with.'

I was going to pick the first name that came into my head but my mind went blank. I knew that anything I said would be wrong. I knew I'd lost it.

'You can't say nothing because you're a phoney,' said the driver. 'You don't belong here. I don't know what you're trying to pull but you'd better fuck off before I lose my temper.'

I crawled back to the classroom with my tail between my legs. Everyone cheered when I opened the door and foul-mouthed Floyd jumped forward, eager to be the first to share his opinion: 'Fuck me,' he said, 'you really fucked that one up, didn't you, mate? You must be fucking gutted. I fucking would be.'

Once the laughter subsided, the instructor, Ken, made me stand up in front of the rest of the class to be debriefed. 'You know where you went wrong, don't you?' he asked. 'You let yourself get in the middle. Once you did that, you were trapped. There was no way out. It was a set-up from the start. They wanted to get you in the middle so they could give you a good grilling. Once you sat down between them it was all over bar the shouting.'

For the next two hours we listened to the tape again and again, going through every single one of my mistakes. I spent the whole time cringing. It was completely humiliating but at least I'd learned my lesson. 'Don't worry, Martin,' said Ken. 'Sometimes it's the best way to learn. At least that's one mistake you'll never make again.'

Ken's words echoed in my head as I got closer to Steve and Mo and that empty chair. I could have fetched another one from somewhere else and sat on that, but the nearest was at least fifteen feet away and then I'd look as if I had something to hide. All I could do was walk right into the lions' den and hope for the best.

Steve did all the talking and his questions started the second I sat down. 'So you're Martin,' he said. 'And you're a friend of Leo, are you?'

'Yeah. That's right. I guess I must have known him a couple of years now. Maybe friends is the wrong word, but I know the guy, we've done the odd bit of business together.'

'And what kind of business is that?'

I was trying to gauge the tone of Steve's voice. He was well spoken but there was still a touch of aggression and a lot of frustration, as if he felt he had better things to do. 'Well, mostly I buy and sell cars,' I replied.

'So what good is that to me? I don't know why you're here. I've got a car. I didn't come here to meet some fucking used car salesman.'

'Look, you and I both know that there's other business that you two are involved in and I . . .'

'What the fuck do you know about our business?' snapped Steve. 'Who have you been talking to?'

'Well, Leo told me about . . .'

'Leo? Leo don't know shit about nothing. The only people who know about our business is me and Mo. That's the way we like to keep it. So tell me, what do you know about our business?'

I was answering his questions but not really answering them. I was trying to bat everything off and Steve just kept probing deeper and deeper. My worst fears were coming home to roost. 'Listen mate, there's no point in having a go at me,' I said. 'Don't shoot the messenger. I'm just trying to do you a favour. I was told you could use some help with your finances.'

Steve was staring at me as I spoke, looking right through me. 'I ain't your mate. I don't know the first thing about you. Where do you live?'

'What?'

'Oh great. Deaf as well as stupid. I said where do you live? I want to know where you live. You know, one of those house things with a roof and windows.'

'What's that got to do with anything?'

'I'm just interested. Indulge me.'

'It's not important.'

'I see. So you want me to trust you with my business but you won't trust me with your address. Well, you can just forget the whole thing.'

'All right. I live down in Brixton, for what it's worth.' I picked Brixton because I'd spent some time working in the area when I was in uniform and knew it well. From what he'd said on the phone before we'd met, I was counting on the fact that it wouldn't be the sort of place he'd go to very often. 'Just off the Atlantic Road. It's an OK area.'

'Brixton. I don't know anyone from that part of town,' he said. 'Don't you know anyone round here? Someone I know? Someone I've worked with?'

'Listen, Steve, I don't really like discussing other people's business without their permission. I don't like it when people do that to me.'

'Fair enough. I'll tell you what. Let me have your home number, I'll call you there tonight,' said Steve.

One of the problems with being the first man in on a job is that you have very little back-up. You are only supposed to be there for one or two brief meetings and then hand things on. If you're in place for a longer run, you would probably set yourself up with a flat somewhere, have another officer posing as a wife or girlfriend. Then you'd be able to give people a number, tell them to meet you somewhere and come across as a real person. As first man in, you're forced to keep your distance.

'No way. I don't work like that,' I replied.

'What? You afraid to give me your number? What you hiding from us? Where do you really live?'

'Listen, I'm here to do business, right? Do you guys want to do business or what?'

'Yeah, we want to do business. That's our thing. We live to do business. It's just that right now, I'm not sure if we want to do business with you. You could be anybody. You could be anything.'

'That's just words. You don't know me – so what? I don't know you. I'm only here because Leo put me in touch, said there might be something in this for me.'

Steve leaned back in his chair. 'Tell me again, how exactly do you know Leo?'

There wasn't much to tell but I tried to give as much detail as I could. Luckily, Leo had some friends in Brixton so the story was that we'd met in a pub there one night, that we'd just got chatting after he'd asked me for a light. We'd realized we both did a bit of shady business and eventually hooked up for a few jobs. We saw each other every now and then, hung out, went drinking and clubbing but mostly it was about business.

When I finished, Steve seemed a little more relaxed but I felt more uncomfortable than ever. I was half turned to the left in my seat, looking directly at Steve. Mo was on the other side of me but he'd pushed his chair back a foot or so. It bugged me that even if I faced forward, I couldn't see what he was getting up to back there. And it was really bothering me that I'd been there for more than fifteen minutes and Mo hadn't said a word the whole time. I tried to put it out of my mind and stayed focused on Steve who slowly seemed to be coming round to the idea that I might be all right.

'OK,' he said thoughtfully. 'Let's just say that I find someone in Brixton who knows you. And let's say that they give you the OK and that I decide to do business with you. What sort of amount can you deal with?'

I looked at Steve long and hard. He was well dressed, well groomed. He was obviously doing very, very well out of his business. Somehow I didn't think the informant had read the situation right at all. Steve was clearly dealing with large amounts of money and £3,500 would probably be small change. I decided to take a chance and up the ante.

'Well, Leo's vouched for you guys but I still don't know you. I wouldn't go any higher than £10,000 for the first cheque.'

Steve exploded into laughter laced with venom. 'Ten grand. Ten fucking grand.' He leaned back on his chair and looked over to Mo. 'Do you hear this guy? Ten grand. Ten fucking grand he says.' Then back at me, 'What are you doing here? Why did you waste your time coming here today, eh? Who the fuck are you? You've got to be taking the piss. Is that what you're trying to do, take the piss out of me?'

I wanted to kick myself. I'd gone too high and made him suspicious. I should have stuck with what Leo had said. It wasn't completely lost though. I could still rescue the situation. I just needed to find a way to go back down to £3,500 without offending them. 'Come on guys, get real. I thought you guys were big time. We can bring it down if you think that's too much.'

'Too much!' Steve's eyes widened until they were the size of saucers. 'Too much!' He grabbed the lapels of my jacket with both hands and pulled me towards him. He spoke slowly and deliberately, pausing between each word, his voice barely more than a whisper. 'I am talking about £750,000 in a single cheque. You hear me? Seven hundred and fifty thousand. And you have the cheek to come here and talk about ten grand. You don't belong here.'

It was then that Mo decided to speak for the first time, his words cutting through me as he set to work on the weakness in my cover. 'What I find strange,' he said in a low drawl with a slight American twang, 'is that I have known Leo for six, maybe seven years. And in all that time, I ain't never seen you.'

I didn't even bother to turn around to look him in the eye before I responded. 'Haven't you? Well, is that my problem, or is that your problem?'

'Right now my friend, it is your problem,' Mo replied, jabbing his index finger into the back of my neck. I could feel his nail digging into the flesh. I felt as if he'd drawn blood.

From then on I had the two of them going at it, giving me a grilling in stereo. Steve still couldn't get over the fact that I thought £10,000 was too much for him. 'Who do you think you're dealing with? What do you think we are? Can't you tell class when you see it?' Mo, on the other hand, was getting weirder by the second. 'Where I come from,' he said, 'we have a thing called *santeria*. Do you know what that is? It's voodoo. Cuban voodoo. We can put spells on people, you know. We can make things happen. Bad things. I'm gonna put a spell on you, Martin.'

I flicked my head round. 'Voodoo. What the fuck are you talking about? Listen man, I ain't having this conversation with you, I'm trying to do some business with Steve.' I was trying to make a last ditch attempt to get the toys back in the pram but the strain was starting to show.

Mo looked me straight in the eyes. 'If I put a curse on you, you could be dead within a week. Maybe even sooner.'

At least we were in public. If we'd been alone, God only knows what they might have done – it was clear that neither would shy away from violence. Mo leaned forward and scrutinized my forehead. 'You're sweating,' he announced. 'You're scared, aren't you?'

I tried to sound as if it was the most ridiculous thing I'd ever heard anyone say. 'Am I? I don't think so.' But I was. Of course I was. I could feel all the beads of sweat queuing up waiting to drop.

Mo spoke again, he was really finding his voice now. 'The other thing I find strange, really strange,' he said, 'is that Leo's in prison. He's been arrested and he's in prison. And all of a sudden, while he's in prison, he comes up with the name of someone who knows him, but who we have never heard of. I find that very, very strange.' I remember thinking to myself, 'Well of course it's strange, you arsehole. It's a fucking set-up. That's why it doesn't make any sense.'

The grilling had been going on for nearly twenty minutes. It was only a matter of time before Steve and Mo came to that conclusion themselves. I had to get out of there. I knew they wouldn't try to stop me, not in public, so I stood up and looked at Mo. 'I don't know who you think you are, talking about voodoo and shit. That ain't no way to do business. You don't want to deal with me? Well, that ain't no problem 'cos I don't want nothing to do with you. Either of you. I'm leaving.' And I stormed off, mustering all the anger and dignity I could manage. Inside it was a different story, I was just relieved to have got out of there in one piece.

I headed straight for Scotland Yard to fill them in. DS Taylor was waiting in the SO10 office. 'Martin. Hi. How did the meeting go?' he asked with a smile.

'Biggest load of shit you ever saw,' I said. 'And as for that informant, you better order an ambulance because I'm going round to the prison right now and I'm going to throttle him. He let me down badly, dumped me right in it. The guys were on to me from the start, they knew there was something. I didn't have a chance. I didn't get anywhere with them. A complete waste of time.'

Chris nodded his head. 'Right. I see. OK. Fine. That's just the way it goes sometimes. Sorry it was a bad meeting though. Anyway, would you mind giving them a quick call and try to get back into them? We really want this job to come off. Maybe if you let them cool off overnight.'

The next day I called Steve's mobile phone. It was answered on the first ring and I recognized the voice instantly. It was Steve. 'Steve, hi it's Martin. How you doing?'

There was a pause. 'If you're after Steve, he's gone away. I'm just looking after his phone for him. I don't know when he's coming back.'

'Look, Steve,' I said, 'I know we kind of got off on the wrong foot but ...'

'I've told you. Steve ain't here. And even if he was here, he wouldn't want to talk to you. You're bad news you are. Don't call this number again.' And he cut me off.

It was the end of my involvement but not the end of SO10's work with Steve and Mo. Like any criminals, they were not about to shut up shop and quit the game just because one deal had fallen through. They simply started looking around for someone else who would be able to launder their profits, so Chris Taylor knew it would only be a matter of time before we got another bite of the cherry.

Leo was totally out of the game. Steve and Mo wouldn't touch him with a bargepole so he was useless. Instead, the squad targeted another minor member of the gang, arrested him and convinced him to introduce a different undercover officer, who in turn introduced our bogus bank manager, Max, to Steve and Mo. Within a month, their entire operation had been closed down and all the main players were behind bars awaiting trial.

6

Philip: Jean might have been approaching middle age but her features were still youthfully soft, her body petite and trim. We had arranged to meet in a mock Tudor pub on the outskirts of Kent and when I spotted her, she gave me a half-smile that lit up her face, and beckoned me over to her table. She seemed uneasy, keen to get right down to business, but having once worked as a nurse, she had this calm, assured way of talking – a way that made you believe everything was going to be OK, that there was nothing to worry about. And that was the voice that this very ordinary mother of two used to tell me, in between tiny sips of white wine, that she wanted me to murder her husband.

The plot had been hatched three weeks earlier as she returned home in a minicab from her weekly 'girls' night out' at a Chiswick bar. Jean always booked the same local firm to take her home to Putney and had become quite friendly and mildly flirtatious with one of the drivers, Perry. As they sped along the banks of the River Thames, their idle conversation inevitably settled on her private life.

'How are things at home?' Perry asked her.

Jean sighed deeply. 'I won't lie to you,' she told him. 'It's worse than ever. I've told Charles that I want to leave him but he won't give me a divorce. He says it's for the sake of the kids but that's just a lie. He won't let me go because he likes to see me suffering. I hate him so much right now, more than ever before. I wish he was dead. Honestly, if I knew I could get away with it, I'd kill him myself.'

Nothing more was said on the matter but two days later, while her kids were still at school, Perry turned up unexpectedly on Jean's doorstep. 'That thing you mentioned in the car,' he whispered over a steaming mug of tea as they sat in her kitchen. 'About getting rid of your old man. The thing is, I know some people. If you're really serious about it, I might know some people who can help you out. I mean, he could just get hit by a bus. It's up to you.'

It had been a particularly bad day. Jean's husband had refused to give her any extra money even though her sister's fortieth birthday was approaching and she wanted to buy her something special. 'I'd love it if the bastard got what was coming to him. That would be better than winning the lottery.'

What Jean didn't know was that Perry was a registered police informer and saw her predicament as a chance to earn himself some brownie points. The minute he got home, he called his police handler and told him everything. That set off a chain reaction that ended with me attending a briefing at Wimbledon station a few hours before Perry had arranged for Jean and I to meet.

Posing as a contract killer is an incredibly delicate task. The biggest danger is that, just by turning up for a meeting with someone, you unintentionally back them into a corner and leave them with no way to back out. It's all too common for people to say the most horrible, hurtful things in the heat of the moment, but that doesn't mean they'd necessarily follow through.

To play the part effectively, you have to look and act as though you are capable of killing someone, as if you've done it dozens of times. But if you do that effectively, it becomes very difficult for the person that you're meeting – who has usually been told that you've had to travel a long way and have gone to a lot of trouble to be there – to tell you that they never really meant it.

There had been a batch of cases at the Court of Appeal in which several people convicted of conspiring to murder their spouses or partners had claimed they had been victims of police entrapment. Each said that they had been intimidated or bullied into making compromising statements after meeting a hitman who turned out to be an undercover police officer. In response, the rules of engagement at SO10 had been tightened up. For us to take things further, Jean would have to leave no doubt that she was prepared to see the murder through to its grisly conclusion.

As Jean was as far from being a hardened criminal as one could imagine, there would be none of the usual precautions: I didn't need a cover story or a back-up team. 'Just try to relax and be yourself,' the detective sergeant in charge of the operation told me when I met him at Wimbledon nick. 'The most important thing is not to push her into anything. Just be businesslike, find out what she wants, what she's willing to pay and just how serious she is.'

'What do you reckon to it from what you've heard?'

'Wouldn't like to put money on it either way. The nark is an ex-little-league blagger, got a fair amount of form but I don't think he makes stuff up for nothing. I'm sure she said to him that she wanted her old man dead, the question is whether she meant it.'

If I could secure solid evidence that Jean was indeed planning to have her husband killed, that she would pay a deposit, assist with the planning and make a final payment after the job had been done, then there would be enough to charge her with conspiracy to commit murder, a serious crime that carried an average prison sentence of between five and ten years. If the first meeting went well, I'd ask her to write down a list of her husband's movements, times and places where he could be found. That would be hard evidence that we could use in court to show a jury that this was more than just an idle notion, that it was a firm plan.

The sergeant and I quickly ran through the latest trends in contract killings – prices, techniques and so on – just so that I would sound realistic. There was always a chance that Jean had made inquiries elsewhere as well and I had to fit in with the rest of the market. 'According to the bods at SO11, the going rate for a hit is ten grand,' he said, reading from a sheet of paper. 'It's been ten grand for years. For some reason, inflation hasn't come to the world of contract killing. You want half the money up front and the other half on completion of the job. No compromises.' And then it was time to get wired up.

People imagine that SO10 has a special cupboard full of incredibly high-tech equipment. Certainly I did before I actually started working for them. When someone talks about getting 'wired up', it conjures up an image of lots of expensive miniaturized recording and surveillance equipment, satellite systems and bugs disguised as buttons, lighters or tie pins. That's about as far from the truth as it is possible to be.

The standard issue bit of kit for covertly taping conversations is the Nagra recorder. The first time I saw one on the training course, I choked so hard I almost swallowed my tongue. At four inches by six and nearly an inch thick, it's like carrying around half a house brick. It's not too bad for the female officers; they can put it inside their purse or, if they're wearing a skirt, it's just about possible to keep it down their knickers. For men, there's only one place it can go. It has to be taped into the small of your back. Once it's in position, the microphones are attached. They are the size of pencil erasers and fit on the end of two long wires attached to the machine. The best place to have them is just above the nipples with the wires trailing over your shoulders and back into the machine.

As Jean wasn't going to be expecting anyone to be taping her, I didn't have to worry about her spotting it, but normally, wearing a Nagra is a real trial. First off, it makes you look like a hunchback. You cannot walk around in a T-shirt, you need something loose that flaps down over your back and conceals the bump. Want to spot a wired-up undercover cop in the summer? He's the one in the trenchcoat when everyone else is in short sleeves.

An undercover officer wearing a Nagra in the small of his back can't afford to let anyone get behind him nor can he bend down for any reason for fear it might show. Most of all, he can't afford to let anyone touch him. In training, one particular situation the officers are taught to watch out for is going through doorways. Lots of people will say 'After you' when they get to a doorway and let the other person go first. And as the other person walks through, they will gently slap their back to see them on their way. Want to spot a wired-up undercover cop going into a pub? He'll be the one letting absolutely everyone else go first.

Nagras record beautifully but that's where all the technological advances begin and end. There's no voice activation and no remote control. The only way to switch the machine on is to click a little hook which sits on top of it. It's an awkward, fiddly move when the Nagra is right in front of you, let alone when it's stuck behind you. It can't be switched on in public without drawing attention to whoever is wearing it so another skill undercover officers have to develop is working out when to start the tape.

Once a Nagra is running, it can't be switched off until the job is completed, not unless the officer using it records the time and reason for switching off and then the time when it's switched on again. But if a recording full of stops and starts is presented in evidence, there's a danger that the case will fall apart the moment it gets to court, no matter what the tape has managed to catch. The defence will claim that anything could have happened during the time the machine was off, so the only safe thing to do is to keep it on all the time.

But that's tricky too because the tapes last only two hours. As soon as the Nagra goes on, the clock starts ticking away. Put the machine on too early and crucial bits of the conversation could be missed when the tape runs out. If an undercover is sitting with a group of villains, talking about nothing in particular, desperately hoping one of them will implicate himself in a crime but he hasn't done so when there's only ten minutes of tape left, the temptation to try to hurry things along is enormous, but it has to be resisted.

It doesn't end there. Once a Nagra has been switched on, there's no way to check whether it's actually running or not. Because it's concealed in the small of the back or somewhere else out of sight, you can't see if the tape is going round at all. The tape can't be taken out and played back to check that everything is working properly because that will taint the evidence and besides there's no play button on the Nagras anyway. They record and that's it.

Throughout the ranks of SO10 there is a regular trade in horror stories of people being at really important meetings with a bunch of dangerous, nasty characters who have been talking about all sorts of amazing things, and getting back to the station only to realize that the machine wasn't working after all or that the tape jammed or that the batteries had run flat.

Then there's the noise. Not while they are recording – thankfully they are almost silent – it's the noise when the tape runs out. All tape recorders make a little click when they shut off and the Nagra is quieter than most, but because you know it's coming and it's attached to your body, you can both hear it and feel it. There have been times when I have been on a job, wearing one, and everything has gone very quiet just at that moment. No one has ever said anything but I always worried that one day someone would.

There is other technology available. Recording equipment can be built into cars or items of luggage, though that only works if you can guarantee that the key conversation is going to occur at a particular place or time. There are also open mikes, miniature radio transmitters the size of a tie pin that come with a tiny battery pack. They work well but you need to have a back-up team in a van fitted with a receiver in order for anything to be picked up. And the van can never be more than 250 metres away. Open mikes are great if the undercover is in a fixed location such as a hotel room, but if they are likely to be on the move, there's nothing quite so flexible or effective as a Nagra. Or at least not yet.

Even if everything works perfectly you're not out of the woods. If the targets start to implicate themselves or say something about a crime that would be good evidence in court, an undercover officer can't ask them to give more information. If they start firing questions and getting the targets to open up, defence lawyers can argue that the conversation constitutes an interview with a police officer. And if a police officer wants to interview someone, they have to read them their rights first. If they haven't done that, then any evidence, no matter how damning, becomes inadmissible.

The most notorious example of this came a few years ago when thirty-nine-year-old mother of two, Patricia Hall, vanished from her home in Pudsey, Leeds on a freezing cold night in January. Although hundreds of people disappear each year, hoping to leave their troubles behind and start over, they almost always leave some kind of trail, take a bunch of personal items with them or stockpile cash beforehand to sustain them. Patricia had done none of these things. She hadn't even taken any warm clothing. Foul play was suspected right from the start.

It didn't take long for the detectives investigating the case to discover that, shortly before she went missing, Patricia had told her husband, Keith, that she was going to leave him for another man, sparking a series of furious arguments. Keith, who insisted that Patricia had simply walked out on him and their two young sons after one particularly nasty row, became the prime suspect in his wife's murder, but not a scrap of evidence could be found to prove he was responsible, or even that she was dead.

Six months on the police investigation was stalling and Keith, a self-employed delivery man, began to rebuild his life, advertising in the lonely hearts column of his local newspaper for a new partner. SO 10 were quickly alerted and a highly qualified female undercover officer named Claire was instructed to make contact.

Keith could hardly believe his luck. Claire was everything he had ever wanted – attractive, intelligent, enormous fun to be with – and most of all she seemed genuinely interested in him. As the weeks passed the pair spoke regularly on the telephone and had a series of intimate meetings; Keith rapidly became besotted. Claire wore a Nagra to every rendezvous and through a little kissing and cuddling – but strictly no sex – gave Keith the impression that she too was developing deep feelings for him.

After four months Keith proposed marriage and asked Claire to move in with him. The only problem, she explained, was that she was terrified his wife would suddenly return. That would simply be too painful to bear and she would rather end the relationship there and then. The only way to go forward would be if she knew the absolute truth about what had happened.

For a while Keith said little, but as they sat in Claire's car which had been fitted with a hidden recording system, he slowly began to open up.

'She's dead,' he said softly.

'How do you know she's dead?' asked Claire.

'How do you think I know? . . . I was sleeping downstairs, then I woke up. I strangled her. There was a voice in my head telling me to do it.'

'What had she done? You wouldn't have done that unless she had done something.'

'She was wanting to cut me out of everything, that's all.'

A week later, Claire pressed Keith about what had happened to his wife's body. She feigned fear that it would be found and he would be taken away from her. 'The police will never find it,' he said coldly. 'I burnt it.'

Three days later Keith Hall was arrested and charged with his wife's murder.

The taped confessions were the only real evidence, but when the case came to trial the judge, Mr Justice Waterhouse, ruled the recordings could not be heard by the jury because they breached the code of practice governing interview procedures with suspects. 'However good the intentions of the police officers involved and however skilful a performer the undercover police officer may have been, the effect of what was done was to negate the defendant's right not to incriminate himself,' he said.

Keith Hall was acquitted of all charges. 'I did not murder my wife,' he said outside the court. 'It remains a mystery to me where she is.'

Patricia Hall is still listed as 'presumed dead' and the whereabouts of her body remain unknown. The local CID are not seeking anyone else in connection with the inquiry.

Using a female undercover officer to elicit a murder confession in this way – a technique known as the 'honeytrap' – is always fraught with difficulty. A few months after the Hall case had been kicked out of court, I popped into the SO10 office and found the place frantic with activity.

A slim blonde woman with big eyes and a sparkling smile sat quietly in one corner while everyone ran around, trying to sort out a safe house and a new identity for her. The woman was an undercover officer who went by the code name Lizzie James, and an hour or so earlier she had been pulled out of a high-risk deep cover operation.

In what turned out to be the most infamous case of its kind, Lizzie had been briefed to act as the ideal partner of a man who was suspected of being a sadistic, sexually deviant killer. His name was Colin Stagg, the chief suspect in the murder of Rachel Nickell, the young woman who had been assaulted and stabbed to death on Wimbledon Common in front of her two-year-old son.

Lizzie was working alone with minimal back-up and special precautions had been taken to ensure her safety. Her coat was lined with stab-proof material and she wore a polo neck jumper fitted with a hidden metal band, protection should Stagg attempt to strangle her.

Throughout the course of the operation, Lizzie pretended to share Stagg's deranged sexual fantasies, writing and talking about a variety of disturbing topics including sadistic hardcore pornography, male domination and sexual violence.

Faced with the prospect of a future with his heart's desire, someone who promised to make all his dreams come true, Stagg had been expected to confess within a few weeks. It was not to be. Lizzie spent seven months on the job, saving every letter that he wrote her and using her Nagra to secretly tape all their conversations. There were plenty of hints, dozens of remarks that could be interpreted a number of ways, but a full-on confession remained elusive.

Lizzie kept on pressing the issue, becoming more and more insistent. Her last-ditch attempt involved implying to the virginal Stagg that she would provide his first full sexual experience. She told him she would be with him for ever, but only if he was the Wimbledon Common murderer. 'I'm sorry,' he told her, 'but I'm not.'

Despite the lack of a confession, the Crown Prosecution Service decided to proceed on the basis of conversations with Lizzie where it was felt Stagg revealed information he couldn't have known without being the murderer. Great importance was also attached to the psychological profile. Stagg was charged with murder and committed to trial, but almost as soon as the case opened at the Old Bailey, the judge, Mr Justice Ognall, threw it out. Criticizing the undercover police operation as 'misconceived, manipulative and deceptive', he said the tapes showed the operation had been nothing but a blatant attempt to trap the suspect into making a confession. He directed the jury to find Stagg not guilty, allowing him to leave court a free man.

Lizzie James herself, until then one of SO10's top performers, felt so bitter and let down by the experience that she stopped doing undercover work and quit the force altogether a couple of years later.

When it comes to tapes obtained by an undercover officer posing as a potential contract killer, the law is slightly more relaxed. Because in theory the recording is not an admission of a previous offence but an offence in itself – the act of soliciting a murder – the evidence is generally allowed. The key difficulty is ensuring that the person being recorded is the one making all the running, that they are not being led along. The role of the undercover has to be that of passive listener, nothing more.

The sergeant finished putting the last of the tape across my back to hold the Nagra in place and I got ready to leave. 'You're all set, Quasimodo,' he said with a grin. 'Do you want to ring the bells now or wait till you get back?'

Jean had picked the pub specially, a place where she felt there was no chance of bumping into anyone she knew. I parked outside and clicked on the Nagra, then made my way inside. Although I'd never even seen a photo of her, I spotted her as soon as I entered. The place was packed with young people in brightly coloured tops drinking bottled lager and swaying in time with the heavy bass beat of the music. And in a corner, through the haze of cigarette smoke, sat this prim-looking schoolteacher type. She stood out like a sore thumb.

Her faded blonde hair was cut into a neat bob and she wore a smart white blouse that was fastened at the neck with a pearl brooch. I walked over and asked if she wanted another drink – she didn't – got myself an orange juice and sat down opposite her. It was obvious that she was in a pensive, serious mood so I decided to play it straight, no small talk. 'Well, you know why I'm here. I understand that there is something you want accomplished.'

Jean shifted uncomfortably in her seat, then looked up at me. 'Is it going to be you? Are you going to be the one that actually does it?' she asked.

'That's my business. That doesn't concern you. All you need to know is that if you're still looking for the same end result, then I can help you out.'

Her eyes fell to the floor. 'Well, I'm not sure if I do now. I mean, I talked to Perry a couple of weeks ago and he said he knew some people but, oh God, I never thought . . . I mean, now you're here, now someone is actually sitting here, right in front of me, well, it takes the whole thing up a level. My heart's in my mouth. I don't know. I just don't know what I'm doing here.'

I settled back and took a long, slow drink. It looked as if this job was going to be over before it had even begun. 'Listen lady,' I said softly. 'If you don't want this thing done, then don't have it done. No one's trying to force you into anything. Take it from me, if you've got reservations, then don't go down that road, because once this thing is set in motion, there's no turning back.'

She looked up at me again and started fiddling nervously with her wedding ring. I could see tears welling up in her eyes. 'We used to have so much fun. It's all over. My marriage. It's not what it used to be. We used to be so good together but now, I just don't think he cares about me any more. I try to look after myself, to keep things special, but he just doesn't appreciate any of it. He treats me like dirt. I can't live with him any more.' She held my gaze, waiting for a response.

'Well, if you don't want to live with him,' I told her, 'then the answer's obvious. Leave him.'

She sighed. 'I want to. I've tried. But it's not that simple. He wouldn't give me any money, he'd cut me off without a penny. And I just can't afford to go on my own. The kids would be devastated. I don't want to do that to the children. They'd end up hating me. You don't know what it's like. Do you have children of your own?'

It was all starting to get a little personal and off target. 'No offence lady, but that really ain't your business. And I ain't Marge fucking Proops. I didn't come here to listen to your problems. I mean, I've got problems of my own but you don't hear me going on about them. Is there any point in me being here? What do you actually want to do about your situation?'

She finished off the last of her wine and took a deep breath. 'I think . . . I think I want him killed.'

I shook my head. 'Think isn't good enough. I can't do jack shit with think. I need a yes or a no. It's not just me involved you know. I'm just here to find out if you want this done, but there are going to be other people I have to get in touch with. They won't all be as patient as I am. They won't take being messed about.'

'I'm sorry,' she said quietly. 'It's just . . . it's on my mind the whole time. It drives me mad. I can't think about anything else other than how miserable I am.' She paused for a second, deep in thought. 'If I do go ahead with this, how does it work?'

'Have you been told how much it's going to cost?'

'Perry said about £10,000.'

'Exactly £10,000, not about. This isn't something you can haggle over.'

'Of course not. I'm sorry, sorry. Ten thousand pounds. Right.'

'Right. And we're going to need half the money up front. Cash. No cheques or anything stupid like that. Preferably tens and twenties.'

'Yes, of course. I've got some savings. I can do that.'

'And then the rest of the money when the job's done.'

'Actually, can I pay you the rest when I get the insurance money? If I give you half up front, then I won't have anything left.'

'What! You're having a laugh, ain't ya? No, no, no, no. It don't work like that. You're not paying for a sofa, you're paying for a service. That's not how we do business. That's not how anybody in this game does business. Do you know how long insurance companies take to pay out? Sometimes they never pay out in cases like this. We have to have the money straight away.'

We could both tell this was going to be a sticking point but Jean chose to ignore it and move on. 'What else? What else would I need to do? I can get you a picture of him. Would that help?'

'Yeah, that will be good. But it's not just as simple as saying "This is what he looks like, off you go". We need to know his movements: what time he leaves for work, what time he gets back, where he drinks, where he hangs out. What car he drives, what clothes he wears, stuff like that.'

'He used to rush home from work, you know. When we first

got married, he couldn't wait to be with me. We spent all our time together. It was so wonderful.'

'I think we're getting off the track here.'

'Of course. I'm sorry. Details of movements. Yes.'

'And then we need to know how you want it done.'

'What do you mean?'

'Well, if we do this thing. How do you want it done?'

It was as if she couldn't quite take in what I'd said. 'You mean, I get to choose? I have a choice?'

'Not necessarily. Some people are happy to leave it up to us. Others, they want to know it's been done in a certain way. I don't know why, I guess it means more to them.'

'How many ways are there?'

'He could just disappear. He could be chopped up. We could wipe him all across the motorway. He can be stabbed, shot, strangled. You name it.' As I spoke, she was looking at me numbly. I was worried that I had started to scare her, that she was imagining the father of her children lying in some field, chopped to pieces. I was wrong.

'I want the bastard to suffer. He's made me suffer and I want him to as well. Right until the last minute.' And then she burst into tears, reached across and clutched my hand. 'I used to love him once you know. It's all wrong now but I used to love him.' Her voice was getting louder and louder, she was wailing uncontrollably, other people in the pub were starting to look over in our direction. 'He used to be such a good man.'

I wrestled myself away from her grip and chanced a look behind me. Only a couple of people were paying us any attention. We probably looked like a couple whose illicit affair was coming to a painful end. 'What do you think you're doing?' I said. 'You're drawing attention to us. Pull yourself together.'

But Jean was in full flow. 'It's his work. It's pressure of work. That's what took him away from me.'

'Listen lady, I don't give a fuck. I just want to know if you want him dead or not.'

I was starting to feel really torn. I wanted to comfort her, help her out. But in my role as a cold ruthless killer, all I could do was try to find out if I was wasting my time or not, whether her husband was genuinely in danger. It meant I couldn't afford to offer her the sympathy that she needed. 'You're making a right prat of yourself and you're not making me look too clever either,' I told her. 'I think you should take yourself off to the toilets and sort yourself out.'

It took nearly fifteen minutes for her to emerge looking a little more composed on the outside but still shaky underneath. I bought her another drink – whisky and ginger ale this time – and tried to get a final answer out of her. We had now been in the pub for just under two hours and I was getting impatient. 'OK. I really need to know. Is this the direction you want to go in?'

She looked up at me. Her eyes were still red and puffy from crying, her make-up had been touched up but you could see the dark half moons under her eyes where it had run. 'I'm so unhappy. He knows how unhappy I am, but he won't give me a divorce. He'll never give me a divorce. He's going to make it last for ever.'

I leaned a little closer to her and lowered my voice. 'What I need to know from you now is whether you actually want this done. Because when I leave here, I'm going to have to start making phone calls and doing things. And once I do that, then the wheels will be in motion. So what's the answer?'

Her silence seemed to go on for hours. In the background I could hear the music from the jukebox, the sounds of the other drinkers chatting. And then, this tiny little click. The tape on the Nagra had run out.

'Yes. Yes, I want it done,' she said at last. I nodded and started to get up. 'But . . .' she said, 'I still love him. I'm still not sure.' I sat back down again.

'So what are you saying? Are you saying yes or are you saying no?'

'I'm saying yes.'

'Are you sure?'

'I don't know how I'm going to raise the money.'

'So you're not sure.'

'I just wish there was some other way, some way to make him love me again.'

'There are always options lady, there's always something you can do.'

'No. Not this time.' She sat up straight and a look of determination came over her face. 'I want this done. I'm 100 per cent sure. I want him dead. I want you to kill the bastard.'

I just couldn't believe the tape had run out at such a crucial moment. I wanted to kick the table in frustration but had to check myself. It was sod's law and there was nothing I could do. It wouldn't have been enough to secure a conviction on its own anyway, I would have needed some corroborating evidence.

We arranged to meet again at the same time the following week with Jean agreeing to bring a list of her husband's movements and other details. If she complied, we'd have all the evidence of intent that we needed. I waited for her to drive off, then I left to head back to Wimbledon.

'I don't know,' I said to the sergeant when he asked me how it had gone. 'I don't know if I scared her into it or what, I have to have a listen to the tape. She seemed pretty determined though. I guess we'll find out the truth next week.'

A week and a day later I returned to Wimbledon for a second briefing and a second session with my good friend Mr Nagra. 'It shouldn't be so much of a problem this time,' said the sergeant as he taped me up. 'If she's serious, she won't mind if you get straight to the point. I don't see any reason to have to keep beating about the bush on a second meeting. Crank it up a notch and we'll see what happens.'

I waited in the pub for an hour but Jean never turned up. We later heard from Perry that she'd changed her mind, she claimed she had been fascinated by the idea and liked fantasizing about the fact that she had the power to do it, but that she'd never go through with it. She had been keen to come to the second meeting and had prepared a list of her husband's movements as asked, but decided that it would be taking her fantasy too far.

We had no choice but to believe it. We had insufficient evidence to prove that she would have taken things further so the investigation had to end there. In many ways I was relieved and anyway, it could be argued that it was still a result. After all, if she had managed to track down some other contract killer, it could have ended very differently.

To this day, poor old Jean has no idea just how close she came to going to prison.

And her husband has no idea just how close he came to being murdered.

7

Martin: Leroy Palmer was SO10's very own Dr Jekyll and Mr Hyde.

A softly spoken, non-smoking, church-going teetotaller, who was intelligent, articulate and fluent in several languages, Leroy had a heart of pure gold and was one of the most popular officers at his station. He always dressed smartly, said grace before meals – even at the police canteen – donated thousands of pounds to charity and spent all his spare time showering his three young children with love and affection. A regular saint.

But when Leroy went undercover, he turned into a creature from another planet. Out went the home counties accent and in came a rough Jamaican patois littered with the grossest expletives; out went the smart suits and sensible shoes and in came ultra-baggy jeans, puffa jackets and oversized designer trainers. But the biggest change of all was to his personality. Out went the gentle giant and in came an intimidating, aggressive street punk. The undercover Leroy would even walk differently, adopting a strange kind of Neanderthal shuffle that made sensible people rush to cross the road whenever he approached.

Leroy was usually kind and courteous; his *alter ego* was incredibly rude, unbelievably arrogant and totally over the top. But he got results and I always felt very comfortable working with him, so long as I could stifle my giggles. When I was asked to set up a long-term operation against a gang of major drug dealers operating out of a barber shop in Catford, I knew that Leroy was the man I wanted by my side.

SO10 operations will usually target only the very highest levels of organized crime so, before an undercover officer can be assigned to a job, it first has to reach a particular grade. There is no point in a local drug squad requesting SO10 support if the person they are after is just some bozo who once a month sells a couple of joints to his best friends; the huge cost and complexity of an undercover operation can only be justified if a major player is involved.

Most of the time the system works, but every now and then a local drug squad will get desperate to tackle someone who has been eluding them. In cases like that there is an enormous temptation to ramp up the job in order to get permission for an undercover to come on board. Instead of grams, they'll start talking about kilos, instead of hundreds of pounds it'll be hundreds of thousands of pounds. By the time the SO10 operative has made their way into the so-called gang and found out the truth – that it's just an ageing hippie with a single well-tended cannabis plant growing on his rooftop – it's too late to do anything about it.

The Catford barber shop job was unusual in that there was no informant. Instead the lowdown on the gang's activities had come from uniformed beat officers talking anonymously to a handful of concerned locals who, while keen to see the gang brought to book, were unwilling to make statements themselves. With no one to introduce us, Leroy and I would be going in cold.

There are few hard and fast rules when it comes to working undercover but one of the cardinal ones is that, unless you're after nothing more than general intelligence, you never go in cold.

One of the difficulties caused by the fact that most working police officers know nothing about SO10 is that it means they also know nothing about working undercover. They assume that, just because a particular pub or club has a reputation as a place where drugs are sold openly, all an undercover needs to do is go there and within a few hours the whole sales team will be identified and behind bars. In reality, a new face on the scene might get offered drugs, but not by anyone operating at a particularly high level. The kind of people who would walk up to a total stranger in their local pub and offer them something are simply not going to have a massive stash of the stuff back home.

There are exceptions to the rule and there are ways round it, but they take time and cost money. And you never know what you're actually going to get. Donnie Brasco, the FBI agent who managed to infiltrate the Mafia in New York and a number of other US cities, did much of his work going in cold, but he spent six years undercover and it took nearly a year before he got his first big break. Furthermore, he never set out to get into the Mafia, he was just targeting some fences.

Putting what little intelligence there was together, it appeared the gang ran an extremely tight ship. There were three main bosses, Garth, Scott and Shaun, who in turn employed at least a dozen foot soldiers to do their bidding. The trio had met a few years earlier at a local boxing club and had developed a fearsome reputation. Stories of their exploits were everywhere; Scott had once beaten a man into a coma after he had insulted his girlfriend, Shaun had served time after stabbing someone in the leg during a bar fight, while Garth had single-handedly wrecked a Chinese restaurant during a night out with friends when the waiters had made the mistake of asking him to hurry up.

The centre of the gang's operations was a barber's bang in the middle of a little shopping parade, along with a fish and chip shop, an off licence and a pub. The parade itself backed on to a gloomy council estate which was so rough it was considered something of a no-go area by the local police. More than once, officers responding to house calls in one of the flats had returned to their patrol cars to find the windows smashed or the vehicle ablaze. The area within the estate up to the end of the parade of shops was considered the gang's territory. They could do pretty much whatever they wanted knowing that none of the locals would dare to complain.

According to the information picked up by the beat officers, most of the drug sales took place at the back of the barber shop, but the gang rarely kept large quantities of drugs there. Instead they had built up a sophisticated network of safe houses throughout the estate. Tenants would be paid a small fee to keep parcels on the dealers' behalf and if a sale was made, the parcel would be retrieved and brought to the barber shop at the last minute.

There was a flat above the barber shop which the gang used as an impromptu meeting place, somewhere they could discuss business and negotiate sales well away from prying eyes. Finally there was the pub. It was a pretty ordinary place, but as with everywhere else in the area they saw it as little more than an extension of their territory. Everybody in the pub knew them and they knew every single person who drank there. Inside the members of the gang would openly smoke joints, talk about people they had cut up, jobs they had planned. They felt they were untouchable. No one would ever complain because everyone in there was vulnerable. Getting into the pub ourselves was going to take time, but it was clearly a key part of the operation.

As far as the actual drugs on offer were concerned, the word was that everything from crack cocaine to speed and ultra-strong skunk cannabis was being traded in significant quantities and that the gang were making profits of at least £10,000 each month. With no test purchases to look back on, it was impossible to gauge exactly how accurate the information being fed through actually was, but Chris Taylor and the rest of the top brass at SO10 came to the conclusion that the likelihood of busting a sizeable operation was high enough to warrant putting a couple of undercovers on the job.

A few days later, I found myself in a tiny wood-panelled meeting room at Catford nick with four members of the local drug squad who were full of enthusiasm and excited about the prospect of finally getting one over the barber shop gang. 'I'm telling you Martin, the sky is the limit on this,' said Ben, a young detective constable with the squad and the man who would be our main point of contact during the operation. 'We know you're not interested in small beer but these blokes are the real thing. We really want to nail them and don't care what it costs or how long it takes. We want you down there virtually full time gathering evidence. Seven days a week if you like. You just go for it. You're the expert so you tell us what you need and how long you need it for and we'll do everything we can to give it to you.'

Although SO10 has a central budget, much of the money for individual operations comes out of the budget assigned to the squad who call the undercovers in. It means that the issue of cost is never too far from the surface.

I leaned forward in my chair and put my elbows on the table. 'I'm glad to hear you say that Ben because if you want us to go in completely cold, no snouts, no introductions, and somehow end up being drinking buddies with these guys, it's going to take time and it's going to take money. We could be talking months. We're going to have to make out that we have just moved into the area. Spend time walking about and being seen, getting to know the local shopkeepers. It's only when they have become completely used to the idea of us being around, when we're getting talked about on the grapevine, that we can start trying to engage them in conversation.'

As I spoke I could see that Ben's 'sky's the limit' talk was already wearing thin. I carried on. 'If we're walking around, we can only be on the street for a certain amount of time before we start to look suspicious. The locals are gonna think we're lost or something. And if someone does say something to us, "Can I help you?" or whatever, it's no good saying, "Oh don't worry about me, I live up in Bethnal Green but I've just come up here for the night to do a bit of walking around." We have to have a reason to be there and a reason to be walking around. That means you're going to have to get us a flat on the estate, a car, stuff like that. I hope you've got deep pockets.'

I knew I was laying it on a bit thick but I got the feeling that Ben and the rest of his team were expecting me and Leroy to work miracles. I felt the best tactic was to be totally honest and tell him in advance what we were going to be asking for, rather than getting a few days into the job and then having to pull out because they suddenly realized they couldn't afford it after all.

Ben came back a couple of days later and said we'd been given the go ahead. They had found us a flat on the estate, rented out in a false name to an untraceable address, but they were not willing to provide us with a car. 'We don't want you to spend all your time driving about,' Ben said. 'We want you on the streets, mingling with the people. And you start at the end of the week.'

The plan for the first night was simple enough. Leroy and I were going to spend an hour or so walking around the estate, have a quick bite to eat in a local café, go in and out of the flat and bang a few doors so that the neighbours knew someone was living there and then go home. It was early days and neither of us felt it was worth actually spending the night in the flat. Besides, Kathy and I had just moved into a flat together and she was becoming increasingly frustrated with my prolonged absences, asking what was the point of us living together if I was never there.

Leroy and I had just arrived at the edge of the estate on that first night and were making our way through to the shopping parade when something across the road caught my eye. Three young black kids were viciously mugging a middle-aged white guy who had been walking along with his wife. I could hardly believe what I was seeing. The two groups had been going in opposite directions, each seemingly minding their own business, but as they had passed each other, two of the boys had lashed out at the man, knocking him to the ground. As his wife screamed at the top of her voice, they rifled his pockets, found his wallet and then took off down the road and vanished.

All this happened while Leroy and I were passing on the other side of the road and there was absolutely nothing we could do about it. It's the kind of crime that you would never see if you were in uniform because people would spot you a mile away and wait until you were out of sight. But in our undercover mode, we were just ordinary members of the public. It was like living in a whole new world.

Apart from the wife who was clearly in deep shock, Leroy and I were the only witnesses. We had a rough description of the boys, we knew which way they had run off and we had seen the whole thing happen. A big part of me wanted to break off and give chase there and then but I didn't. We knew the police were going to turn up at any minute so we went around the corner and back to our flat to wait for the incident to blow over.

The problem was we were undercover; to intervene would have blown everything we were working towards. Robbery was just part of life on that estate. We couldn't even risk going across the road and being good Samaritans by giving the man first aid and comforting his wife. If one of the targets saw us do that and we bumped into them later, they'd be suspicious of us and would never trust us. Your average criminal won't do anything for anyone unless they think they're going to benefit from it.

And while the drug squad were aware that there was an undercover team working in the area, that knowledge wouldn't have been spread among the beat officers. If one of them called me in as a witness, I would have to admit who I really was and I didn't want that. Some cops have big mouths and when you're on a job, you never trust more people than you absolutely have to.

Once I was on an undercover job in Shepherd's Bush posing as a man interested in buying a couple of kilos of amphetamine. I was on my way to a meeting, driving a Porsche which I'd picked up from the SO10 car pool, when I got pulled up by two local traffic cops.

It was close to midnight and there I was, wearing my NUFF RESPECT hat, driving a flashy car through a run-down part of town and I just happened to have £2,000 – money for a test purchase – in an envelope in the glove compartment. They were convinced I was up to no good and insisted on taking me back to the station.

Once there, I was subjected to a strip search and questioned for half an hour before they had to let me go as I hadn't actually done anything wrong. To this day, those two cops have no idea that I was a fellow police officer. I could have ended it all with a swift phone call to SO10 but the rule is that you never declare who you really are unless you absolutely have to. Until that happens, you just front it out or, better still, avoid the attention of the police in the first place.

As soon as we heard the police sirens, Leroy and I vanished into the estate leaving them to sort out the mugging on their own.

Our flat was a pretty grotty place. Ben said it would be great if we could get to know some of the locals and invite them back to ours. He obviously hadn't seen the place himself. It was three floors up on one of those long, narrow buildings with a balcony. The view was pretty good – providing you were tall enough to see over the roofs of the other blocks of flats – but the inside was dingy and smelly. It was also incredibly noisy: during the day and night screaming gangs of local kids would play cricket or rounders on the square patch of grass outside in defiance of the 'no ball games' signs.

Although it was cut short by the mugging, Leroy and I had managed a quick walk around the area. We sat down to work out a plan of action, particularly for getting into the pub.

Even without going inside it, I knew exactly what it was going to be like. It would be a scene straight out of one of those old westerns where there is a guy playing the piano and everyone is singing, dancing and having a good time. Then the doors open and everything stops and everyone stares. The minute we walked into the pub it would be just like that, which made it all the more important that we made sure we were seen in the area as much as possible.

Leroy and I figured out that the best way to progress was to do the complete opposite of what we had been taught in training school. One thing they teach you about is the phenomenon called trigger points. If some guy walks around wearing a white T-shirt with a big orange splash on the front of it, that's a trigger point. Even if people on the streets aren't paying much attention to anything, when the orange splash passes by it will register in their minds because it stands out so much.

If the same bloke walks back a short while later, people will see the trigger point again and they'll start thinking, 'Now where have I seen that guy before, what is going on here?'

Ideally, undercover officers go out of their way to avoid wearing trigger points but Leroy and I knew we had to do the complete opposite. We wanted to be noticed as much as possible. With all the pressure we were under from the drug squad, it had to happen as quickly as possible.

Leroy, being Leroy, had his own ways of being noticed which were guaranteed to keep me amused during those long, boring days and nights establishing our cover.

Walking alongside Leroy through the estate in the middle of the afternoon, I turned to say something and he wasn't there. I looked back and spotted him at the foot of a block of brownstone flats squinting at the upper floors and shouting, 'Rose, Rose. Are you there, Rose?' at the top of his voice.

'What the hell are you doing?' I said. 'Who the fuck's Rose?'

'No idea,' Leroy replied.

'Then what are you calling her for?'

'I tell you, Martin. Every single time I come through an estate like this, there is always some bloke shouting up for Rose. Every time. So I'm just making like. I'm just helping the two of us to fit in. Now people are going to think I know Rose. They'll know we belong here.'

Another time we were sitting on a bench in a square of grass opposite the pub. There was no one around and Leroy was being himself, speaking in his usual, cultured voice, telling me all his plans to take the sergeants' exam and build up a career in the force. Midway through a sentence, Leroy snapped back into Jamaican patois.

'Bwoy I just take the gun, and I just lick him like dat with it, lick 'im,' he said, waving his hands around to imitate the act of giving someone a pistol whipping. I was totally confused. It had come out of nowhere. I didn't know what was going on. But at that same moment, this big Rastafarian walked past my shoulder on his way to the pub. Leroy had seen him coming out of the corner of his eye and slipped into undercover mode in an instant.

As soon as the man was out of earshot, Leroy said, 'Sorry about that. Didn't want to give anything away. He just came up behind us and I had to change. So about being a sergeant . . .' And he carried on about the exams without missing a beat.

Leroy was a real one-off.

At the end of our first week Leroy and I were back in the meeting room at Catford nick for our first debriefing.

'So, who have you met?' asked Ben.

'No one,' I replied.

'No one? What do you mean no one?'

'Just that. No one. We've just been walking around.'

We'd only spoken a few words but already Ben was growing red with frustration. 'Walking around! You mean you haven't spoken to anyone?'

'Well, I suppose we've spoken to a couple of people,' I said, trying to placate him. Leroy looked over at me and nodded solemnly in agreement.

'Thank God for that,' said Ben. 'Who? What did you find out?'

'Well, I spoke to the guy in the chip shop,' said Leroy.

'Right, yeah, and what did he say?'

'Well,' Leroy continued, trying to stifle a giggle. 'He asked me if I wanted a large or small portion and whether I wanted them open or wrapped, salt and . . .'

'I'm not in the mood for any stupid jokes,' Ben cut him off. 'I want to know what you've done.'

'Look Ben,' I said, trying to restore a bit of calm. 'This is the way it's going to have to work. All we've done is wander around for the past week. You can't expect us to do anything more than that. We're going in cold. It just ain't going to work any other way. We've been up and down the road, in and out of the estate, we've had bits to eat here and there. Sometimes I go there during the day for a quick walk, sometimes Leroy goes on his own, some-times we go together. But all we've been doing is walking around.'

'Walking around! Just walking around. For a week! Jesus. Is that what we're paying you for? What about the barber shop, haven't you gone in there?'

'No, not yet.'

'But that's the main target. That's where it all happens. Why haven't you gone in there yet?'

'Well Ben, it's a barber shop. And I don't need a haircut.'

As far as I was concerned, we were still weeks away from first contact but the pressure from the squad was getting too much so Leroy and I made the decision to hit the pub. The compromise was that we would do it during the day rather than at night. It was much quieter during the day and it was unlikely that any of the targets would be there. Going in at that time would give us a chance to get to know the layout of the place and ensure our faces were familiar to the landlord and a handful of customers.

I pushed back the heavy wooden door covered in cracked black paint and stepped inside. Every pair of eyes in the place instantly fell on me, but only for a second. It was pretty much what I had expected. There was a pool table to the left, alcoves with bench seating in each of the corners and a large square bar in the centre. There were big picture windows on both sides of the bar and, despite the heavy curtains, enough light streamed in to stop the place looking too threatening.

Propped up on stools alongside the bar were two old men nursing halves of Guinness. A couple of younger lads who looked as if they might be on their lunch break were having a quick game of pool.

The landlord was probably in his early fifties, short and hard looking with just a monk's fringe of grey hair around his ears. He was the only other person there. 'What'll it be, gentlemen?' he asked, greeting us in his chirpy Irish accent.

We ordered a couple of bottles of beer and sat at the bar. Inevitably, it was only a few minutes before Freddy, as the landlord was called, began to try to satisfy his curiosity. 'Haven't seen you two before. New round here?'

I felt as if I was reciting the script to a play I'd written. 'Yeah, I moved into a place on the estate last week.'

'Work round here, do you?' asked Freddy.

'Nah. I've got a week off to help me sort out the move. Thought I'd take the opportunity to get to know my local.'

Over the next few days I popped into the pub most afternoons, sometimes with Leroy, sometimes on my own. By the end of the week we felt confident enough to try going in during the evening.

Even though we'd been there in the afternoon, night time was always going to be trickier. The second we opened the door on that first Friday night, the whole place went quiet, the pool balls stopped clattering into the pockets and everyone turned and stared. Luckily my attempts to bond with Freddy had paid off handsomely. 'Martin,' he called out as soon as he saw me. 'The usual?' he asked, already reaching for the fridge. I could feel the whole pub relax.

As we moved towards the bar, I had a good look around. I could see the three main targets gathered at the pool table. Perfect. All

Leroy and I had to do was play pool with one another, show them we had a bit of skill, then challenge them to a game and we were bound to end up talking. I put a couple of pound coins down on the side of the table and went to the bar to wait for our turn.

There was already money down before us and some of the targets also put money down after us, but they all kept on playing and our money never seemed to move. It was not even acknowledged. In a normal pub you would walk up to the table and ask 'Is it my go or what?' but here that simply wasn't going to work. We just had to wait.

When they'd finally had enough, Leroy rushed up and grabbed the cue as I began resetting the balls. The targets sat on the window sill by the door watching us suspiciously. And that's when Leroy leaned over to me and whispered in my ear, 'Martin. How do you play this game again?' I knew we were in for a performance. He had no idea what he was doing. While I tried to concentrate on getting half decent shots, Leroy was dancing around, whacking everything as hard as he could and yelling out 'What a shot!' at the top of his voice every time he made contact with a ball. It was embarrassing but very deliberate.

Soon the whole pub was watching his antics. He'd made an impression that wouldn't quickly be forgotten. I could tell that the targets found Leroy amusing and enjoyed watching him make a fool of himself, but it wasn't enough for them to want to come and start talking to us. We needed to find another way in.

Over the next couple of weeks Leroy and I made a number of evening visits to the pub. Once we took two female undercover officers with us, posing as our girlfriends. One was Helen, the woman I'd met on my course, and the other was her friend Esther. We never spoke to anyone else that night but I believed it was good for the image Leroy and I were trying to portray for people to see that we didn't only have each other for company.

It did make me wonder whether we should have used a female officer right from the start. Although there had been a lot of fuss with the Lizzie James case, female undercovers are always worth their weight in gold. There are at least thirty on the books of SO 10 and they do everything from posing as prospective girlfriends of suspects in major crimes to working as secretaries in offices. A former henchman of the Kray twins, and one of the most notorious and dangerous gangsters of recent times, was put away by an undercover called Lucy who, acting as his secretary, bugged his telephone as he arranged drug deals with the New York Mafia from his office in London.

A couple of weeks later, feeling more confident, I went into the pub on my own one afternoon and started chatting to Freddy. It was pretty obvious that, although not a fully fledged gangster himself, he wouldn't say no to the odd piece of criminal indulgence. I decided to use him as my way in. One thing about undercover cops is that they always buy, they never sell. But I decided to offer him something none the less, something I hoped he might want to pass on to the targets, to see what happened. A good word from him would be priceless.

I sat at the bar and produced a manila envelope from my jacket pocket. Inside were two blank passports. Freddy inspected them closely and whistled in admiration. 'Nice work. Do that yourself?'

'Nah, man. This is the real thing. I've got a man down at the passport office who gets me the odd blank one. I know you've got connections and I wondered if you knew anybody who might be able to make use of this kind of stuff.'

'Leave it with me, Martin, I'll see what I can do.'

The truth was, with SO10's contacts down at the passport office, we could get as many blank passports as we wanted, so long as we could justify having them. What I wouldn't be able to do was actually let any of them go or hand over any samples. It would just become self-defeating, providing one more opportunity for someone to flee the country under a false name or sneak in undetected.

Like the flat though, it was all about creating an illusion. I had to give the impression that I could and would supply passports. And that would be my ticket into the gang. I even gave Freddy my phone number for the flat on the estate, though it was actually connected to a second line at the home I shared with Kathy, just in case he wanted to get in touch.

Two days later, I was back in the pub and Freddy came down and sat at my table. 'I was talking to this guy I know, you've probably seen him in here. Name's Garth. He does a lot of business in the area, if you know what I mean. He told me to call the next time you were in. He wants to talk. He'll be here in ten minutes.'

Garth arrived and picked up a large port and blackcurrant from the bar before joining me.

'Where's your friend?'

'I don't know. Off with some woman probably.'

'He's a funny guy. Very funny.'

Garth was eyeing me suspiciously the whole time. There was no trust in his eyes at all.

'So, I understand you are the man with the passports.'

'Well, it's not exactly me. I have a friend who can get them. I could introduce you if you like.'

'What do you get out of it?'

'That's between me and him. Let's just say there's a kind of finders' fee involved. It's worth my while to find him new customers.'

'So, if you don't do passports, what do you do?'

'I don't know if I want to talk about my business with someone I don't know.'

He took a large swig of his drink and nodded, acknowledging the point. 'OK, but I've got contacts of my own. Might be able to find customers for you too, for a fee of course,' he added mimicking me. 'How much do you want for them?'

I scratched my chin for a second. 'The price is £7,500 each.' It was over the odds, not way over the odds but certainly more than any self-respecting crook would be willing to pay. I knew I had to pitch it just right, not so much that I would look like a greedy idiot but enough so that I looked like I knew what I was talking about. If Garth really wanted a passport, I knew he'd be able to get one elsewhere and cheaper.

'That's too much, man. I ain't paying half that.' He was trying it on, trying to beat the price down. All I had to do was stand firm.

'That's the price my friend needs. If I don't get that much for them, it's not worth my while.'

We didn't do business that day, and when Scott arrived a few minutes later Garth went off to join him. But at least I had made the first contact. Now that my presence had been acknowledged, I could move on to the next stage.

Six weeks into the operation, I was finally ready to go into the barber shop. On a Saturday afternoon I pushed back the glass door and walked in, tingling with anticipation. To the left, under a mirrored wall, was a lime green Formica worktop punctuated with three porcelain sinks. To the right was a bench where waiting customers sat and flicked their way through piles of out-of-date magazines and newspapers. The second I walked in the whole place went quiet and the three leather barber's chairs swung round to face the door and see who was arriving. It was actually a more intimidating experience than going into the pub.

I didn't make eye contact with anyone, I just hurried to a space on the bench between the two other waiting customers and sat down. The silence didn't last. They had obviously been midway through an animated conversation about who was the better fighter, Jackie Chan or Bruce Lee, and it was soon in full flow once more.

'Jackie Chan's nothing but a slitty eyed comedian,' said the eldest of the three barbers, a black guy in his early thirties with tiny dreadlocks and a prominent gold tooth. 'He's just the Chinese Charlie Chaplin. I'm telling you, one on one, no camera tricks, no stunts, Bruce Lee would kick Jackie Chan's fucking arse right off.'

'You're talking bollocks man,' came the reply from the barber nearest me. His hair had been straightened and given the wet look treatment. Little curls flicked around his face as he spoke. 'You know how tall Bruce Lee was? Five foot nothing. The man was a fucking dwarf. Couldn't have weighed more than eight stone. They used to speed up the camera to make him look good. My sister could take him.'

'That ain't no boast,' said Mr Gold Tooth, 'your sister could take fucking Mike Tyson. She's an animal.'

It was as if they were oblivious to the fact that they had customers. From there they went on to act out scenes from their favourite kung fu films, kicking and punching at the air around them while still holding the scissors, clippers and cut-throat razors they were using. At one point the man with the wet look hair attempted to do a high kick which put such strain on his groin it left him limping for the rest of the time I was there.

The customers sitting in the chairs were clearly used to it, either remaining still or joining in the conversation themselves. I thought about joining in but decided against it. The other two people waiting on the bench beside me had said nothing until their own turns came. It seemed to be some kind of etiquette that you only spoke or were spoken to while actually having your hair cut.

When my turn came round, I sat down, told him I wanted a trim and waited until he put a giant bib over my clothes and began cutting. Then at last, 'How are you then, mate?'

'I'm fine,' I said, relaxing into the role. I had to stay cool. This was the big moment, this was the break we'd been waiting for. I had as long as it took this guy to cut my hair to find out as much as I could about who was behind the trade in drugs. 'I've just moved a few weeks ago,' I continued, as casually as I could. 'I've got a little flat on the estate that I share with my mate.'

'Oh yeah. I think I seen you around. Been in the pub too.'

'Probably, I'm in there every now and then. So . . . what's your name?'

'All done.'

'What?'

'All done, your hair is finished, man.'

These guys may have been bullshit when it came to the martial arts film industry, but they sure knew how to cut hair. He had finished me to perfection in less than three minutes. We hadn't even broached the subject I wanted to talk about. I needed to buy more time in the chair.

On the wall, fastened with Sellotape, there was a curling photo of a geezer with a really sad haircut, diamonds shaved into the back of his head.

'Actually, I've always wanted a cut like that.'

The barber looked at me, just to make sure I wasn't actually a fourteen-year-old boy. 'OK. You're the customer,' he said.

For the next hour or so, while I underwent the greatest humiliation of my life, I chatted to this guy about kung fu, cars, music, girls, pork ribs. Every subject in the world you could think of apart from drugs. Every time we shifted anywhere near it, he would enthusiastically and automatically start talking about something else.

I was back at work the following day, where I had to face the CID office in my suit, tie and stupid diamond-patterned hair. It took two weeks to grow out.

At the end of two months, it was pretty clear to Leroy and myself that these blokes didn't have any drugs, or at least not in the kind of quantities that would interest SO10. The budget for the operation was going through the roof. Leroy and I had been at the pub or on the estate on all our days off, during evenings and weekends, and we were just wasting time. We called a meeting at the local police station and told them frankly the one thing they did not want to hear: that they were pissing in the wind.

Their response was to declare that we were wrong, that we were simply trying to cover up the fact that we hadn't been good enough to get to the drugs, despite all the time we had taken and all the money we had spent.

In one last desperate bid, the drug squad planned a massive raid. I wasn't around for it but I heard all about it afterwards. They had ordered a furniture truck and box vans, all loaded up with police officers. The raid had taken place simultaneously at the flat, the barber shop and the off licence. And the pub. From the four places all they came away with was a Hoover bag full of home-grown cannabis with a street value of less than nothing.

8

Philip: The air was heavy with the stench of cannabis and cigar smoke, the stinking once-grey carpet was stained with a mixture of blood, beer and cigarette ash and each and every chair was smashed, slashed or broken. You couldn't take more than a couple of steps without crunching a bit of broken glass underfoot, the legacy of a thousand bar fights. I'd been to a few dives in my time but this one was in a class of its own. I was in the snooker hall from hell, just off Brentford high street, sipping from a frosted bottled beer and knocking a few balls around with Danny, the informant on the job, while we waited for the targets to arrive.

As I looked down the narrow room at the groups of men huddled around the tables, I recognized at least a dozen faces from the drug squad mug shot files. The place was heaving with big league gangsters who ran the place like a private club. To get in you either had to be a member or a member had to call up in advance and leave your name at the door. Danny and I had arrived early, much to the dismay of the shaven-headed gorillas in suits guarding the door who were halfway through throwing us out when they realized they would have to let us in.

We had not been there for twenty minutes, impatiently awaiting the arrival of Jack, Matt and Andrew, a group of likely lads who were looking to sell on a heap of high-quality cocaine. We had a table to ourselves but the place was so crowded that every now and then we'd accidentally bump into the people playing next to us who mumbled under their breath and scowled at us. Like everyone else there, the men on the next table had broken noses or cauliflower ears. It wasn't the sort of place you'd want to start trouble in.

There was a little garage music in the background, courtesy of a local pirate radio station, mixed with the hum of conversation and the sound of snooker balls cracking into one another. As I lined up my next shot, Danny looked up at me, chalking his cue as he spoke, 'When do you think I'll get my reward money for this job then, Philip?'

I didn't look at him, I didn't react at all. It was as if he had never spoken. I just played the next shot, then edged around the table. I had no idea whether or not anyone had overheard but I could feel his gaze burning into the side of my head. I knew he was looking at me, wondering if I'd missed his question. I knew he was thinking about how long he should wait before asking again.

'Philip . . .' he began.

I snapped off my next shot, moved round the table and put myself right at his side: 'For fuck's sake,' I whispered in his ear as loudly and fiercely as I could, 'don't go mouthing off. What the fuck do you think you're playing at?'

Danny's face crumpled. 'Oh shit. Sorry mate. I just kinda forgot myself for a second.'

'Forgot yourself? Well for fuck's sake try to remember, and fast. I mean, are you sure you're all right with this? Are you going to be able to cope when these guys get here? These are some bad men we're dealing with you know.'

'Yeah, yeah. I'll be fine. I just lost it for a minute but I'm back now. I'm concentrating. Sorry, I was out on the razzle last night and my head's all over the shop. I'll be all right in two ticks. I need a cup of coffee.'

I've never had a lot of time for informants and Danny was proving to be no exception.

If there's one lesson that they drum into you above all others at undercover training school, it is that informants are the most dangerous people on earth. Of course, they are valuable and much of our work couldn't be done without them, but they are also incredibly unreliable. Basically they are crooks buying their freedom with information, all of which means there's always the temptation for them to ramp up the information in order to get a better deal or a bigger pay off.

More often than not they are stuck between a rock and a hard place. The only way they can get access to information that is of use is by being actively involved in lots of crimes and scams. Informing is a little insurance policy. It means that when they get caught, they've got a decent chance of avoiding prison by ratting on a few colleagues. But it's a high risk game. They're living among these people twenty-four hours a day, seven days a week. There is no escape if it all comes on top.

The number one rule is to get rid of the informant as soon as possible. Once they have done their bit and introduced you to the bad guys, you try to get them out of the picture. The trouble is, a lot of them don't want to go. They are excited by what is going on, they get a terrific buzz from setting people up and they want to see it through to the end.

And it's always your arse on the line. If they screw up, and they often do, it's the undercover that ends up paying the price. Some of the informants are complete loose cannons. You have to ensure that you are always in control of them rather than vice versa. There are rules that have to be stuck to. They are not allowed to lead the targets on and act as *agents provocateurs*. They are not allowed to build a job out of nothing, not allowed to get them to do other things for us. The informant's part is strictly to introduce you to the targets he has nominated. Not to arrange the supply of the commodities, nor to discuss prices and make arrangements. His part is strictly to introduce the undercover to a scene and then make an exit.

Danny was a specialist jewel thief. He would target large homes in affluent areas, break in, and make his way directly to the master bedroom to steal a selection of the best rings, necklaces and bracelets that he came across. Because he left the house mostly undisturbed, it would often be days or even weeks before the owners realized that the items were missing, let alone that they had been stolen rather than simply misplaced.

Danny was in his mid-twenties with floppy brown hair in a pudding bowl cut that would have made him look like a gawky nerd if he hadn't been quite so stocky. He first signed up as an informant after being grassed up himself. One of his fences had been raided and offered up his name in the hope of having his own sentence reduced. When the police burst into Danny's Ealing maisonette, they found enough stolen gear to send him to prison for a very long stretch and it was only a matter of time before he began talking.

For once, however, the informant on the case wasn't looking for someone to put a good word in the ear of the trial judge. Instead, Danny was looking for hard cash. He was friendly with a group of former armed robbers who had invested their hard-won cash in a couple of clubs and now ran a series of protection rackets across south-west London.

A team of them would go into a rival pub or club and cause as much trouble as they could, smashing the place up and threatening the staff and customers. They would go back a week later and tell the manager that if he wanted the trouble to stop, he would have to take them on as partners. Otherwise his business would have to shut down within a week.

Danny had worked as getaway driver on one of their early robberies, had provided cars for a couple of the later ones and had remained friendly with them since. They had recently confided to him that they had come into possession of a sizeable amount of high-quality cocaine and they were looking for a buyer. One of their 'clients' had been unable to pay cash and had offered them drugs instead. Danny was convinced that the gang had cheated him out of his full share in the previous job. He was also pissed off because one of the main men, Keith, had made a pass at his girl-friend during a Christmas party. It was all the motivation Danny needed to pass the information on to his local drugs squad.

He was introduced to me by his police handler and I warmed to him immediately. I quickly learned that while he hadn't actually seen the drugs himself, several members of the gang had spoken to him about them on a number of occasions. The plan was that he would introduce me as a potential buyer so we sat down to work out a scenario of where we knew each other from.

Coming up with a good cover story can be a tricky business. Sometimes it takes only a few minutes before you crack it, other times you can spend all day working at it and still be struggling.

The idea is to find some way that the two of you can join at the hip, something plausible that people will take at face value without feeling they've got to go off and check it for themselves.

You start by asking a series of basic questions: where did you go to school, what is on your criminal record, what places have you visited, what sort of women you're attracted to, music, sport. Stuff like that. Danny had grown up in Acton and still lived in nearby Ealing. I knew practically nothing about both areas so that was no good. After nearly an hour's conversation, he started telling me about a girl he had gone out with some years earlier who lived in Liverpool and how he had spent the best part of six months travelling there every weekend.

I had a cousin in Merseyside and had been going up to see him once or twice a year since I was a teenager. In that time I'd got to know the place pretty well and could rattle off the names of pubs, streets and clubs. I could easily pass as someone who had lived there, especially to a London villain.

On the bigger, long-term jobs like the one with Skank, you might go as far as having a false passport printed up and opening a new bank account, all to back up the idea that you are who you say you are, but on something like this one, I just needed something to use as a quick introduction.

The final scenario was that we'd met in Liverpool in a club called Kirklands. We'd got chatting at the bar and done a bit of work together since then. Nothing major, he'd sold me some jewellery, I'd set him up with some cars stolen in Liverpool. Danny was happy. 'I know loads of people who I've met like that. And it sounds just the kind of stuff I'm into. I'm always the middle-man, taking a cut from all sides, know what I mean? It's perfect, mate.'

You don't always need to use your cover story. Some people are not at all interested, they just want to do business and all they care about is what you've come for and how much money you are going to be spending. Others are the complete opposite, often simply because they are naturally curious. The second you sit down they'll ask, 'So how do you two know each other then?' It's idle banter but potentially dangerous all the same. Worst of all are those who are curious and also absent-minded. They can ask you how you met three or four times during the course of an evening. It could just be the effect of too much dope on their short-term memory but you can't help but suspect that they're making sure the story stays the same each time.

Of course, all this can work to your advantage when you need to put other people at ease. In a pub with an informant you can always fall back on, 'Hey, remember the first time we met?' and chat naturally for ten minutes about where it was, what you did and the fun you had. Anyone watching or listening has no reason to think it's anything but genuine. But it does highlight the importance of getting it right.

Once a scenario is established, it needs to be drilled time and time again with the informant, making sure you and they know it inside out. At the end of the day, the environment you are going into is extremely hostile and sometimes the plausibility of the legend you create is your only defence.

After two more games of snooker during which Danny managed to keep his mouth shut, the targets finally turned up.

Jack, the self-professed leader of the gang, was clearly a bit of a head case. He was about 5ft 8 tall with wide shoulders and a short neck that made him resemble a human pit bull. Andrew, his right-hand man, was taller, leaner and seemed more approachable, while Matt, the muscle man, looked like a Chippendales extra. All three were casually dressed in Armani jeans and Versace shirts that said far more than words ever could about how much money they were making. Danny made the introductions and then got back to the game with Matt while I sat down to one side with Andrew and Jack to discuss business.

'So, I understand you're looking for someone to buy some goods,' I said.

'Yeah,' said Jack. 'But listen, before we talk about anything, I want to pat you down.'

'You what?'

'You might have something on you.'

I wasn't wired up with a Nagra so in theory I should have been happy to be checked out. But at the same time I couldn't agree to it too easily, and it wasn't just to avoid losing face. Suppose I had to wear a Nagra at a future meeting or the next undercover in the chain was wearing one? The only thing to do was make it such a pain in the neck for them that they never wanted to do it again. 'You're having a laugh, ain't you? There's no way you're putting your hands anywhere near me.'

'We just want to be safe,' said Jack. 'You could be anyone, carrying anything. It won't take a second.'

'I don't fucking believe this. All I've got is my bus pass, car keys and a bit of cash and you want to fucking touch me up.'

'Look, either you let us pat you down or we don't talk. The choice is yours.'

'All right. But if you search me, I search you.'

It was his turn to look surprised. 'What? You can't do that.'

'And why not?'

'Man, this is our manor. This is our snooker hall. Everyone knows us. If you start patting us down they'll think you're Old Bill or something.'

'That's exactly my point.'

We settled for a mutual quick patting session but his heart wasn't in it. We must have looked like prats but it established that neither of us was wearing tape recorders, or carrying hidden weapons, which I was far more concerned about. Then we got down to business.

'The price of the merchandise is £32,000 per kilo,' he said firmly.

I shook my head. 'No way, mate. It's way too much. You've got to come down on that.'

'That's what we're asking and that's what we'll take.'

'Forget it. No one's going to buy at that price. Now maybe if I was just after one ki', maybe I'd go for it, but when it comes to five, I want a discount, my friend.'

'What? You want to take all five kilos?' His eyes widened.

I paused for a split second. Jack's forehead had creased up in disbelief and the tone of his voice made me think I'd said the wrong thing. I ran over it in my mind and couldn't see what the problem was. There was no reason for him to be suspicious at me wanting to take all the drugs. 'Yeah,' I said slowly as if talking to a moron. 'I want the whole lot, which is why I want a discount.'

Jack turned to Matt and Andrew and shrugged his shoulders. 'We'll come back to you, through Danny, yeah?'

I wanted to say no, not through my dozy informant, but it would have come across as too eager. 'Yeah, through Danny is fine.'

We arranged to meet back at the snooker hall two days later and this time I left Danny behind. It made me feel safer. Arriving alone I buzzed at the fortified door and the voice of the guard crackled back at me. 'I was here before with Danny,' I said. 'The name's Philip, I'm meeting someone.'

There was a short silence. 'It's a members-only club and I don't see your name down.'

'I'm meeting Jack and Andrew,' I said.

This time the response was immediate. 'You shoulda said. If you're meeting those two you'd better come right in and wait inside.'

Ten minutes later Jack turned up with another member of his gang, Dave, who was keen to check me out for himself. I didn't like the look of him at all. He was a wiry, tough-looking man with a face full of scars and scratches that said don't mess. A wispy beard and moustache hung from his lower jaw and upper lip and his greasy black hair stuck out in clumps around his ears. Even though the club was dark, he kept his sunglasses on. I could feel him watching me the whole time.

'So, you bring a sample?' I asked.

Jack and Dave both shook their heads. 'Actually,' said Dave, 'I wanted to ask you about how you know Danny.'

I looked at Jack. 'Why the fuck didn't you ask me that the other night rather than dragging me back here?'

'Well, you can't be too careful.'

'Yeah, you said last time. But the point is I've turned up. I'm here, ready to do business. What I want to know is whether I'm wasting my fucking time or not.'

Jack chipped in. 'Nah, you're not wasting your time. We've got some stuff for you.'

'Great. You've got the stuff. Is it here?'

'No, it's not here.'

'But I can see it tonight?'

Jack looked at Dave then back at me. 'No, not tonight.'

The conversation was going nowhere but I managed to move it on to discussing the price, trying to negotiate a discount. I soon realized where their suspicions were coming from. They were new to the drug dealing game and were surprised to have met someone so quickly who had access to sufficient funds to buy their whole stock in one go. I was making them very jumpy.

'Are you the man with the money then?' Dave asked.

'That's not really any of your business. All you need to know is that I can do this deal.'

The plan had been to follow standard procedure and introduce one or two other undercovers, but as the evening wore on, so Jack and Dave made it clear that, having met me and sussed me out for themselves, they would not then want to deal with anyone else. Unless I could persuade them otherwise, I would be taking the job right through from first introduction to final bust, something that would put Danny's life in extreme danger as it would be obvious he was the informant.

The only way to try to convince them otherwise was to have yet another meeting with them. This time the venue was a house in Wood Green at the end of Saxon Road next to a set of pastel-coloured garages. It was one of those roads where every car was a battered Escort or Cavalier and every fifth vehicle was a Transit van. The Mercedes I was driving would have looked out of place were it not for the nearly identical model parked halfway down the road. I guessed correctly that it belonged to Jack.

I'd given the address to DS Taylor as soon as I'd got it and he'd run it through the computer to ensure it had not been the scene of any previous drug busts or arrests and that no major villains had ever lived there, just as an extra precaution. It came back clean. As I'd met the same guys twice before on their own patch, there was no cause for concern. In Taylor's opinion the job was going pretty well. He wanted me to press to make a test purchase, show the guys that we had access to money, and then push for a meeting with a second undercover for a bigger deal.

Two days before my next meeting with Jack, I was enjoying a day off when Chris Taylor called me on my covert line at home. 'I've given this number to a regular informant who has come forward with what sounds like a top-notch gun job. Loads of them available. Anything you're after. I want you to set up a meeting and see if you can move it forward. He should call later today.'

It's quite common for SO 10 officers to be asked to work on more than one job at the same time. They can find themselves posing as contract killers during the day, then adopting a completely different personality in order to try to buy child pornography in the evening. The ability to keep tabs on who you are supposed to be and when is another prime requirement for the potential undercover.

I spent most of the rest of the afternoon sitting within reaching distance of the phone. Even though my covert land line was usually hidden away, my son was now old enough to go rooting around for it whenever it rang. Although I knew he couldn't give much away, I didn't want anyone to know more about me than they had to. You make a far less convincing playboy drug dealer with a flash car and loads of spending money if people find out that you've got a wife and young kid at home.

Two hours later the informant, Toby, called up. His youthful voice was squeaking with enthusiasm. 'What I'm saying is, whatever you want, this guy can get it for you. Revolvers, automatics, Uzis, AK47s, fucking bazookas. You name it, man. It's just a phone call away.'

'So you've seen this stuff yourself then?'

'No, not myself, but a mate of mine hangs out with this bloke and that's what he told me.'

No one knows for sure just how many illegal guns there are in circulation in Britain. The best estimates vary between 500,000 and 2 million. Whatever the real number, one thing is certain: whereas guns used to be reserved for the criminal élite, today everyone who wants one can get hold of one. An old revolver can be had for £150 to £300, a newish semi-automatic runs to £700 or so while fully automatic machine guns or assault rifles start at around £1,500.

The popularity of weapons varies according to popular culture. When the *Dirty Harry* films were doing big business, everyone wanted a .44 Magnum. Then *Lethal Weapon* became a box office smash and everyone wanted a 9mm automatic Beretta. Black gangster films like *Boyz 'n' the Hood* and *Colors* boosted the popularity of the Uzi sub-machine gun, a pint-sized weapon capable of spitting out 600 rounds per minute, especially in Yardie circles.

James Bond's gun of choice, the Walther PPK, never took off. Although it looks stylish and fires 9mm ammunition, it has none of the stopping power of larger, more sophisticated weapons. The most highly sought after black market weapon of the moment owes its popularity to a myth. The Glock 17 L (the same gun favoured by members of SO19) is a 9mm, seventeen-shot semi-automatic pistol renowned for its high accuracy and immense 'put down' power. The gun is almost entirely made of high-tensile plastic rather than steel. The myth that makes it so popular is that it is the only gun in the world which will not set off an airport metal detector. But it's just a myth.

For up and coming criminals who don't want to risk keeping a weapon with them all the time, guns can be 'hired' from gangland armouries. The terms vary but generally involve a fee plus a returnable deposit. If the gun is fired, the deposit is retained and the renter is obliged to dispose of the weapon themselves. The reason for this is that no one wants to pick up someone else's history. Modern forensic techniques make it easy to match bullet fragments or shells to a particular gun. An unlucky armed robber with a hired gun could easily find himself charged with a murder he knew nothing about. Consequently great importance is attached to whether a gun is 'clean' or 'dirty'.

Chris Taylor had got very excited about Toby the informant. Although guns are recovered all the time in police operations, tracking down the illegal armourers remains a rare occurrence. Quite often, an armourer won't have a criminal record, will live in a respectable area and not be the sort of person who is known for hanging about in criminal circles which can make tracking them down almost impossible. But one such operator can be responsible for holding or providing guns for dozens, even hundreds of criminals involved in a range of crimes.

From the information Toby had given to Chris Taylor and then to me, it seemed we had latched on to one of the biggest armourers operating in south London.

The plan was that I would meet Woody, the armourer, and try to win his confidence with a small test purchase. I would then introduce him to a series of other undercover officers to help distance Toby from the final bust. Chris Taylor envisaged it as a very long-term operation. He hoped that we would not only be able to take all Woody's guns out of circulation but also gain valuable intelligence about the people he was dealing with.

Guns are a huge priority within SO10 so after speaking to Toby, I called Chris Taylor back and got the authorization to meet up with Woody that same evening. I went down to the pound to pick out a car for the job. I decided the Porsche 911 would be too flashy for a criminal of the level I was trying to portray, the same went for the BMW 535 which was less than a year old. I settled for a two-year-old Toyota Celica and was soon heading off for the meeting, due to take place in a diner in New Cross Gate.

I picked Toby up from the station half an hour before we were set to meet Woody. Because there was no time for us to work out a scenario from scratch, I adapted one that he and Chris Taylor had used on a job a few years earlier when Chris was still on 'active' duty. Basically the story was that I had been introduced to Toby by a mutual friend and had bought a gun from him a year or so earlier. Now I was looking to buy more.

Toby was twenty-two years old but looked far younger, dressed in typical skateboarder gear with a side-on baseball cap and tufts of untidy afro hair sticking out above his ears. My first impression was that he looked far too innocent to be a gangster, let alone an informant. His voice had not yet broken properly and whenever he tried to shout or got excited, it would jump an octave or two.

We met Woody in the corner of a fifties' style diner round the back of the tube station. He stood out immediately, his own ragamuffin street clothes in startling contrast with the acres of gleaming glass and chrome. He was tall and slim with several large gold rings hanging from each of his ears.

We sat in a booth tucked away in a corner, ordered a round of coffees, and began talking.

'OK, I'm not here to fuck about,' I said, getting into character. 'I understand you've got something you want to sell.'

Woody smiled. 'Yeah, man,' he said with the merest trace of a West Indian accent that showed he had spent most of his life in the UK. 'Got some guns, innit.'

'So what are we talking about? What kind of choice?'

'Choice?' Woody took a big slug of his coffee and eyed me as if I had suddenly begun speaking a foreign language. 'Ain't no choice, man. I just got two.'

I fought the temptation to grab Toby and ask him what the hell was going on and tried to carry on without showing my disappointment. 'What, so this is just a one-off then?'

'Yeah. Look, if you don't want them, I can get rid of them with someone else. Not a problem.'

It was a typical case of SO10 Chinese whispers. An informant hears one thing, passes it on to a friend who adds a bit and then passes it on to someone else, who adds a bit more until it becomes completely unrecognizable from the truth.

'So what have you actually got?' I asked.

Woody wiped his mouth on his sleeve before he spoke. 'Got a short barrel Smith and Wesson .32 and a .357 Magnum Python. You can have them both for £500.'

'Are they clean?'

'The Python's never been fired. The Smith was used to teach someone a lesson a couple of months ago.'

'What do you mean, teach them a lesson?'

'You know man, put one in someone. Wound them.'

'But what does that mean? Wound them in the foot or wound them in the head? It's gonna make a difference to how much I pay for it.'

After twenty minutes of haggling, we settled on a price of £400 for the two with the sale arranged for the following evening, one night before I was due to meet up with Jack and the others.

I called Chris Taylor after the meeting and he agreed that we were doing the right thing. Although he was disappointed that the job hadn't turned out how he'd expected, taking two guns off the streets was still better than nothing.

The following night I drove the Toyota down to a car park at the back of New Cross Gate tube station just as it was getting dark. I'd been there ten minutes when Woody turned up in a battered BMW and parked alongside me.

The back-up team were secreted in the bushes and abandoned railway arches at the far end of the car park but there was to be no raid. Arresting Woody would make it obvious that Toby was an informant and Chris Taylor felt he was too well connected and too valuable to risk that. Instead, Woody was going to be allowed to walk away with £400 of police money none the wiser. And there would be two fewer guns on the streets that night.

Woody pulled a canvas holdall out of the boot of his car and laid it on the ground in front of the Toyota so it was illuminated by the headlights.

'You wanna check them?' he asked me.

It suddenly occurred to me that I had no idea how to check a gun. I had never even held one before. 'You go first,' I said.

Woody reached into the bag and pulled out the Smith and Wesson. I watched closely as he opened the barrel revealing the cylinder. He span it a couple of times, then looked through to make sure it was empty. Before he had finished, I reached into the bag to pick up the Python to begin doing the same.

The first surprise was just how heavy it was. It felt like a solid lump of iron and at first I thought it might be caught on something. I soon adjusted my grip and followed Woody's actions, confirming that this gun was also empty before firing the empty chamber into the ground a few times to ensure the action worked properly.

Satisfied, I handed over £400 in £20 notes and shook Woody's hand. 'I can always use good guns,' I told him as he headed back to his car. 'If you get any more, give me a call.'

★

I arrived to keep my appointment with Jack and his boys. Both sides of the road were lined with beech trees pruned back so high that their first branches didn't spread out below about fifteen feet. Jack's house was right at the far end with unpainted dark bricks ingrained with dirt, three narrow sash windows on the upper floor and a front garden so small it was filled by his wheelie bin. I rang the doorbell and Jack opened up, revealing a large steel portcullis on the other side, held in place with a giant padlock.

'Don't mind the precautions,' he said casually. 'You can never be too careful around here.'

'Yeah, yeah.' By now I was used to the fact that Jack and the others were super cautious so it didn't faze me at all. Jack set about opening the security gate and, as Matt hovered around in the background, we stood in the hallway arranging the next stage of the deal.

'I think we're going to be able to do something this week,' said Jack.

'Right. And what about the discount?'

'Well, I've talked with the others and it won't be a problem. We just need to sort out exactly how much. You still want to take it all?'

'Yeah. But I want to make a test purchase first, check how pure it is. And there's no point in you bringing me a wrap with a couple of grams in it. You need to bring a full ki' over and we'll choose the point to take the sample from together. It's not that I don't trust you, it's just that . . .'

'You can't be too careful, yeah, I know,' said Jack, finishing my sentence with a smile. 'Can't argue with that. Come through and have a seat while we sort it out.'

Leaving Jack to lock up behind me, I stepped into the hallway, pushed back a heavy wooden door and took the first right into the living room. Matt was there along with Andrew and another man I didn't recognize. A wave of unease washed over me. 'All right lads, how's things?' sounding more confident than I felt.

Matt was about to answer but was distracted by Jack viciously slamming the door shut behind me. And that's when the shouting started.

'Who are you?' spat Jack, his face inflamed with sudden anger and viciousness.

'Where are you from?' Matt and Andrew joined in the barrage of demands. 'Who do you work for?'

They were getting overheated, gabbling at the top of their voices, then they started pushing me back into a corner.

'We're gonna fucking cut you up unless you tell us what we want to know.'

'You're dead you motherfucker. We're gonna fuck you up big time.'

I glanced around the room, taking in the situation quickly. All the windows were barred and the front door had been locked. And there was no way I could get past the three of them. But worse, I didn't understand what the hell was going on. 'For fuck's sake, will just one of you talk at a time. What the fuck's going on?' I yelled back. That just made them more angry.

'Are you trying to tell us what to do?' Jack sneered, poking me hard with his index finger, obviously provoked by my efforts to try to get a handle on things.

'Who do you think you fucking are?' said Matt.

Matt took a step forward and pushed me so hard I stumbled backwards. 'You stupid fuck,' he hissed. Instinctively I pushed back, sparking an even greater rage. Matt raised his fist. 'You want some of this? C'mon. You want a piece?'

Then Jack's voice cut through the others', lowering the tempo a little, but still loaded with menace. 'The thing is, mate, we're not happy with you. We need to check you out.'

'What do you mean you're not fucking happy with me?'

'You could be anyone. You could be police. You could be the man sent here to kill us.'

I laughed. 'Yeah right, like I'd really come down to kill the three of you on my own. Anyway you checked me out, you met me with Danny, patted me down.'

They were so jittery and they didn't know what they were

doing. It was as if they had bought a book on how to be a drug dealer and they were going through the chapter entitled 'How to check your sources'. It was pathetic.

'Look. Just tell me exactly what you want.'

'We need references,' said Matt enjoying his choice of words. 'We want to know how you know Danny.'

I took them through the whole scenario, how I'd met the guy in Liverpool, how we had started doing a bit of work together and so on. 'Look lads, we can get in a car and I'll take you to Liverpool and you can see for yourselves.'

Andrew sucked his teeth. 'You're just trying to be flash now, you wanker. You're just taking the piss.'

'I'm just trying to help. Let's face it, the mood you guys are in, I'm fucked whatever I say.'

I was waiting for them to start pounding me. Instead they sat me down in a chair and tried to tie my hands together. 'What the fuck do you think you're doing? No way, get the fuck off!' I shouted, fighting wildly.

And they just bottled it. Matt gave up trying to grab my flailing elbows. 'OK, we won't tie you', trying to sound in charge. 'But just sit there. We're going to go and check you out.' Andrew couldn't resist an extra dig, 'And if you don't check out, then the only way you're leaving here is rolled up in a rug.'

With that the three of them slammed and locked the living room door.

I leapt up, ready to force the door and make my escape but I caught myself just in time. Although I'd heard the front door open and shut, I had no way of knowing if all three of my captors had left the house. As I stopped to think, I heard soft footfalls and muffled voices from upstairs. I kicked myself for not paying enough attention when I came in to notice whether it was all one house or two separate flats. Either way, with the security gate on the front door, there was no way at all I'd be able to get out that way.

I checked the windows at the front of the living room. They too had bars across them, far too narrow for me to be able to slip through. There was no doubt about it. I was trapped.

I took a deep breath, sat back down and thought about what was likely to happen next. Technically, I couldn't see that I had anything to hide. I'd established a cover as a legitimate buyer and showed enough interest in buying their drugs to keep them keen. The big problem, of course, was Danny. He was so flaky he was likely to let the truth slip after a couple of pints, let alone a thorough beating.

If by some miracle he held out, it would look really odd if they came back after half an hour and found me trying to squeeze out of a barred window. That would give the game away that I had something to hide. On the other hand, if Danny cracked, and I had no reason to believe that he wouldn't, then the second they opened the door they would either put a bullet in my head or begin torturing me for information. I'd dealt with dozens of cases of gangland torture during my time in the CID and it wasn't something I relished the idea of experiencing first hand.

The days of the Krays, when your bollocks would be wired up to a car battery, seemed tame compared to some of the modern methods. In the East End the favourite torture technique was to take a hammer drill and make a 5mm hole in the top of someone's big toe, right through the nail, drilling straight down until the bit hits the ground underneath, spraying blood and gristle around the room every inch of the way. One south London gang liked to tie people face down on the floor, rip their shirt so their back is exposed, and then place an iron between their shoulder blades. The iron is plugged in and switched to maximum heat. Within seconds it begins scorching and melting the flesh beneath it. The pain is enough to make even the strongest pass out within seconds. When this happens, the iron is switched off (but not removed) and the victim revived with a bucket of cold water. Then the iron is switched back on. Even thinking about it made me shudder.

I was trying not to allow myself to panic, not to think about other 'treats' they might have in store for me, but I couldn't help it. I looked at my watch. An hour had passed and there was still no sign.

I was dying for a slash but there was nothing around. I worried about my family. My wife knew I was working but had no idea where I actually was. The SO10 operations team's first thought was unlikely to be that the meeting had gone wrong. After all, I'd met the same guys twice before without any problems.

Like an insomniac's in the early hours, my mind flicked from subject to subject but always came back to the worst that could happen. In theory SO10 officers are trained to cope with every conceivable situation but there was no way to prepare for a reality like this. We'd covered kidnap and hostage negotiation as a part of the training course but the scenario had ended so badly, I was struggling vainly to keep the memory of it out of my mind.

It started with a class outing to a farm in Bedfordshire to work a scenario about a major drugs buy. As often happened, the dealers were being portrayed by two SAS men, drafted in from their base in Herefordshire especially for the day. My classmate Tim was to be the undercover buyer while the rest of the class played the roles of the back-up and arrest team.

During the pre-bust briefing Ken, our instructor, had sat us down and set out the conditions under which the deal would take place. 'This is a really important buy,' he explained, seeking to make the scenario as realistic as possible. 'We've been working on this gang for months and we're all set to take them out. The armed back-up are already in position, you guys are the arrest team.'

He pulled out a map of the farm. 'The back-up will be in two vans parked here and here. Tim, you're going to make your way to this barn next to the main farm house here. That's where the targets will be waiting. From our observation point, we can cover you only outside the building. If you go inside, we won't have a clue what's going on. What you want to do is, as soon as the targets open the door, get them to come out to your car to look at the money. The attack signal will be you opening the boot. As soon as you do that, stard back and watch the cavalry arrive.'

Half an hour later I was one of five officers squeezed into the back of a Transit van tucked into the side of a barn off the main dirt track leading to the farm. Through a rear peephole I watched Tim drive past in a Range Rover and started flexing my legs, ready for the arrest.

Tim was wearing an open-mike radio transmitter fitted to a speaker in the van so we could all hear what was going on. We listened as he parked the car in the farmhouse driveway and got out.

'Testing, testing,' he said softly as he made his way across the gravel path to the barn. 'Hope I'm coming through loud and clear.' As he reached the door, Tim came back into our narrow field of view and we looked on as he rang the doorbell.

And that's when all hell broke loose. The heavy wooden door was whipped open and a burly forearm reached out, grabbed Tim by the scruff of the neck and dragged him inside. We winced in sympathy as we heard the kicks and punches hitting his body, accompanied by his muffled screams.

Cutting through the racket a new voice shouted out of the upper floor of the barn, 'We know you're listening. Don't try nothing, we've got your man and we're gonna kill him.'

What should have been a simple drug buy had turned into a desperate hostage situation.

Within ten minutes a superintendent who was attending a nearby training course on hostage negotiation was brought in to practise his skills. 'OK, get me a phone link with the people inside the building. I want to see plans of the entire area, and I want the head of the armed response team here right now.'

The farm was transformed into a flurry of activity as, desperately trying to keep out of sight of the main building where the hostage was being held, we took up support positions according to the Super's wishes.

The soldiers refused to answer the phone, so the Super was forced to crawl up the muddy path to the edge of a drystone wall and begin the negotiations using a megaphone. 'Don't make a bad situation worse,' he began. 'Let him go now and things will be better for you.'

'Fuck off!' came the reply. 'We're gonna kill him.'

The Super cleared his throat. 'There's no need to kill him. Tell us what you want.'

'We just want to kill this bloke,' a voice shouted back.

'Surely you must want something.'

'We've got everything we need: guns, knives, the lot.'

'Well, can we swap that hostage for someone else?'

'Why? We want to kill this fucker, not anyone else.'

An hour passed with no sign of movement from the captors. Apart from the occasional scream which seemed to be coming from Tim, the farmhouse was silent.

'Look, you're going to need food and water at some point,' said the Super, trying a new tack.

'No, we don't.'

'Surely you must need food at some point.'

'No, 'cos when we kill him, we're gonna eat him.'

And so it went on. After two and a half hours of getting nowhere, the Super conceded that there was no way to negotiate with the captors. The only thing to do was send in an assault team to stage a rescue bid. 'The problem here,' Ken explained, 'is that the captors feel they have nothing to lose. They might as well be hung for a sheep as a lamb so they might as well kill the hostage.'

Minutes before the assault was to be launched, the barn door suddenly opened a little and Tim stepped out. The poor bloke was completely naked, with a length of cheesewire around his neck and the sharp edge of a Bowie knife resting a fraction of an inch under his testicles. His hands were tied behind his back and he genuinely looked absolutely terrified, almost weeping with fear and shivering with cold.

'Come on then you bastards,' said a voice. 'Come and get him. We'll see how much is left by the time you get here.'

Not before time, Ken, breaking with protocol, quickly called the training exercise to a halt. 'I think this one is getting just a little bit out of hand.' He couldn't suppress a thin smile at how things had turned out.

As I sat in Jack's living room waiting for him and the others to return, Ken's words were echoing through my mind. If Danny had cracked and admitted I was a copper, the gang would almost certainly have to kill him. And once they did that, they'd have nothing to lose. They might as well kill me too.

I glanced down at my watch. Three hours had gone by. I started to sweat and looked out of the window again. I couldn't allow myself to panic. There was no way to break past the grille but I could at least smash the window and shout for help. The problem was that in doing so I would be completely changing the dynamic of the situation, placing myself in the centre of a siege, the last thing I wanted to do.

Four hours. My imagination played cruel tricks on me. I wondered how they would do it. Would they throw the door open and quickly fire a couple of silenced rounds into the back of my head? Would Jack use a blade? Maybe Matt and Andrew would hold me down while Jack kicked me in the face until I passed out. It was always Jack finishing me off.

Five hours. My stomach lurched and rumbled with nerves and hunger as time dragged on. I knew my head was twisting everything, making it seem a hundred times worse but I couldn't stop myself. I wanted to get out of there so desperately. I pulled up the carpets, looking for loose floorboards, looked in drawers and corners for some kind of weapon. Anything I might use to defend myself. If I'd had it, I didn't want it to happen without putting up some kind of fight. But there was nothing, nothing apart from the chair which looked as if it would fall to bits if I picked it up, let alone hit anyone with it.

After six desperate hours, I heard the key slot into the lock and turn. The door slowly swung open and the trio swaggered in. 'We've checked you out,' said Jack. 'And you're cool.'

But I was still in character. And now my character was fucking furious. I couldn't let that be the end of it. You can't go through something like that and then say, 'Well, thanks very much, I told you I was OK.' You have to show the indignity, you have to show strength. I leapt up from the chair and punched Jack square in the mouth sending him reeling back against the door frame, his eyes wide with pain and shock. I scrambled on top of him and hit him, smacking him in the face, his head slamming against the floor, before Matt reacted by grabbing me from behind and hauling me off. 'You fucking bunch of wankers!' I raged, trying to wriggle out of Matt's grip. 'I'm gonna come back here and kill the fucking lot of you. You guys are bang out of order. I'm gonna fucking tear you apart.'

Andrew jumped in to break up the fight while Jack picked himself up and tried to defuse things. His apology came through his rapidly swelling cut mouth. 'I'm sorry, easy, hey, easy. Fuck. We just had to be sure. We were just being careful, man.'

'Fuck that,' I shouted in his face. I was ranting now but I didn't care. 'You guys are fucking amateurs and I'll be back. You cunts are history.' Then I bundled past them and stormed off fuelled by a potent mixture of anger and fear.

Contrary to my expectations, the operations team were tearing their hair out with worry by the time I got back to the station. They'd received a telephone call from the informant a couple of hours earlier. Jack, Matt and Andrew had gone round to his house and beaten the crap out of him in an effort to find out if I was who I said I was.

Danny had been left with a broken leg, a fractured pelvis and a cracked vertebra. Despite the ferocity of the beating, he had refused to say anything other than the scenario that we had prepared. Although I gave him full credit for that, it's not as if he had much choice. If he had admitted that I was a police officer, Jack and the others would have killed him on the spot before returning to the farm to do the same to me.

The DS from the drug squad was furious with himself. 'We should have followed you, we should have fucking followed you,' he kept saying.

I put a reassuring arm on his shoulder. 'Don't worry about it. It's just one of those things. It could have happened on the first night, it could have happened after I'd spent a week with them.'

It was lucky that I had been dealing with a group who were clearly out of their depth. They weren't used to the ways of the drugs underworld. I still couldn't get over the fact that when I told them to fuck off and not tie me up, they had just left. It made me lose all respect for them. It was also about the only cause for optimism at all while I was locked up in that room. If you're going to do something in this company, you have to do it 100 per cent. Never back down.

I got on the phone to DS Taylor that afternoon and told him what had happened.

'I'm well pissed off about this,' he said. 'Talk about the wheels coming off. You've had six hours in solitary, the informant's had a beating and we still ain't got no drugs. So how did you leave it?'

'I threw a few fucks around, pushed one of them about a bit, told them they were all a bunch of cunts and walked out.'

'Right,' he paused for a moment. 'So you didn't get a number then?'

I could picture him smiling at his own wit. He was joking but as far as he was concerned the job was toast and the only way to get it going again would be to find a brand-new informant and start afresh. As for my involvement, there was no way I could go back to the gang, not unless DS Taylor was willing to sanction murder.

I was playing the part of a hardened drug dealer and the only way to respond would be in character – to go back there with a 9mm to blow their heads off. They wouldn't expect anything less.

9

Martin: The Johnston brothers were international car thieves at the highest level, running a hugely profitable, tight-knit firm which specialized in ringing high-quality motors. They didn't bother with Escorts, Astras or ten-a-penny family runarounds; instead they restricted themselves to the likes of BMW, Mercedes and all the big four-wheel-drive machines, Range Rovers, Cherokees and Land Cruisers, and they worked to order.

A typical scam would start with the gang using their network of contacts to find a nearly new BMW 3- or 5-series that had been involved in a big collision, preferably smashed up at the rear, and declared a write-off. They would buy that for peanuts – often as little as £500 – from an unsuspecting scrap dealer, claiming they wanted it for a few spare parts, and as a matter of course would be given the car's log book and paperwork. The brothers employed a small group of highly experienced teenage car thieves and one of those would then be instructed to go out and steal an identical BMW from the same year and in the same colour. The thief would get a few hundred pounds for their trouble – not bad for what was often little more than an hour's work.

The stolen BMW would be taken to a scrapyard controlled by the brothers. Sometimes it would be literally chopped in half and the good end of the write-off welded on to the matching end of the stolen car. Other times they would simply remove the chassis and engine numbers from the write-off and weld them to the stolen vehicle. Either way, the end result would be a car that, although officially declared a write-off, had somehow miraculously been repaired. With all the necessary paperwork to show that the 'new' car was legitimate, the final stage in the scam would involve the brothers hiring someone to pose as a private seller to advertise the car in a local newspaper, at an average 'bargain' price of around £15,000 but often much more.

While most car theft gangs went around in T-shirts and jeans, the brothers preferred smart suits and ran their operation like a multinational corporation. They appointed individual 'executives' to take charge of areas such as advertising and sales, research and development – even personnel. They also operated a bonus system for the employees who distinguished themselves each month. The techniques more than paid off. In a good week, they would steal at least five cars and were believed to be earning close to a million pounds a year.

I learned all this while sitting in a quiet corner of an upmarket seafood restaurant in south London with Nick, an informant, and his friend Bernard, a former associate of the Johnston brothers. Nick was in his mid-twenties and a bit of a south London lad who, with his shoulder-length blond hair, sparkling green eyes and barrow boy charm, wouldn't have looked out of place in a boy band. He had his own motor repair shop but ran a business on the side which specialized in ringing convertible BMWs. A week earlier he'd been caught red-handed with six partially stripped down models in his lock-up garage and now faced going down for a hefty chunk of bird.

In a desperate bid to keep his freedom, Nick had approached the Met's car crime squad and offered to grass up some of his competitors. He'd done it a couple of times before and escaped custody as a result but this time was a little different. The squad pointed out that his offences were so serious that his only chance of staying out of the slammer was to assist in bringing down a team of heavy villains. The Johnston brothers fitted the bill perfectly.

The world of the professional car thief is a relatively small one – there are only so many scrapyards to go round – and whenever one of their number gets collared, no matter how minor the offence, word travels through the grapevine like wildfire. If the arrested person gets released on bail there follows an unofficial period of exile during which no other car thieves will make contact or return calls. Everyone is familiar with the way that police recruit their informants and knows only too well that someone who has just been arrested is a prime candidate for turning grass.

Because of this Nick was doing his best to keep his latest trip to the courts as quiet as possible. As he worked mostly alone and stole each of the cars himself, he didn't have to worry about suppliers coming by and asking for payment. The Johnston brothers were known to employ a 'security consultant' who looked through the court listings each day and made a note of any familiar names, but Nick had a ten-day window of opportunity until his first appearance at the magistrates' court.

Despite his precautions, a few people harboured suspicions about Nick simply because he had been arrested and charged on a number of occasions and had yet to serve any time in prison. But some people are just lucky like that. Nick seemed to have been given the benefit of the doubt, but he knew that his luck couldn't hold out for ever. If it happened again he'd have no chance of pulling the same trick. This was his last chance to stay out of jail.

I got assigned to the job because of my obsession with cars. During my time on the crime squad, before I joined up with SO 10, I specialized in chasing car thieves. I knew pretty much every technique there was for ringing a car and I knew the location of every engine number and security device on most of the major models. I'd be able to talk comfortably about the art of car theft until the cows came home and would therefore find it easy to fit in.

Although also a professional car thief, Bernard was about as different from Nick as it was possible to be. He used to work for the international division of the Johnston brothers' corporate crime machine. Orders would be received from as far afield as Spain, Pakistan and Thailand for prestige cars which would then be stolen to order.

'It was dead simple,' he said, sucking the meat out of a bright red lobster claw. 'We'd go around the West End late on Friday night or during the small hours of Saturday morning, picking up Porsches, Range Rovers and whatever else we had orders for. The ones for the Far East had to be shipped out in containers but if they were for Spain or Ibiza, you'd just pack up your luggage that same night, load it in the back of the nicked car and set off. You're well on your way before it's even been reported stolen. You always paid cash on the ferry so they could never trace you and you had to remember to buy a return ticket so you avoided suspicion.

'Once you were there, you delivered the car and then took a flight back. Couldn't be easier. Best job in the world. And I'll tell you another thing, Martin,' he said with a chuckle, 'there aren't many people who get paid to go on holiday.'

Bernard was in his early sixties with a mop of grey hair that barely covered his fast-growing bald patch and a deep tan from all the time he had spent on Spanish beaches in between 'working'. Although he was a master craftsman when it came to car theft, he realized he was getting a bit long in the tooth. He had officially retired from the game and was planning to move to Tenerife to see out his days there.

Nick was hoping to use his friendship with Bernard as a way in to the brothers. He had brought me along for Bernard to suss me out, see if I knew what I was talking about so that he could put in a good word for me. As we chatted away, it became clear that the pair were obviously extremely close.

'Bernard's like a second father to me,' Nick said with a smile. 'You've known me since I was what, nine years old or something.'

'No, don't,' said Bernard giggling. 'You're making me feel old. I don't want to feel old. It's bad enough thinking about retirement.'

As I was sitting there in this lovely restaurant, with the sun streaming through the curtains, eating my lobster and joking with the others about the silly plastic bibs that they had insisted we wear, I was actually having a pretty good time on this undercover assignment.

Bernard started talking about car ringing, some of the things he had got up to in the past. He was explaining to Nick about using an angle grinder to erase the chassis number on a car then stamping a new one on by hand as a way of disguising its identity. I thought it was time I threw in my ha'penny's worth.

'You have to watch out though,' I told him. 'The police have these X-ray machines and they can scan the number and tell if it's been tampered with.'

Bernard nodded brightly. 'You're right. That's true. I know a couple of people who have been caught out that way. You're better off removing those sections altogether and welding in the bit from the other car. As long as you do a good enough job, hide the joints, you can get away with it.'

We talked about the finer points of ringing and twinning – a process whereby a car is stolen and given the identity of an identical car in a different part of the country. The owner of the original usually only finds out this has happened when they receive a parking ticket or speeding fine intended for the owner of the counterfeit.

We talked about using 'grabbers', electronic devices that picked up the signals from infra-red door openers. You could stand 200 yards away from a car and, while the real owner locked it, use the grabber to pick up the code and then open the doors at your leisure. If you were also armed with a set of false keys – widely available in the right circles – it meant you could steal some of the flashiest, most lucrative cars on the market without so much as scratching the paintwork.

We chatted about the way that some manufacturers were trying to catch the ringers out. They had started adding extra chassis numbers in odd places that, if you weren't aware of them, would immediately point back to the car's true origin. One company had even inserted a tiny slip of paper with the chassis number into the springs under the back seat, a pretty sneaky trick but a simple and incredibly effective way of catching out all but the most accomplished car thieves.

As I'd suspected, I wasn't telling Bernard anything he didn't already know, but by sharing information about my supposedly criminal past, I put him at his ease and showed that I knew what I was talking about. It seemed a dead cert that I was going to get a first class recommendation. What I didn't know at the time was that the brothers had already decided that Bernard was dead wood. He may have been as sharp as a tack but he might just as well have been senile for all the notice they took of him.

The trouble was that Bernard was of the old school, a dying breed, the sort of bloke who would never hit a woman and hated kids who mugged old ladies or burgled the houses of people who had nothing worth stealing. The sort of bloke for whom grasses were the scum of the earth and who would rather go to prison for a crime he didn't commit than co-operate with the police.

Although villains like to think the notion of honour among thieves still exists, it's just a load of hot air. All of the biggest, best-known and most dangerous criminals around, from Kenneth Noye and the Yardie Aldridge Clarke to Great Train Robber Charlie Wilson, have informed on those around them when it suited them to do so.

Of course, Bernard had no idea that Nick had become an informant, or that I was an undercover police officer. In fact, I soon realized that Nick had another agenda: he was anxious to ensure that Bernard had truly retired from the game so that there was no chance he could get caught up in any subsequent raid. Or find out what Nick was up to. 'I'm telling you Martin, I'm glad he's moving abroad,' he had told me as we made our way to the restaurant earlier that day, 'it would kill me if Bernard went down for something. The Johnston brothers are bad news, no one is going to miss them if they get put away, but Bernard, he's virtually family. I wish I could tell him the truth about what I'm doing. Deep down, I know he'd agree. But at the same time, I know he'd never understand, he's old school. He'd cut me out of his life completely and that would be too much to take.'

Before he left for the Canaries, Bernard had put in a few calls to the brothers but they had refused to talk to him. Nick phoned me a couple of days later sounding more anxious than ever, 'I think we're back to square one.' He knew that time was running out. His court appearance was looming, and once his name was listed it would be only a matter of time before the brothers found out and he would have no chance of stitching them up. The following week all was quiet and I thought the job was going to come to nothing.

Then one afternoon as I sat in the Plaistow CID office, Nick called me out of the blue. 'I think I've cracked it, Martin,' he said cheerfully. 'Can we meet up?'

This time the venue was a grotty pub in Streatham. The bar was a tiny semicircle up by the door and the seating was split into individual booths along both walls. At the far end a giant TV screen was showing highlights of an obscure Nationwide league football match. Nick was already there when I arrived, sitting in a booth and knocking back his second bottle of lager. I got myself an orange juice and joined him. 'OK, what have you got?' I asked him.

'It's good stuff, Martin. Basically I put the word out that I knew someone who was interested in getting his hands on some tasty motors with a view to sending them overseas. And I've hit gold. It just so happens that the brothers are looking for some new people who they can offload and sell stuff to. I've spoken to someone really close to them, they say they've heard my name and they've agreed to meet up with the two of us. I'll call you later in the week, let you know where and when.' I'd never seen him look so happy – and relieved.

Most of the time Nick was a bit of a hard nut. You could tell, just by looking at him, that he could take care of himself and there was no doubt that he'd been in plenty of scrapes to prove it. But every now and then, a softer side would emerge. 'Hey, Martin. Do you want to see something really special,' he said as I drove him home after our meeting.

'It's not illegal, is it? I'm not going to have to nick you for it, am I?'

Nick laughed. 'Don't think so. Not unless you've started moonlighting for the CSA.'

He reached into his back pocket and pulled out a tiny gold heart-shaped locket. Inside was a picture of a baby, no more than eight weeks old.

'I didn't know you had a kid,' I said.

'That's because I don't really. This is Holly. She must be five years old now but this is the only picture of her that I've got. Things between me and her mum didn't work out. She buggered off to Essex. I think she's with someone else now, got other kids an' all.

Don't think Holly knows anything about me, probably thinks this other bloke is her dad and that really pisses me off. But when I look at her picture, I dunno, it just makes me think that one day something good might be round the corner. Things might turn out OK.'

'Let me give you a tip then, give you a head start. Stop nicking stuff.'

Nick slapped his forehead and smiled. 'Shit. Hadn't thought of that. I was thinking more along the lines of pulling off one really big job and then retiring, but giving up – yeah, that's good too.'

We spent most of the following day together, going over the scenario we had created, working out the best way of introducing me to the brothers and so on. Usually, I didn't have a lot of time for informants but I found Nick fascinating. So we chatted easily about how he had got into crime – 'It just happened. One day I found myself with no money and then I saw some car with a handbag on the back seat. I only made £40 but it seemed like a fortune. It was downhill all the way after that' – and about his struggles to go straight.

'God knows I've tried, but it just follows you around. The problem is, when you run a motor shop, people know that you've got access to tools and other bits and pieces. At least twice a week I get offered something dodgy – switching the numbers on something that's been stolen, changing the locks because the owner has "lost the keys", that kind of thing. It's all very well taking the high moral ground and turning it down but when you're working for yourself, there are bills to pay and it's the only work around, it's a lot harder to say no. After a while you just think fuck it, if I'm gonna break the law, I may as well make proper money out of it rather than just peanuts. So that was when I started stealing motors myself.'

Despite his youth, Nick had already managed to pack into his life a variety of experiences from the joy of fatherhood to the despair of drug addiction. 'I started off with weed because everyone I knew was doing it. I liked it, it helped me relax, so when other things came along I tried them all, just to see what they were like.

LSD was a blast, watching buildings walk around and shit like that but mostly I just took speed 'cos it was cheap and let me party all night. I never touched heroin though – can't stand needles – and that made me think I'd never become a real addict. But then crack came along.

'The first time is always the best time. It felt like the top of my head had come clean off. Every other time you do it, you're just trying to repeat that first high. Spent a fortune on the stuff. It was only when Holly's mum left me that I realized how much it had taken over and that I had to clean myself up. I ended up moving back in with my parents. They practically locked me up. Banned me from seeing all my old friends for three months until I'd got my head straight.

'Coming off crack was the hardest thing I've ever done in my life but having done it, it kind of gives me hope. I think if I can do that, I can do anything. I know I keep fucking up every now and then, but I've had enough of this game. I mean, Bernard's a great bloke an' all, but I don't want to end up like him, an old has-been always wondering what might have been.'

'What made you become an informant then?' I wanted to know more.

'It all happened four years ago. I'd been caught with my paws on a couple of well-dodgy motors. I knew that I was looking at some serious time. I'd got out only three months earlier and I just couldn't face going back again. It's rubbish when people say they can do their bird standing on their heads. It grinds you down. The detective who arrested me, he seemed like an all-right bloke. I saw the chance of doing a bit of business and told him about one or two things that I'd heard. He said he'd follow them up and put a word in for me at court. I ended up getting off with a fine. After that it was easy. I knew the kind of stuff he was interested in and I'd pass on bits of information. Sometimes for a leg up, sometimes for a bit of cash, sometimes just for a laugh.'

Officially informants are supposed to refrain from getting involved in crime themselves but everyone ignores that. The only way they can get to hear of anything that is of any use is if they are living the life themselves. So every now and then they pass stuff on to the police, and every now and then they do the job without telling anyone and line their pockets. And it's the times when they get caught that they come running to the police to try to set someone else up.

Depending on how well connected they are and what sort of information they are willing to provide, informants can earn pretty good money. A day-to-day snout who does little more than keep a local CID officer up to date on who has burgled what might earn around £20 a time. An informant on a bigger, one-off job will probably command a fee of a couple of thousand pounds. When it comes to providing information on bank robberies or jewel thefts, the informants are entitled to a share of whatever reward money is on offer, usually 10 per cent of the value of the haul which can often amount to tens of thousands of pounds.

The really big money is where the really big risks are: informing to Customs and Excise about major drug importations. For class A drugs like heroin or cocaine, Customs will pay a reward of £1,000 per kilo of drugs recovered. If an informant can get a tip about a large-scale shipment, they can set themselves up for life. More often than not, they also sign their own death warrants. When a gang loses out on a big shipment, they don't rest until someone has been made to pay.

Nick, however, was only in it for beer money and a kind word to the judge. During the day, he had repeatedly been trying to make contact with the Johnston brothers but drawn a blank. Although, like all good villains, they had mobile phones permanently clamped to their ears, they gave out their numbers only to a handful of people. Information about cars, deals, payments and the like had to be made through a series of intermediaries – the brothers' corporate communications division if you like – and confirmation or instructions would come back via the same route. Direct contact with the brothers was so rare that some people wondered whether they really existed at all.

In all we spent four hours making constant phone calls and hanging out in two Southwark pubs in the hope that one of the brothers or one of their associates might happen past. One place in particular, the Marquis of Granby, seemed to serve as an unofficial messaging centre. As we sat nursing our pints we watched a succession of villains come in and ask the barman, Mark, if the brothers had been in. And every few minutes the phone would ring and Mark would take messages clearly intended for members of the gang.

That afternoon, as we were driving along the south bank of the River Thames, Nick's patience finally paid off. He gave me a thumbs-up sign while chatting on his mobile and set up an arrangement to meet with the brothers the following evening.

'These guys are really ultra fucking cautious,' said Nick as he came off the phone. 'They want to know what car I'm going to be driving and everything. I don't think they'll like it if we suddenly turn up in a different one. I'll pick you up outside the station at six.'

I shook my head. 'Don't be a twat Nick, don't turn up at the police station. Park down the high street, outside the post office, and I'll meet you there.'

I went back to the CID office alone and spent the next couple of hours finishing off paperwork for an assault case that I was investigating. Just before 5 p.m., I went to the locker room to get changed. I'd just taken off my suit and was pulling on my lucky NUFF RESPECT cap when the inspector came running down the corridor and stuck his head round the door.

'Where do you think you're going?' he asked.

'Told you earlier, guv. I've got a meet with an informant. It's an SO 10 job. I'm being picked up in an hour.'

'Not any more you're not,' he didn't sound as if he was going to be open to persuasion. 'Half the relief's off sick and the CID office is like a fucking ghost town. Cancel it. I really need you to work late otherwise we're all going to be in the shit.'

'Leave off guv, it's taken for ever to set this up.'

'You think they're going to give crime the elbow overnight and go into pizza delivery? It'll hold.'

That was that then. I got on the phone to Nick. I knew my

words upset him. 'Fuck! I don't fucking believe it,' he said. 'They just called me up about five minutes ago to confirm the whole thing was still on. They're dead keen. They'll be well pissed off if I cancel on them now. Is there really no way you can make it, even for a bit?'

'No can do. Not at all. Sorry, mate. See if they can do it tomorrow.'

Three minutes later Nick called back. 'They must think I'm all right. They said no problem at all, we can do it same time, same place tomorrow. But they want me to go along tonight anyway, talk over a few bits and pieces. They probably want to know a bit more about you as well.'

'That's fine. Just stick to the scenario.'

'Leave it to me. I'm going to big you up big time.'

It turned out my guvnor was telling the truth. We really were short staffed and I ended up staying at the office until well past ten, transcribing interview tapes, collating paperwork and checking statements. By the time I got home I was so exhausted that all I could do was go straight to bed. It was just as well. Kathy had got fed up waiting for me and gone to bed herself, but at least it meant the night didn't end in yet another row about whether my work was more important than she was.

I woke up the following morning feeling as if I hadn't had any sleep at all and arrived back at the CID office feeling as if I'd never left. I was looking forward to having an early night but then I remembered that I'd rearranged the meeting with Nick for that evening. Somehow I didn't have the heart to cancel him again – especially as his court appearance was only three days away. Sleep would have to wait.

I was on my third cup of tea of the morning when DS Taylor called. 'Hey Martin, how's it hanging?'

'A bit lopsided Chris, but it's nothing a week's sleep wouldn't put right. What can I do for you?'

'Well, you know you're supposed to have a meeting with an informant tonight, well he's not going to be able to make it. He's put on a bit of weight.'

'Chris, you're not making sense. I don't know what you're talking about.'

'Didn't think you would. You better have a look at the papers.'

Still confused I put the phone down and reached for the *Daily Telegraph*, the nearest paper to hand, and began flicking through, scanning the columns. It didn't take long to find the story.

An unidentified man was last night in critical condition in hospital after being shot six times while waiting in his car close to a set of railway arches in Southwark, south London. Witnesses to the attack say two men in their mid-twenties walked up to the driver's side of the car, produced handguns and fired repeatedly without warning. The man was hit in the chest, shoulder and leg. He was taken by air ambulance to St Thomas's hospital where he is under armed guard. Police are keeping an open mind about a possible motive.

As I read I could feel myself getting more and more short of breath as my chest tightened. A wave of nausea surged through me and I scrambled to the toilet, locked myself in a cubicle, and crouched panting over the bowl for ten minutes. Once I realized I wasn't going to throw up, I slumped on the pan with my head in my hands, thinking about Nick's shooting and how close I'd come to being there with him.

When I eventually got back to my desk, there were half a dozen messages from Chris Taylor to check I was OK. Naturally I was taken off the Johnston case immediately. In fact all undercover operations linked to the gang were stopped. It was just too dangerous. For all we knew, Nick might have been threatened before he was shot and blabbed details of the police operation against the brothers.

We were still as busy as hell in the CID office but my guvnor said I could take the rest of the day off. I refused. I wanted to keep myself occupied and was grateful for the chance to throw myself into my work.

I felt numb for the next three days. The news dented my confidence alarmingly. I felt I had no right to be doing that kind of work if people were getting killed as a result. I wondered if I could ever work undercover again or whether I'd lost my bottle. But after two or three more days, the feelings began to subside and I started to recover. I figured that, when you looked at the case closely, all the signs were there. The targets had been far too accommodating, far too eager to meet on their own turf. Nick had come across as being desperate, and with his past record that could mean only one thing. He had paid the price for playing out of his league.

The Johnston brothers and a couple of their associates were brought in for questioning but they all had rock solid alibis for the time of the shooting. We learned from other informants that they had hired a couple of gunmen from Manchester and brought them down especially to do the job. It seemed they didn't know what Nick was planning, just that he seemed too eager to meet up with them. Confident that the chances of them ever being convicted of anything to do with the attack were almost zero, the brothers decided the easiest option was to take him out of the equation altogether.

By the following Friday, ten days after the shooting, I had been assigned to a new undercover job, to bring down a gang that was stealing luxury rugs and carpets from factories off Brick Lane and shipping them to Europe.

Nick died in hospital two days later.

10

Philip: 'Their names are Philip and Martin and they are right evil bastards,' said the voice on the Nagra tape. 'Believe me, you don't want to cross either of them. For fuck's sake don't piss them off, otherwise, and I ain't messing about here, otherwise you could die on the street. They'll blow you away in a heartbeat.' The voice belonged to Christian, an undercover detective operating out of Southgate. He had spent three months working his way into a gang of cannabis smugglers in Walthamstow and was setting them up for the final bust.

The leaders of the gang were originally from Pakistan and had been using their contacts across the border in Afghanistan to purchase large loads of cannabis which were then being shipped to Britain hidden in containers supposedly of dried fruits.

Martin and I had never met but we had been picked by DS Chris Taylor to play the role of the drugs checkers. While Christian met up with some of the smugglers to show them the money, Martin and I would meet up with their main courier, Clint, to check the merchandise before the money was handed over. But of course the exchange would never take place and all members of the gang were set to be arrested.

Working undercover is never easy, but every now and then a job comes along where all the hard work has already been done and everything has been set up in advance. Over the months, Christian had done such a good job of building the two of us up to be a pair of such ruthless killers that poor old Clint, a fairly low-ranking member of the gang, was absolutely terrified.

The meeting took place just after 9 p.m. in a little car park off Plevna Road at the back of the Edmonton Green shopping centre. Martin and I were driving this huge Mercedes. We had only met about twenty minutes earlier and were still getting to know one another when we arrived at the plot and parked. Five minutes later, a battered Transit van turned up and a little weasel of a man clambered out and waved at our car. His lower body was silhouetted by our headlights; I could see his knees were shaking.

'Are you . . . are you the geezers?' he stammered.

Martin and I got out of the car and strode over to him. As I got nearer, I could see he was as white as a sheet and sweating.

'You all right, mate? You don't look well. What is it?'

'Nothing. I just don't want to get on the wrong side of you guys.'

'Well, just so long as the drugs check out OK, you won't, will you? Show us what you've got.'

Clint shuffled over to the back of the Transit and opened the doors. Inside, packed in neat blocks from the floor to the ceiling, were huge lumps of cannabis wrapped in brown plastic. There were 100 kilos in all, a deal worth £180,000.

'OK,' said Clint, moving to close the doors again.

'Hey, not so fast,' said Martin. 'There could be any old crap in those packages. Open a couple of them up so we can have a look.'

Clint let out a sigh. He was obviously hoping that he would be able to get out of there as quickly as possible. From the way he was walking, it looked as if he desperately needed a piss and we were holding him up. He reached into his back pocket and pulled out a small flick knife, then reached into the van and cut a sliver off the corner of the nearest block.

I took a sniff and passed it to Martin, who rubbed it between his fingers and held it up to the light. We knew this bloke was completely in our power and we wanted to play around with him as much as we could. As Martin acted the part of cannabis connoisseur, I could tell he was having a hard time keeping a straight face. After what seemed like ages, he passed the sample back to me, nodding sagely.

'My man says it's acceptable,' I said. 'Open up a couple more.'

Clint couldn't believe it. 'You want me to open up a couple more?'

'Yeah. That's what I said. Obviously we ain't got time to look at all of them, but we're certainly going to look at a few. That's the way it's going to work so you'd better open up a couple more. You got a problem with that?'

'No. Sure, whatever you say. Sorry, I didn't mean nothing by it.'

This time, when the guy took his knife to the slab his hand was shaking so much he could barely keep his aim.

'Do you want me to do that for you, mate?'

'*No!* I mean no, it's OK.' He was clearly unhappy at the idea of letting me anywhere near the knife.

'Sort yourself out or this is going to take for ever. Just steady your hand and cut the damn thing, will you?'

With each new sample, Martin and I went through the same routine. We were starting to enjoy ourselves, and couldn't resist upping the ante. It wasn't just about being cruel, there was real novelty in doing a deal when the gangsters were scared of *us*. Usually it's the other way around.

'You know . . . I'm not sure about this one,' I said when it came to the third sample, turning to Martin. 'What do you think?'

Out of the corner of my eye, I looked across at Clint. I could see his knees wobble as I spoke. I was sure he was about to faint. Martin took the bait immediately. 'What, you think it's fake? You think this geezer could be trying to rip us off?'

Clint staggered backwards, trying to get to the safety of his van. 'Oh Jesus. No. It can't be. It's all good stuff. Oh shit. Let me check. Please, just give me a minute.'

By now Martin had taken the sliver of cannabis and run it under his nose. 'Actually, I think it might just about be OK. It's not what we're used to, but it'll do.'

Ten minutes later and well aware that Christian would be getting impatient, we decided to put Clint out of his misery. 'OK, it's fine. It's good stuff. We'll take it.'

Even from where I was standing I could almost feel the relief sweeping over him. 'Really? That's it? You don't need to talk any more, you don't need to see any more?'

'No, that's it. You just go and sit in your van and I'll tell my people that it's OK to hand the money over.'

The bloke rushed to me and grabbed my hand with both of his, shaking vigorously. 'Thank you, thank you so much. I really mean it. Cheers, mate. Thanks. Really appreciate this. Pleasure doing business with you, a real pleasure. Thanks. You're a real gentleman. Both of you, real gentlemen.'

He held on to my hand just a little too long and shook just a little too hard. 'All right. OK, mate,' I said. 'Sure. Yeah, OK. Now just get the fuck off my hand, get back in your van and wait, will you?'

While Martin made a quick call to Christian, I gave the attack signal, taking off my coat and swinging it over my shoulder. That same instant a dozen bright red pinpricks began dancing on Clint's chest as the SO19 sharpshooters trained the laser sights of their weapons on him.

As he climbed into the driver's seat of his van he didn't notice the members of the arrest team sprinting out of the darkness across the car park towards him. He only spotted them after the first shout of 'Armed police, you're under arrest!' echoed through the night air. Clint froze with fear, standing open-mouthed and staring at the screaming bodies running towards him. As one officer got within range, he dived at Clint, grabbing him round the neck and dragging him to the ground. Martin and I climbed back into the Merc and drove off in the opposite direction, bursting into laughter at how Clint had been so intimidated by us.

We met up with Christian and the rest of the squad later that evening for a celebratory drink and, while everyone else took part in a contest to see who could drink the most pints of lager in the shortest possible time, Martin and I sat in a corner with a bottle of beer each and pissed ourselves laughing about how much fun we'd had.

Through the jokes and reminiscences, we discovered we had loads in common: neither of us had harboured a long-term ambition to join the police and we both found the overtly macho canteen culture difficult to take at times. On the other hand we both loved police work, especially the jobs for SO10, and couldn't imagine doing anything else with our lives.

Martin told me about the first time he bought a gun. He'd met up in a car park with this shady bloke who pulled a .38 Smith and Wesson out of the folds of his jacket. 'How much do you want for it?' asked Martin. 'It's a two-er,' replied the bloke. Never having bought a gun before, Martin thought the man meant £2,000 and started trying to beat him down – to £1,500 – until he realized he meant £200.

I told him of the time I was in the back of a taxi with a major coke dealer, being followed by an arrest team. The attack signal was that I would put my arm across the back of the rear seat. Once I was sure the bloke had the drugs on him, I gave the signal. Nothing happened. So I put my arm down then gave the signal again. Still nothing. It turned out that the arrest team had been caught up in traffic and were so far behind, they couldn't see me signalling. I had to stall the bloke, who was wondering why I wasn't handing over the money, until they finally caught up and made the arrest.

The more we talked the clearer it became that we would enjoy working together again.

Three weeks later we found ourselves behind the counter of a second-hand goods store in Walthamstow. It wasn't just any old store. The place had been set up especially by the Met as part of the anti-burglary initiative, Operation Bumblebee. The staff were two SO10 officers who had spent three weeks letting it be known that they were willing to buy pretty much everything and anything, regardless of where it came from. The word spread like wildfire, and within days local criminals were virtually queuing up around the block to offload their stolen booty.

Every new sale was damning evidence. The shop had a hidden video camera positioned over the entrance and three more covering every square inch of the inside. Covert tape recorders automatically switched on every time the door opened, capturing every word.

The two original SO10 officers, Jeff and Pete, had to attend a court hearing halfway through the operation so Martin and I were drafted in to cover for them. It was enormous fun. All day long groups of muggers, car thieves, ram raiders, burglars and lorry hijackers would come along and ask us to take a look at what they had.

For once, it made sense for us to offer over the odds. We knew we'd get the money back once the criminals were arrested and, more importantly, it meant the owners of the stolen property would get it returned to them. Right from the start we believed the villains would think it was all too good to be true but no one suspected. They were probably blinded by greed and the chance to make a fast buck.

The only time anyone expressed any doubts was on the second day when a boy of no more than fourteen who had sold Jeff and Pete a Rolex the week before came sidling into the shop and nervously inspected the walls and ceiling.

'Can I help you?' I asked.

He squinted at me, then approached the counter. 'Are you two police?'

I feigned genuine surprise. 'Now how could we be police? If we was police, would we be buying all this stuff, giving you good money an' all?'

The boy scratched his head. 'Nah. I guess you wouldn't.' Then he turned and walked off.

Ten minutes later he returned with a video recorder.

The operation ended a few days later and was pronounced a resounding success. In three weeks almost 400 local criminals walked into the shop with stolen goods valued at more than £500,000. One gang of ram raiders brought designer clothes worth £80,000 while a single teenage thief produce thirty car radios in less than twenty-four hours.

Martin: Two months after the cannabis job and a week after we'd finished working in the shop, I was asked to infiltrate a gang of armed robbers whose glory days were rooted firmly in the seventies. They were real throwbacks who had done loads of time, then come out and decided to move into dealing ecstasy. As soon as I heard about it, I called Philip and made sure he was available to be the money man on the operation. I really looked forward to working with him once more.

It was a job where the informant was more of a liability than anything else, far more dangerous that the gangsters I was going to be dealing with. He looked and sounded just like Shaggy of *Scooby Doo*, a gangling figure well over six feet tall with thin straggly hair, a wispy beard and beady little eyes. He was such a slippery customer he all but left a trail of slime wherever he went. At the time he was up before the court for a load of burglary with a long list of other offences being taken into consideration and was desperate to avoid being locked up.

The first night I met him, in a pub in Thamesmead, he seemed to forget completely what his role was. 'Hey, Martin, when we get this thing off the ground I've got an idea. You're gonna get all this police money to buy these tabs right? Well, we should split them. Give me half the tabs. I know someone I can sell them on to. I can get a really good price and then we can share the money out. No problem. What d'you say?'

Jesus! This guy was a fruitcake. I took a long sip of my drink, then looked him right in the eye. 'Mate, there's something I should point out to you right now just to ensure there is no confusion later. I am a policeman, you are an informant. I put that to you right now. Forget all the undercover crap and the buy and the money. The only thing you need to remember is that I am the policeman and you are the informant. I don't need to be here, you do. I can go home at any time I want, you can't because you've got a problem. So just leave out all this crap about taking some of the drugs and selling them on. Just stick with what you're supposed to be doing and we'll get along fine.'

Shaggy winked at me. 'I know what you're worried about. It's that Roger Cook, ain't it? You think I might be setting you up and stuff. Thinking about what's going to happen to your kiddies if you get sent away and lose your job. Nah man, this is cool. Just you and me involved. Big money. We can clean up.'

I couldn't believe this space cadet. He was like something out of a bad dream. 'Listen, mate. You don't know jack shit about me, you don't even know if I've got a family. I'm here because I've got a job to do. And that job is being a policeman. And your job is being an informant. Anything other than that, just forget it right now.'

I hoped I'd got my message across but Shaggy was in a world of his own.

The first time we met the targets was in a pub in Welling. I was seriously worried that Shaggy was going to say something idiotic and give away the fact that I was a policeman and was relieved when, after a few minutes of conversation with the two former robbers, he got up and wandered off to do his own thing.

Graham and Hugh were both in their mid-fifties with lank grey hair falling over their foreheads. Graham had a noticeably bigger than average jawbone that made him look like another cartoon character, Desperate Dan. Hugh was the younger of the two but looked much older. His face was so covered in lines that he looked worried even when he was perfectly happy.

The pub was enormous with one long wooden bar with a brass foot rail along its length, but managed to feel cosy because it had a number of wood and glass partitions splitting it into small sections. We were sitting around a square table beside the unlit fireplace. At first the two blokes seemed a little intimidated by me, particularly Hugh who hardly spoke a word all evening, but as the number of pints of bitter consumed went up, so they began to relax.

'We're both a bit new to this game,' Graham confided.

'Oh yeah?'

'Yeah. I think we're more from the old school. We've both done a bit of time for armed robbery. I tell you Martin, when I started out, none of the blokes I knew would touch drugs. You wouldn't even have a drink before you went out on a job. Nowadays, everyone's at it.'

'True, it's where the money is, mate. Always follow the money.'

Graham settled back in his chair. He was feeling more comfortable now and wanted to open up to me, to share his philosophy on the criminal life. 'The whole world has changed, and not necessarily for the better. Running into a bank with a shotgun, it used to be something that only professionals did, and you could earn good money out of it. I've done bank jobs and come away with eighty or ninety grand. It might not sound like a lot to a youngster like yourself but back in the seventies, that was a fortune.

'Today all the gaffs have security cameras, exploding bags, time lock safes – all sorts of shit. If you're really lucky and have a blinding day, you might come away with, what, two grand. Two grand. I ask you. I mean, if you do things properly, it just ain't worth it.'

'Properly?' I said, genuinely interested in what he was saying and the chance to have a history lesson in organized crime. 'What do you mean by properly?'

'In my day, you didn't just have your best mate driving the car, you had a wheelman, a proper getaway driver. Then you'd have a couple of lookouts down each end of the road that the bank was on and then you'd have at least one other bloke inside there with you to watch your back, make sure none of those have-a-go heroes tried to get in the way. But all that costs money. It means you do a bit of work, you get two grand and you have to split it five ways.

'If you look on *Crimewatch* these days, the bit where they have all the film of blokes and even birds doing bank jobs, they're always on their tod. The money they're getting, it's not worth their while otherwise. And they don't even take guns no more. No one with any sense does 'cos you know what's gonna happen. You're gonna get yourself killed.'

He was now getting into his stride, warming to the theme. 'My mate Tony Ashe, I shared a cell with him at Parkhurst, he did a job a few years ago just to try to get a bit of money to pay for some Christmas presents for his kids. He was working with this other geezer, Ronnie Easterbrook, nasty piece of work. Anyway, they plan a hit on this security van in Woolwich, just round the corner, and because they're all from the old school, it's all set up properly, two getaway cars, face masks, the lot. Only the bloke who is looking after one of the cars for them, this little shit called Seamus Ray, he decides to grass them up.

'The job goes off without a hitch, they've got £10,000 on them, but then they get to the spot where they're changing cars and that's where the ambush goes down. Dozens of police, all armed, yelling through their megaphones to put the guns down and all that. Easterbrook, nutter that he is, points his gun and is about to let one off when he gets hit in the shoulder. The getaway driver takes one in the hand and poor old Tony, he gets it through the heart. Dies on the spot. Fucking tragedy it was.

'In the old days the police didn't have to bother with guns because it wasn't about hurting people. It was never about hurting people, just getting the money. I used to load the sawn-off with cartridges filled with rice. You'd run in, shout out that it was a stick-up and fire a shot at the ceiling. There'd be a hell of a bang and the lights would go out, so everyone would think it was the real thing, but if you ever got caught the judge would give you time off because he'd know you were never going to kill no one.'

I looked at him, wondering if he realized just how terrified the people he had robbed would have been, regardless of his efforts to do no harm.

'It's not the same now though. That's why when I came out, I decided to knock it on the head. I may not understand all this drug stuff and I'd certainly never take it myself, but selling it is a hell of a lot safer than what I used to do.'

I'm sure Graham's tale of gangland woe could have gone on all night. He didn't get a chance to continue, silenced by a huge commotion from the direction of the toilets. I could hear a familiar voice shouting, 'I ain't done nothing. Fuck off you big ape. I ain't done nothing.' Predictably enough it was Shaggy, having a fight with the landlord of the pub who was manhandling him towards the front door.

Shaggy's fists and feet were flailing all over the place but the landlord, who indeed was something of an ape, was much too strong for him. Every now and then he'd sock him in the side of the head to shut him up but mostly he just dragged him through the crowded bar. It turned out that Shaggy had vanished off to the gents where he had proceeded to try to sell dope to anyone who came in, usually while they were having a slash.

Shaggy's bruised and battered body was being dragged not more than five yards from where Graham, Hugh and I were sitting, but we all chose to ignore him. 'That man is a prize prat,' said Hugh.

'You got that right,' said Graham.

I said nothing. Unfortunately the scenario that Shaggy and I had come up with made out that the two of us had been friends for some time. I was hoping I wasn't going to screw up the deal by being associated with such a tosspot.

'I'd better go and check that he's all right,' I said reluctantly, getting up to leave.

'I'm sure he's fine,' said Graham with a smirk. 'He's probably learning a valuable lesson. Best let him get on with it. Have another drink.'

I left the pub half an hour later and found Shaggy sitting on the kerb, tending to his wounds and waiting for me. 'There you are Martin. I thought I'd lost you.'

'Maybe next time,' I whispered under my breath.

Just when I thought things couldn't possibly get any worse, Shaggy started trying to hitch the two of us a ride home. Typically his technique left a lot to be desired. He would stand in the middle of the road, both his hands out in front of him and scream, 'Give us a lift, you bastard!' to every car that went past. He succeeded only in terrifying several lone female drivers and causing lots of boy racers in their souped-up GTis to swerve at the last minute to avoid running him down.

I'd arranged a second meeting with Graham for later that same week and made a mental note to do my best to get rid of Shaggy as quickly as possible. I arrived at the pub and found Graham at the bar, but there was no sign of Shaggy. After waiting for half an hour, Graham had had enough. 'I'll tell you what, Martin,' he said. 'If it's all the same to you, I think we should cut the guy out of the deal. He's unreliable, he's unprofessional and he's a fucking idiot. If we take him out it'll be better for all of us. What do you say?'

'You took the words right out of my mouth.'

We soon got down to business. Graham might have been new to the drug game but he was intending to start pretty near the top. I was posing as a man who controlled a network of doormen who worked at clubs across the country and therefore had the ability to sell drugs undetected. It was a plausible cover because that's exactly how it works. It's the only way you can have clubs where everyone gets searched at the door but somehow drugs are freely available when you're inside.

In most cases, doormen will confiscate any drugs they find and pass them on to their own dealer. The going rate is £1 per tab sold. In many cases, the money doormen make from their drug racket is many times what they earn from their day jobs, let alone what they're being paid for spending a night on a door.

Graham offered me 25,000 tabs to start and the plan was that I would take 25,000 every week after that. 'Come on Graham, there's no way I'm going to take that many off you when I don't know you. No offence, but I think we need to start on a smaller number first and then build up. If the product is good, then I'll happily place a regular order.'

We eventually settled on 5,000 for the first run, priced at £6 each, which on approval would lead to far bigger, weekly orders. The deal was set up for the following week.

As well as Philip, who was going to be the money man, I had taken on Leroy Palmer. Along with a female detective who was posing as his girlfriend (just to make the whole thing seem even more legitimate) Leroy would be the man who would go and check the drugs, the same way Philip and I had done with the cannabis. Leroy would also be the one wearing the Nagra and would record Graham or Hugh talking about the drugs while they were being verified.

We arrived at the venue in two cars, Philip and I in a two-litre BMW, Leroy and Mo, his girlfriend for the night, in a convertible Saab, and parked round the back. Leaving the others in place, I walked into the main bar where, once again, Graham and Hugh were already waiting for me. They both seemed very excited to see me. Even Hugh seemed much more talkative than usual.

'OK,' said Graham after we had got the small talk out of the way. 'Let's do it. Let's go get the stuff and sort it. You've got the money on you, haven't you?'

I looked at Graham. 'You are new to this, aren't you? It don't work like that. What is gonna happen is that I have a man outside, an expert, who is gonna go and look at your drugs. If he is happy, he will come back and give me the OK to hand over the money.'

Graham's face fell. 'I don't know about that,' he said. 'I don't really want to get anyone else involved. I'm happy dealing with you. Why can't you come with us?'

'If I come with you that means leaving the money,' I explained, 'and that's something I'm just not prepared to do. OK, how about this: my man will go and look at the drugs with you. If you are happy, you can all come back here, with the drugs, and we will do the exchange right here.'

This time Graham was happy. His main concern seemed to be the idea of handing over the drugs to anyone but me. He obviously felt comfortable with me but was still uneasy in his new role.

'Well if that's all OK, you'd better come outside and look at the money.'

Graham's face fell again, this time a little further. 'I ain't going outside with you. Can't you bring the money in here?'

By now I was laughing inside once again. He was obviously scared shitless. He was convinced he was going to be shot in the head and robbed the second we got him into the car park.

After a few seconds of dithering, Hugh stepped forward, nervously. 'Come on Graham,' he whispered, but loud enough for me to hear. 'We'll both go.'

We walked over to the BMW. It was a cold night and Philip was sitting there in a couple of coats with jumpers on underneath. He looked absolutely huge, like one of TV's gladiators or something. Graham and Hugh were taking little pigeon steps towards the car, flicking their heads round at every little sound. As they got close, the electric window of the Beamer hissed down and Philip leaned out.

'Y'all right?' he growled. He might just as well have been eating raw meat off the barrel of a gun. He couldn't have looked tougher and meaner if he tried. The money was in a plastic bag on the seat right between his legs. 'Here it is,' he said. 'What do you want to do? You want to sniff it? You want to touch it, feel it? What you want to do?'

Graham and Hugh were at least ten feet away when they raised themselves up on their toes so that they could just barely see into the BMW. 'That's fine,' said Hugh. 'Looks like £30,000 to me,' he said.

'I agree,' said Graham, lowering himself back down. 'I'm sure it's all there.'

Philip leaned his head out a little more and raised the bag a little higher. 'Yeah, but what do you want to do? Don't you want to count it?'

'Nah,' said Hugh, backing off now. 'We'll take your word on that, mate. We'll be off now.'

The geezers were being so obliging, so eager to do business that for a while it crossed my mind that perhaps there had been an almighty cock-up somewhere. Perhaps rather than being a former armed robber, Graham was really a member of another undercover squad and we were targeting each other. It hasn't happened yet but what with Customs, MI5 and other agencies all running their own undercover operations, it is bound to happen one day.

I dismissed the thought – if they were another squad they would be trying to buy, not sell – and got on with the task ahead, resting my hand gently on Graham's shoulder. 'OK, you see that car over there?' I said, pointing to the Saab. 'That's our man. He's going to look at the drugs. He has just come over from another bit of business and he has his woman with him. If he doesn't come and see the stuff now, it ain't going to happen. If he says the stuff is good, then we will crack on, if he says it's shit, then the deal is off. So you go over and see him and then we can do business.'

What happened next surprised us all when we eventually found out. Graham and Hugh invited Leroy and his girlfriend into their car and took off down the road. They stopped outside a three-bedroomed semi which turned out to be Graham's family home. After introducing a bemused Leroy to his equally bemused wife and kids, Graham led him out to the garage where he produced a large bag of ecstasy tablets.

If Graham was scared of me and Philip, what sort of state was he going to be in after an encounter with Leroy? I had returned to the car with Philip and we had decided to move away from the pub car park, just in case Graham had hatched a plan to send a team to rob us of the money.

We were parked on the side of a hill up the high road overlooking the pub when we saw Leroy and the others return. Once inside and with the drugs in a little rucksack, Hugh and Graham helped themselves to a much needed drink and told Leroy that they would wait inside while he went out to fetch me and the money. As Leroy left the pub, he took his hat off. That was the signal.

From our vantage point we could see dozens of shadowy figures running towards the pub and a sea of blue flashing lights burst into life.

The best part of the job was that Graham and Hugh never suspected that they had been set up. When they were arrested they told the police that they had been in the pub having a quiet drink when they had noticed this rucksack on the floor. They opened it up and saw the drugs inside and were just about to hand it in to the barman when the raid took place.

They changed their minds and pleaded guilty once they heard Leroy's Nagra tapes.

Martin: As Philip and I cheerfully chalked up our biggest joint success, we were blissfully unaware that just over 100 miles away, an insignificant little man we had never heard of and would never meet was about to set off a chain reaction that would ultimately lead to disaster.

It all started in late February in Handsworth, Birmingham, when Del Jones, an informant for the West Midlands Police drug squad, passed on a tip that his former friend, twenty-three-year-old Carl Marshall, was well on his way to becoming one of the biggest crack dealers in the north west.

Crack cocaine is usually sold in 'rocks' costing around £20 or £25 each and even the most active dealers tend to have only a few rocks on them at any one time. Marshall, however, was selling the stuff in lumps the size of house bricks, each with a wholesale price of up to £90,000. Broken up into street deals, the same crack would be worth more than £500,000. Jamaica-born Marshall, a stocky six-footer, worked closely with his older brother, Lenny, a tough ex-soldier, and the pair had established a crack manufacturing plant in the basement of a house in Grovehill Road. The remainder of the house operated as a brothel with both Carl and Lenny acting as pimps, each controlling a string of prostitutes.

The head of the drug squad, Detective Chief Inspector Charles Morton, immediately set about gathering more information about the Marshall operation. Both brothers had previous convictions for drugs offences and the experience had made them extremely wary. They would now deal only with black buyers and insisted that customers travelled to Birmingham in order to do business. The Marshalls employed an extensive team of lookouts and assistants who had somehow managed to identify virtually all the officers in the local drug squad as well as all their unmarked vehicles. The whole gang would vanish at the first sign of a police presence.

As well as the crack factory in Grovehill Road, the brothers used properties in Victoria Road and Stafford Road. Pinning down their home address was impossible as they moved around constantly in order to frustrate attempts to observe their activities.

By May, as more and more information about the targets flowed into his office, it became increasingly clear to DCI Morton that standard police tactics would not suffice and the only hope of success against the Marshall brothers would be to launch a covert operation. One man who was the obvious choice – none other than foul-mouthed Floyd, the mixed-race, mole-faced detective I'd met during my SO10 training course. Floyd was the best man for the job because he was easily the most experienced black undercover in the area. It just so happened that he was also the only experienced black undercover working in the West Midlands at the time. With his appointment to the team, the operation code-named 'Marine' was born.

Posing as a crack user hunting for a £25 rock, Floyd set off in a taxi with Del on the evening of 24 June, hoping for an introduction to the Marshall brothers. The pair toured a couple of pubs and several key crack dens in the Handsworth area with Floyd waiting in the car while Del went inside to check who was about. Each time he returned saying that neither Carl nor Lenny were there but that he had been given another address to try. After an hour or so, Floyd was beginning to believe the whole thing was a wild goose chase when they decided to try the house in Stafford Road.

This time Del came back after five minutes with a big smile on his face. 'Lenny is home,' he said, 'he's going to come down and see you.' A few minutes later a short and skinny black man with close-cropped hair and a bright orange top leaned out of an upstairs window and waved to the taxi before running down and climbing into the back alongside Floyd.

'I'm Lenny,' he said breathlessly, his voice a harsh mix of Birmingham street slang and Jamaican patois. 'Do you want a two "o" or a two five?'

'Gimme a two five.'

'OK, no problem. Driver. Take us to Victoria Road. Now listen, Floyd, when we get there, you're gonna have to wait outside. I don't know you so you can't come in. Maybe next time. You got the money?'

Floyd handed over £25 as they arrived and Lenny disappeared for a while then returned with a paper wrap with a single rock of crack inside which he immediately handed over.

'Later, Floyd,' said Lenny and slipped away into the night.

With limited resources at his disposal, DCI Morton knew there was no point in rushing the operation. Unless he could find other undercover officers to introduce to the gang it would be blindingly obvious that Del had made the initial introduction and his life wouldn't be worth tuppence. And while Frank's test buy showed that drugs were readily available, Operation Marine had yet to establish that the brothers were indeed dealing in large quantities of crack.

While he considered his options, he ordered Floyd to take a 'softly, softly' approach, waiting several months until he next made contact with the Marshalls. The plan was that he would gradually ask for larger amounts of crack hoping the brothers would slowly come to trust him, so that when he introduced a 'friend' who had plenty of money to spend, their greed would be aroused and they would offer to supply a large quantity.

On the evening of 16 September, Floyd and Del drove to Stafford Road and waited until a cautious-looking Lenny appeared and quickly climbed in the back of the car.

'Hi, Floyd. How's things? What can I do for you?' he said.

'Fucking excellent, mate. Can you do me a fifty rock?'

'No problem. Do you know Soho Road? Go there and stop outside the two phone boxes opposite the Kentucky Fried Chicken.'

Soho Road was right in the heart of the Marshall gang's territory and was their preferred location for dealing. There were dozens of hiding places for their lookouts and it was easy to check whether a potential customer was being followed, had brought reinforcements or was under police surveillance.

When they arrived Lenny clambered out and made a phone call from the nearest call box, then got back in and gave Floyd directions to a cul de sac by Westminster Road. 'Wait here,' said Lenny, vanishing for a few minutes into a new terraced house and returning with a second man sporting short dreadlocks and a soft black leather jacket.

The man climbed into the back and spoke to Floyd without introducing himself. 'How much do you want?'

'I want a fifty rock now and a half ounce later.'

'OK. What do you pay per ounce?'

'About £1,200,' replied Floyd.

'Well, it's expensive here. It'll cost you £1,850 an ounce.'

'Forget it, I don't pay fucking silly money.'

No one in their right mind would pay that price for an ounce of crack and Floyd knew it. If he'd agreed, he might just as well have taken out his warrant card and stuck it to his forehead. Every buying operation is about balance. You're keen to make sure the job comes off and you're under pressure from the squad that set it up. That can lead you to offer over and above street value to ensure the deal goes ahead and that the sellers don't go elsewhere. But once you go beyond an amount that any dealer would consider reasonable, all you do is arouse suspicion.

In the drug world everything has its price and everyone knows exactly what that price is. There might be minor variations from town to town, from supplier to supplier, but you have to learn what those are before you go to make a buy, otherwise you can put yourself at risk of being robbed. The notion that a fool and his money are soon parted is never more true than when applied to drug dealers.

'OK,' said Lenny, 'I know somewhere else we can try, someone who might do you a better deal.'

Lenny told Floyd to drive back to Stafford Road. When they arrived at the house there was a BMW parked outside. 'Come on,' said Lenny, 'let's go.'

Floyd quickly realized that this had always been the intended place for the deal. The trip to Westminster Road had been purely for the benefit of the Marshall gang lookouts who were checking if anyone was tailing Floyd's car. It had also been a test to see how he would react to an offer to buy at way over the odds.

Floyd crossed the road and climbed into the BMW's passenger seat and Lenny got in the back alongside a man with long dreadlocks and a strong Birmingham accent who held out his hand. 'You wanted a fifty rock. Here it is.'

'Floyd wants a half. How much?' asked Lenny.

'How much do you pay for it?'

'I hear it's expensive here,' said Floyd, pocketing the wrap of crack. 'I'm not fucking paying over £1,400 an ounce.'

'I can do you half for £850. Take it or leave it.'

'OK. I'll take it. But if I want a larger amount, I want some kind of fucking discount.'

'We'll talk about it.'

Floyd handed over £50. 'Can we say a half in about two weeks' time?'

'Sure. Speak to Lenny. He'll sort it.'

Later that night, while the details of the meeting were still fresh in his mind, Floyd wrote up his notes in his undercover report book and submitted them to DCI Morton. It was clear that the Marshalls were intimating that they could supply larger quantities and he felt that the time had come to move the operation on to the next phase. That meant finding a new team of undercover officers who could be introduced to the gang and lead them through to the final bust.

On Thursday 13 October, a month after Frank's last undercover buy, I was off duty and relaxing at home when, out of the blue, the mobile phone that I used for all my covert operations burst into life.

'Martin? Hi, this is Detective Inspector Nigel Powell from West Midlands Police. I got your name from your old friend Floyd. He said you might be able to help us out with a job we've got running.'

DI Powell went on to explain the basics of Operation Marine, the fact that the targets had mastered the art of anti-surveillance, that they liked to do business in their own area and refused to deal with whites, that there weren't any other black undercover officers in Birmingham so they were having to recruit from outside the force in order to complete the job.

Although large crack seizures were becoming a regular occurrence in London, they were at the time still extremely rare outside the capital so the Marshalls were unknown territory. While nothing DI Powell had said made me think the job wouldn't be possible, it was crystal clear that I'd have to have my wits about me to bring it to a successful conclusion.

It just so happened that Floyd was due in London the following day for a meeting with the local Regional Crime Squad so I arranged to see him there and travel back to Birmingham with him. It was the first time I'd met him since the course, but as we got into his battered Vauxhall Cavalier, the car he used for all his undercover operations, I realized that he hadn't changed a bit.

'Fucking good to see you again, Martin,' he said. 'This job is going to be fucking great. Basically it's a couple of black guys selling crack as regular as clockwork. I've been into them a couple of times already. I've bought a two five rock and a fifty rock. Now they are looking to make a bigger sale. They think I'm just some fucking scumbag user but they know I've got connections to real money. We need someone who can play the part of a proper dealer. And that's where you come in.'

The journey up the M1 seemed to take for ever. The stereo in the car wasn't working so once Floyd had filled me in on more of the background to the job, I had no choice but to listen as he told me his adventures in the years since the course. I just switched off and watched the landscape until we got closer to Birmingham and started talking about the plan for the rest of the day. Initially I had just planned to meet with the senior officers in the case and then return to London, but Floyd had other ideas. 'Well, as you're all the way up here, do you fancy going out and seeing if we can meet the bad boys? We could knock on a few fucking doors, see who's about. Might even be able to get you the first introduction tonight.'

I agreed. To be honest, I was keen to get that first contact out of the way as soon as possible because that would mean I'd be able to take Floyd out of the equation. The two of us obviously had very different ways of working and the idea of trying to do things together didn't appeal to me one little bit.

I'd never been to Birmingham before and as we turned off the motorway, I idly gazed out of the window, taking in the sights and sounds. Within minutes we had arrived at the police station at Thornhill Road, a solid-looking red-brick affair on the edge of Handsworth and, much to my amazement, Floyd drove straight inside. I was speechless. I couldn't believe that Floyd would risk taking the same car he used for undercover work straight into the police station. It was ridiculous. I didn't like it at all. I didn't know the area or the people, I had no idea who might be watching. Especially when you considered how surveillance-savvy the targets were, it made me feel very uneasy. 'This is crazy, I'd never do this,' I gasped.

Floyd just looked at me, completely unconcerned, 'Relax. I do it all the fucking time. It's fine.'

I met with DI Powell who reiterated most of the things Floyd had told me on the road. Going out on a scouting mission meant that I was officially starting my undercover role, something I could do only after following protocol, so another senior officer read out the 'instructions to undercover officers' and handed me my official undercover report book.

I asked about getting expenses to cover my train fare back to London but the officer told me they had run out of petty cash. 'The best thing to do,' he said, 'is pay for it yourself and then claim it once you're back in London.'

It was turning out to be a pretty shitty day. I didn't imagine for a moment that it was only going to get worse. At just after 4.30 p.m. Floyd and I left the station just in time to see the bright winter sky cloud over and catch the first drops of a miserable drizzle that would fall for the rest of the evening. We climbed back into his crappy car to go looking for the brothers, drove out of the main gate, right at the end of the road, right again at some traffic lights and then pulled over. We had travelled less than a quarter of a mile. At first I thought that Floyd must have forgotten something, but then he switched the engine off. 'Here we are,' he announced. 'This is Stafford Road. This is where they live.' It was only when I saw the street sign that I realized he wasn't making a bad joke.

'I don't believe this. I don't believe this at all. We've only just come out of the police station and we're here already! This is the plot! You've got to be kidding.'

Floyd looked at me blankly, as if I was speaking a foreign language or something. 'Don't sweat. It's not a fucking problem. Come on, let's see if they're in.'

I'd complained about virtually everything Floyd had done since we'd met earlier that day and it was clearly getting to him but I didn't care. All I could think was that the sooner I got Floyd out of the picture the better.

Stafford Road was rubbish-strewn and run down. The smell of urine and rotting food hung heavy in the air – there was a public toilet at the top of the road, opposite a pub called the Frightened Horse, but no one seemed to use it, preferring a nearby wall. There were a few trees but all had rings of split rubbish bags growing around their base.

I couldn't believe that anyone, even a drug dealer, would want to live in a place like this. We walked up to a house with a solid wooden door, one of a tight row of nasty nut-brown semis, all topped with pointed attics that made them resemble witches' hats. Floyd rang the bell. There was no answer. He rang again and again and finally a sash cord window from the top room flew open.

A painfully thin, pasty-faced white girl poked her head out. She looked like a typical crack addict, the type that uses heroin to ease the trauma of coming down from a cocaine high and as a result spends the whole time completely strung out on gear of one kind or another. She looked down at us with her big hollow eyes. 'What?'

'I'm looking for Lenny,' said Floyd.

'He's not in. He hasn't been here all day,' the girl replied, her eyes rolling around in her head.

'Well, what fucking time will he be here then?'

'How the hell am I supposed to know? It's Friday. He could be anywhere. Try coming back around 6 p.m., he might be here then.'

For the next hour or so, Floyd and I drove around Handsworth aimlessly, killing time and trying in vain not to get on each other's nerves. At ten minutes to six we returned to Stafford Road.

Floyd rang the bell again and the same girl answered from the same window, looking even more wasted than before. 'Lenny hasn't come round. Haven't seen him all day. I don't know where he is,' she said, seemingly forgetting that she had told us the same thing earlier. 'Try his brother.'

'How the fuck do we get hold of him?' asked Floyd.

The girl sighed heavily and told us to hold on. A few minutes later she appeared at the front door and handed over a piece of paper with the words 'Carl, brother' and a mobile phone number scrawled on it. We took it and headed back to the car as the girl returned into the flat. A few seconds later, she came drifting out across the road and waved us down. 'Tell him you spoke to Rachel,' she said. 'He won't talk unless he knows where you got his number from.'

We tried the number several times that night but never managed to get through to anyone. Floyd and I also tried a few of the pubs and clubs the Marshalls were known to frequent but we failed to make contact. Sometimes we were told that we'd just missed them, other times that they hadn't been seen for days. A few people refused to say anything at all, obviously wary of falling out with the brothers by giving away details of their movements.

At 10.30 p.m. I was sitting opposite Floyd in a filthy pub close to Stafford Road eating a couple of slices of pizza – the only thing on the menu that looked vaguely edible – and drinking orange juice. Floyd suggested that I stay the night as it was getting late. I looked around. Every seat in the place had been slashed or broken, the carpet was stained with spilt beer and food. None of the other drinkers seemed to be smiling or even talking, except for an old black guy in one corner who was having an animated conversation with himself. I couldn't face spending any more time in such a depressing environment and I was due to start work at six the following morning. Once we'd finished I got him to take me to

New Street station and caught the first train back to London.

Although I'd managed to get a phone number for one of the main targets, I still felt incredibly frustrated. Because I had not been properly introduced, it was unlikely that Carl or Lenny would speak to me, even on the phone. It meant that I had to continue working with Floyd.

The following Tuesday afternoon, as I carried on with my normal CID duties back in London, not really thinking too much about Operation Marine at all, Floyd finally made a telephone break-through.

'Is that Lenny?'

'Who's this?'

'It's Floyd.'

There was a pause. 'I don't know you.'

'Is that Carl?'

'Yeah.'

'All right. At last. Is Lenny there? I'm trying to sort some fucking business out with him.'

'Who gave you this number? Where did you get this number from?'

'Some fucking bird called Rachel, Lenny's bird I think.'

'Describe her to me.'

'Fucking skinny thing, dark hair. I don't fucking know.'

'What colour is she?'

'She's a white fucking bird.'

Carl put his hand over the receiver but Floyd could still hear him speak to someone else in the room. 'Do you know some bloke called Floyd?' A female voice answered yes. 'Well, fucking speak to him,' said Carl.

The woman took up the receiver. 'Hello,' she said weakly.

'It's Floyd. Where is Lenny?'

'Hello, Floyd. I don't know, I haven't seen him.'

Carl snatched the phone away and came back on the line. 'Listen, what business are you doing with Lenny?'

'At this rate fucking none. He's an amateur.'

'Have you done business before?'

'Yeah, yeah. And now he's sorting me out a half of rock.'

'When?'

'I'm looking at this Friday. Do you know if he can do it?'

'All his business comes through me so I'll say yes.'

'We've agreed the price, £850. I'll ring you later in the week to make sure you can still do it.'

'OK, Floyd. I'll talk to you later.'

Over the next couple of days, Floyd made further phone calls and told Carl and Lenny that he was representing a gang from London who were keen to purchase large amounts of crack cocaine. Floyd explained that the London team were cautious and wanted a sample in order to check the quality of the goods on offer before committing to a large amount. If the test went well, there was a good chance of regular, substantial deals. The idea was to entice the gang into a situation where their greed got in the way of their better judgement. If we could get them to let their guard down, we could catch them all red-handed.

The promise of a big payday was too much for the Marshall brothers to resist and on Wednesday I finally managed to get through myself.

'Carl. It's Martin. Floyd gave me your number. I want to do some business with you.'

'OK. I know all about it. You have to come up here.' His voice was like his brother's but deeper and harsher in keeping with his considerably larger frame.

'Yeah, that's not a problem. I was going to be up there on Friday. Where shall I meet you?'

'Call me when you get here. We'll sort it out.'

The operation was now advancing far more quickly than I would have expected. At the time I was unaware of the amount of time and effort that the West Midlands had put into trying to catch the Marshall brothers. The police couldn't afford to hang about much longer and had to know for sure if the gang was able to supply large quantities of crack or not. They insisted that the next buy had to be for a substantial amount and asked that I set up a deal for later that same month for an even greater amount. It would be this second, larger buy that would form the backdrop to the raid when an armed team would swoop down and Carl and Lenny would be taken out of the game.

With so much riding on the operation, Floyd was eager to ensure that there would be no problems. On Thursday, the day before the deal was due to take place, he called Carl's number once again. This time it was Lenny who answered.

'Lenny. It's Floyd. You OK?'

'Yeah. You?'

'I'm all right, mate. Look, are we still on for Friday?'

'Yeah man, no problem. Just ring me when you get here.'

'I don't want any fucking about when I get there. I want my stuff and I'm fucking off.'

'No worries.'

On Friday I took the early train to Birmingham and met up with the members of the drug squad. They seemed keen to bring the Marshall gang to book and were obviously grateful for my assistance. They made available £850 of police money to finance the first big test buy. 'Better make sure there's no uniform or plain clothes in the area, I don't want to spook these geezers,' I told them when Floyd and I were about to leave. 'It's not worth their while to cause any trouble for such a small amount of money. It's better if Floyd and I are there on our own.'

At 5.30 p.m., as we sat in the car park of a pub near the brothers' home, Floyd called Carl's mobile. 'Carl, it's Floyd. I'm here, are you ready?

'Look, ring back in ten minutes.'

'Are you pissing about? Do you want my business or what? OK, I'll ring back but you better fucking be ready to talk.'

Ten minutes later, Floyd tried again. The number was engaged. He left it another ten minutes and tried once more. Still engaged. Perhaps he was doing it on purpose to avoid our call. By now the two of us were getting a little tense and very pissed off.

At 6 p.m. Floyd finally got through. 'Carl, what the fuck's going on?'

'Where are you, Floyd?'

'We are at the Hawthorns pub. If you want this money you better get your arse up here so we can fuck off.'

The suggestion that Carl should move away from his usual stomping ground made him instantly agitated. 'No way man, no way. I'm not coming up there. You come to Lenny's.'

'Fuck off,' said Floyd, not wanting to give in too easily, no matter how desperate he was for the job to come off. 'I'll see you at the phone boxes at the end of his street about half six. And don't be late.'

'I won't. See you then.'

Floyd was about to switch the phone off when he suddenly whipped it back to his ear, catching Carl just in time. 'Hey, what do you look like so I know who to look for?'

'Just stay in the car,' said Carl, coolly. 'I'll find you.'

It was nearly 6.40 p.m. and getting very dark when we pulled up outside the phone boxes. Neither of us was surprised that there was no one about so Floyd called Carl once more. 'Carl, it's Floyd. We're here. Where the fuck are you?'

'I'm trying to get into the house. I'll be with you in a minute.'

Ten minutes later, a shabby-looking Lenny Marshall came out of the shadows, whistling, his warm breath forming thin streaks of steam that hung in the air. He got into the back of the car and Floyd followed him, leaving me in the front passenger seat.

'Hi Lenny, this is Martin. The money's his. Now tell me, just what the fuck is going on?'

'Don't worry, I've spoken to the man, he's on his way.'

I needed to join in the conversation. After all, I was supposed to be the one in charge. 'I don't like being fucked around when doing business,' I said firmly.

Lenny met my gaze. 'I'm telling you, he'll be here soon. If you park outside the Frightened Horse pub I'll get him to speak to you as soon as he's here. He'll be in a white Golf.'

Based on what Floyd had told me, I figured the man in the Golf was probably another decoy, an excuse for Lenny to drive around with us and make sure that we weren't being followed. Floyd got back in the driver's seat and set off for the pub which was just around the corner.

We arrived and sat in complete silence until 7.20 p.m. when a white Golf finally showed up. As I made a mental note of the registration, the driver got out and walked away while talking into a mobile phone.

Floyd turned to Lenny. 'Where's the gear?'

Lenny shrugged his shoulders. He seemed genuinely confused. 'I . . . I don't know. The man's walked off.'

Floyd hit the roof. 'Well, fuck this! We're off and tell him he's a cunt.'

Lenny started to panic at the thought of missing out on a substantial payday.

'He was right here . . . fucking eight fifty lost. Give him ten minutes . . .'

I jumped in. 'Fucking bollocks, we've been fucked around since six o'clock. What sort of cunts do you take us for? Do you want to do business or what?'

Lenny was sitting in the middle of the back seat with his head poked forward between the front seats. Suddenly, he pushed his hand through the gap and pointed at a large red Peugeot parked in a bay at the side of the road a little way in front but facing towards us. He had suddenly realized why the job wasn't coming together.

'They're from The Lane,' he said.

'What?'

'Over there. They're all police. Babylon.'

I followed his gaze and peered into the car as we slowly drove past. In the midst of this mostly black area was a large car with four white men, two sitting in the front and two in the back. They all had neat, short hair and sat in silence, casually looking around. I recognized them instantly as four of the drug squad officers that I had been introduced to earlier that day. They could not have been more obvious if they tried. They might just as well have turned up in full uniform in a squad car with the blue lights flashing.

I couldn't believe it. I had specifically told them to stay away but they had turned up anyway and almost certainly blown the job as a result. They spotted us as we passed by and had the typical plain clothes reaction of doing a double take then trying not to look at us. It's like when kids think that if they can't see you, they can't be seen themselves. They just ended up looking incredibly shifty. It's only when you're working undercover that you can ignore things. If you're in plain clothes and see a crime being committed, your instinctive reactions make you stand out a mile.

Behind me I could feel Lenny getting agitated, wondering if we would think he was leading us into some kind of trap. I had to act fast and decided to exploit his fears and turn the tables on him. Spinning around to face him on the back seat I launched into a torrent of abuse. 'What the fuck do you think you're playing at?' I screamed. 'You've brought me here to meet police? If that's the police and you know it then you must be with the police. You can just fuck right off right now. Get out of the car. Move it man, we're going.'

Then it was Floyd's turn to get a bollocking. 'What you playing at, Floyd? Are you some kind of idiot? I thought you said you knew this man, that he was safe. But we ain't been here five minutes and already the police are on to us. What the hell did you bring me here for? I didn't ask to be introduced to no fucking idiots.'

It was working perfectly, the more furious I got over the police presence the more sure Lenny became that I was bona fide. 'Hey it's OK man,' he pleaded. 'We can still sort something out. We can still do business.'

It was a gamble but I had to stand my ground. No self-respecting drug dealer would do anything else. 'Forget it Lenny,' I said ending it. 'Just get out right now and tell your police friends that it's over. I ain't doing nothing with you.' We pulled over and gave him just enough time to reluctantly get out of the car, humiliated, before we drove off at speed.

Floyd and I were on our way back to Walsall Road to give the drug squad a piece of my mind when my mobile rang. It was Carl, almost begging us to come back and complete the deal. The police had gone, the area was secure, they had the drugs in position. He wanted to do business.

We turned around and headed back to Soho Road, arriving ten minutes later and parking alongside the telephone boxes once more.

The police car was nowhere to be seen but the white Golf was opposite and Lenny and another man I hadn't seen before got out, walked over and got into the back of our car. The new man was at least six feet tall and powerfully built. He had short dreadlocks piled on the top of his head, barely visible under the hood of his tracksuit top, and a massive scar down one side of his face that caught the light every time he moved his head. A dangerous-looking character.

'Not here,' he said to Floyd, giving him directions to Union Road, a narrow, poorly lit alleyway just around the corner, barely wide enough for one car at a time. Down one side were the high walls and fences that protected the back entrances of the shops on the main road, on the other was an abandoned building, soon to be converted into a giant temple. We parked directly in the middle. Through the windscreen, I could see the white Golf blocking one end of the alleyway. I glanced in the rear view mirror and saw another car behind us with its interior light on. The driver had long dreadlocks and was smoking a big fat spliff. They could have been lookouts or they could have been reinforcements. Either way, we were surrounded.

'Who's this, Lenny,' asked Floyd, 'Is it Carl?'

'Yeah, I'm Carl,' the man replied. 'Sorry for the delay. I was being careful.'

I spoke up again. 'Careful? How fucking careful are you being if you've got police all over you? You've kept me waiting around for ages. If you're gonna do business, sort yourself out. I don't like waiting. I trade and fuck off.' I could see I was winding him up, that he was struggling to stay calm. I could sense the aggression building up inside him.

'D'you want this half ounce or what?'

'Yeah, but I'm not coming all the way up here and putting up with all this shit again for a half ounce.'

Lenny broke into the conversation. 'We can do ounces in the future.'

'I hope so. Money is no problem.'

Floyd produced a set of electric scales. 'Put the fucker on here then.'

Carl put a white rock wrapped in clingfilm on the balance. The readout said 12 grams.

'Are you taking the piss?' said Floyd. 'It's fucking light.'

'This is the fucking limit man!' I snapped. 'I can't believe you're trying to rip us off.'

Carl attempted to look genuinely surprised and embarrassed but failed. He'd obviously been trying to pull a fast one and hadn't expected us to have scales. 'Sorry. I'll make it up,' he said quickly, reaching into his pocket to pull a second, smaller rock from his other pocket and adding it to the first. The scales read 14 grams – exactly half an ounce.

I handed over the money, which was all in ten pound notes, and Carl and Lenny began counting it. I don't know whether they were doing it deliberately slowly but it seemed to take them ages. They kept messing it up and having to start over again. I could see the lookouts getting out of their cars and walking about to stretch their legs, wondering what was holding things up. It was too dark to see behind clearly but the bloke in front of us was about six feet tall and wearing a dark pinstripe jacket with the sleeves rolled up over a dark woollen jumper and a pair of jeans. As he walked back and forth in front of the street lights I could see a set of gold medallions hanging from thin chains around his neck, glinting again and again. He wore an oversize beige beret on his head, obviously holding in a mass of dreadlocks, and had a neatly trimmed beard and moustache. At one point he started walking towards the car, trying to figure out the delay before Carl caught his eye and reassured him with a nod of his head.

I glanced at the clock on the dashboard. Ten minutes had passed since they began counting and they still showed no signs of finishing. The engine had been switched off and with four of us in the car, the windows were steaming up so badly that little streaks of condensation were running down the inside. I could feel myself starting to sweat.

At that point, Carl messed up the count again. 'For fuck's sake,' said Floyd. 'Did you guys forget to go to school or what? Do you want me to do it for you?' For once Floyd wasn't trying to be hard

– the increasing tension in the car was getting to him just as it was to me. We both wanted to get the hell out of there but the ball was firmly in Carl and Lenny's court.

Carl fixed Floyd with a hard stare and began counting even more slowly than before, licking his thumb before sliding each note from the pile and planting it on his knee. There was nothing to do but wait. I had to stay wary but remain confident that they wouldn't try to rob me, especially when I was talking about spending significantly more in another week or so. I just had to be patient.

The money finally counted, we gave the brothers a lift back to Stafford Road and were followed by the Golf all the way.

'Carl, can we do some proper business next Friday?' I called after him as he walked up the path to his front door.

'No problem. Ring me and we'll do whatever you want.'

'Is that the same number as earlier?'

'Yeah, you can always get me on that number.'

'OK, but don't mess around next time or it's your loss.'

'Don't worry,' said Carl, smiling for the first time that evening and tapping the pocket where he'd stuffed the £850. 'No delays next time. Just give me a day's notice.'

12

Philip: By October, Martin and I were becoming good friends, at least during office hours. We'd worked together on half a dozen varied jobs but had yet to socialize outside the workplace. Each time we met, we'd always end up saying we must get together, go out for an evening with our partners, but somehow we never got round to it. I also got the feeling that Martin's girlfriend wasn't particularly keen on the idea of meeting me, the person who was at least partly responsible for keeping her man away from home so much of the time. Even though my own marriage was pretty solid, there were times when the strain of trying to lead a double life got too much for my wife too.

So when Martin called me up towards the end of the month I knew right away that it was going to be business. 'I'm doing a job for the West Midlands police,' he explained, 'and I'm getting a team together to pose as a serious gang of drug dealers and buy four ounces of crack. I wondered if you'd be available to help me out. Either Thursday or Friday this week.'

I had a look in my diary and saw that I was free. Providing that I could get permission from my boss, I told him I'd be there. 'Who else have you got in mind?'

'Big Des and Leroy Palmer. I did a test buy last week and the targets are a pretty nasty bunch. All combat trousers and hoods up over their heads. The main villain has this big cutlass scar down the side of his face. You know the sort. I want us to look pretty intimidating so that they don't even think about starting trouble. I want to run it the same way we did the ecstasy job. Either all four of us in one vehicle or two each in two cars.'

'Sounds good. I know the type you mean – typical crack heads. Lovely charming people. Sometimes I think they just cast them all out of the same mould. I take it we've got guns on the job?'

'Of course.'

'No problem then. If it all goes tits up, we'll just pull out and let the glory boys sort it out.'

'Too right.'

Two days later, Martin called me back. I could hear in his voice that things weren't right. He told me the West Midlands police had sucked their teeth at the escalating cost of the operation and decided that they could only afford to hire one other Met officer. Martin was going to have to choose one of the three of us. In the end the decision was made for him.

Big Des was refused permission to take part – his boss had said he was getting too old for undercover work and that messing about with a bunch of crack dealers was simply out of the question. Leroy Palmer couldn't get away either – the CID office he was working in was already short staffed and another absence would mean too many jobs would end up grinding to a halt. Having already agreed the time off with my guvnor, I was the one left holding the winning ticket.

Martin: I went back to the West Midlands and explained that the job wouldn't be feasible with just the two of us, we would need at least three people. I don't know what I expected them to reply but when they came back and said they'd found a third black under-cover officer from their own ranks to make up the numbers, it took me completely by surprise.

I couldn't help wondering why, if this new undercover was any good, he hadn't been in on it right from the start of the operation and why they had ended up recruiting from an outside force. But there's no way you can question everything. The West Midlands team were in charge and they had spent months and months on the job. On any undercover operation there will always be information that you are not entitled to know because it could compromise you.

There was also the fact that SO10 had authorized my release. When an outside force makes a request, they have to send SO10 details of the job and of the informant and whether they are suitable.

They have to outline what the job will involve and explain why it will not breach guidelines on the use of undercover officers. For SO10 to have given the OK for me to get involved, the job must have looked pretty solid, on paper at least.

The strike was set for Friday 28 October. The briefing was to take place at 9 a.m. at Walsall Road station. West Midlands booked Philip and I into a motel just off the motorway for the night before to ensure we were well rested before tackling the day's work.

Two days before we were due to leave we heard that the rooms had been cancelled because of budgetary constraints. A worrying pattern was starting to emerge.

I'd specified that in order to bring the job off successfully, we'd need a big, flashy motor like a large BMW or a Mercedes to portray the right image. SO10 has a sizeable car pool with everything from Porsches to Jags, but the West Midlands police didn't have access to anything like that themselves. They said their budget wouldn't stretch to the cost of hiring one so they asked us to go back to SO10 to see if we could get a suitable car from there.

There was one last BMW available but when I went to pick it up on the Thursday evening, it had been booked out for the weekend. It wasn't even for an official job – someone had just taken it out for the weekend to show off to his girlfriend. I was given a Mondeo and told it was the only car available. It was totally unsuitable, nowhere near flash enough. After all, if I had ten grand to spend on crack, then why couldn't I get myself a decent motor – but it was all that was left and would have to do.

On a more positive note, I was making fantastic progress with the targets. The once elusive Carl had started calling me regularly, trying his best to push up the amount of crack I was set to buy.

I made a series of phone calls to Carl, often from home using the Cascade phone, so I'd always try to make sure the background noise was right. Eager to come across as a tough crack dealer as I negotiated a price for the crack that we were going to buy on Friday night, I ensured that even my telephone calls fitted in with the image.

On one occasion it happened by accident. I was at home playing with my turntables, spinning a couple of ragga tracks from Jamaica I'd picked up. As soon as I realized who was calling, I cranked the volume up and told Carl I was in a shebeen. He'd never have guessed I was actually in a three-bedroomed semi in the suburbs.

Carl was keen to make a huge sale, up to half a pound of crack, but I wanted to keep it relatively small. I told him I would take four ounces on this occasion and increase it the next time. As well as being more comfortable with a smaller deal, I also felt it gave me a safety net as Carl would believe that an even bigger payday was just around the corner. In theory, he'd only try to rip us off if he saw nothing more for himself in the future.

Philip: The hotel we had planned to stay in was pretty cheap, around £60 a night, and I couldn't believe it when they cancelled it. We even offered to share a room but they still said no. The only reason we wanted to do it was to avoid having to get up at the crack of dawn in order to drive all the way from London, but in the end that was exactly what we had to do.

It got worse. At the last minute someone from the West Midlands called Martin and said there was a WPC from the East End who was due to have a meeting with the drug squad the same morning. They wondered if we could take her up in our car and save them even more money.

And worse. The night before, Martin spoke to Floyd who said he had heard from DI Powell that they were thinking of cancelling the armed support for the job. 'Don't worry,' he told Martin. 'We'll iron it all out when you get here. I'm sure it will be fine.'

Martin and I talked it over. We were both uneasy and we decided to take our concerns over the way the job was going to SO10. There was a feeling, however, that we should just go ahead and get it out of the way. No one ever expects things to go wrong and we had done plenty of jobs in the past which were every bit as risky. We decided to get this one out of the way and have words in the appropriate ears afterwards.

Martin turned up on my doorstep just after 4 a.m. on Friday morning. I took over driving the car because I wanted to get used to it. As I was trying to make them believe it was my vehicle, I didn't want to embarrass myself by not knowing where the lights switch was or something when the targets were around.

We picked up the WPC and headed straight for Birmingham. We had arranged to meet Floyd outside West Bromwich Albion football ground. The moment I saw him, I almost screamed out loud. I had always thought that Martin had been joking when he said Floyd had a mole the size of a small asteroid clinging to his cheek, but it was true. I couldn't believe that someone so distinctive had been picked out to work undercover. As for his nickname, it only took one sentence to see how that came about.

'So you're the other fucking undercover then,' he said, bounding over with a toothy smile.

'That's right. And you must be Floyd.'

'Good guess.'

Floyd got in his car and we followed him back to Walsall Road station. He drove right in, Martin and I parked a good quarter of a mile down the road and then walked back. I was becoming more and more apprehensive by the minute. It wasn't so much a feeling of impending doom, more that I kept thinking there must be something wrong with me. Nothing was happening quite the way I expected it to and I was starting to doubt myself. Far from an ideal state of mind.

We arrived at the station only to discover that the briefing had been put back until 11 a.m. We could have stayed in bed a little longer.

Martin and I went off for a big fry-up breakfast, then returned and met with DCI Morton and the others. 'It's all looking pretty good, lads,' the detective in charge of the arrest team told us. 'We've found a good OP and, based on Martin's previous experience, we expect the deal to take place in or around the vicinity of the Kentucky. The only snag is that the back-up team can only observe a few feet either way. If the targets try to take you off somewhere else to make the deal, you're going to have to find some way to discourage them, otherwise we won't be able to make the strike and you'll have the Chief Constable up your arses trying to get his ten grand back.'

Morton smiled at his good humour but I didn't feel like laughing. 'When is the head of the firearms unit getting here?' I asked. 'We've got to make sure they know what we're wearing and what we'll be driving, just so there are no mistakes.'

DCI Morton shifted uneasily in his chair and cast his eyes down. 'There isn't going to be a firearms team involved,' he said softly. 'We don't need one. We have got special equipment which shows that they are not armed, they don't have guns. They are going to be going to the plot, handing over the drugs, taking the money and that's that. No guns, no firearms unit.'

From the way he had used the phrase 'special equipment' both Martin and I assumed that they had planted bugging devices in the targets' homes and maybe their cars, but even then I was surprised that they had placed so much confidence in what had been said. People can change their minds overnight. Even if they had been listening to the drug dealers an hour before they left for the job, it wouldn't mean anything.

'It's not really good enough,' I said. 'I could say one thing now then go out the door and say something else. You've simply got to have armed back-up on this kind of job. I've been in exactly this situation before and it turned into a total fucking nightmare.' And I told him the story of Ryan Reid.

In the early part of 1991, twenty-three-year-old Ryan Reid was widely believed to be the biggest supplier of crack cocaine in London. He lived in Kilburn and had dealers working for him all over the capital, but his main 'shop' was on the notorious Stonebridge Park estate in Harlesden, a place so rough that taxis would not pick up or drop off there and postmen were forced to make their morning deliveries in pairs.

A major anti-crack initiative, Operation Howitzer, had been launched with Reid as its main target and I had been one of the first men in on the job. I'd been introduced to him by an informant and had spent just under a month getting to know him at his makeshift crack house – a two-bedroomed flat in the centre of the estate.

That first night I bought a £20 rock. Although lots of the buyers would smoke their rocks there and then, there was never any pressure to smoke at the flat. I would always make the excuse that I was buying my rock and heading home to share it with my girlfriend and no one seemed to mind. At the end of the day they were just interested in getting the money and very little else.

I took the rock I'd bought back to the local police station. Crack was still new at the time and most of the other officers had never seen it before. They all wanted to look at it and smell it, while I explained how you smoked it and how it got its name.

I went back with the informants and bought crack on two more occasions before I started going in on my own. By then I'd just knock on the door and the geezer acting as a guard would recognize me and let me in. Slowly but surely I began to gain Ryan's confidence and he'd welcome me like an old friend. 'Philip, my brother, how you doing?' he said, greeting me with a hug on my fifth visit. Ryan dressed in classic 'black gangster' style – baggy jeans, T-shirt and baggy patterned overshirt, a ploy to make his skinny frame seem more imposing – but when he spoke his voice was pure north London. His show of affection was strictly in the pursuit of business. I'd hinted that I had friends from up north who were interested in selling crack and needed a reliable supplier. Once he took the bait, it was my cue to introduce him to the next undercover officer in the chain.

'Philip, I want to give you a treat tomorrow. Business is good and I'm getting myself a new car. I wanted to give you a ride. You know, if you spent less time smoking this shit and more time selling it, you could have all this too.' Ryan wasn't feeling charitable, he just wanted me to join his band of merry salesmen.

The following day, as arranged, he picked me up from Stone-bridge Park tube station in an immaculate flame red BMW 535i. Financially it was just a drop in the ocean – he was making £2,000 a week profit from his trade and was eager to make more. But today he just wanted as much of the world as possible to see him in his new car. He drove so slowly up and down Harlesden high street that we were being overtaken by push bikes. Every now and then someone on the street would recognize him and wave. Ryan was in his element. 'I don't live like the people on this estate. I have a whole house, not a flat. My hi-fi is pure Kenwood, my TV is pure Sony. Nothing but the best.' He was revelling in it but eventually he calmed down enough to get back to the business in hand.

'So Philip, tell me about your friend. He wants to sell crack. No, it's better than that, isn't it? He wants to buy my crack and sell that. How much do you think he can shift?'

'I dunno, you'll have to ask him. He's coming down next week. I'll bring him round if you want.'

Ryan's face erupted into a broad smile. 'Excellent. You've got my mobile number. Give me a call and we'll fix something up. Now I've got some other important business to attend to, where can I drop you off?'

Over the next week Ryan's business grew but so did his paranoia. Although he never suspected that he was being targeted by an undercover team, he was becoming more cautious. He had been stopped at random by a team from the local drug squad a couple of weeks earlier and, though he didn't have any gear on him, the incident led to him upping the level of security at his crack house.

He also began paying friends to drive his new beamer around during the day, hoping to distract any surveillance teams while he himself continued selling crack. He cut back on the number of people he was dealing with, at least in part because he hoped to make up the difference by offloading crack to markets outside London.

The following day I met Duncan, an undercover from the West Midlands who was playing the part of my friend. After being briefed at Paddington Green station we went to Stonebridge so that I could introduce him to Ryan. The sun was beating down but it was still freezing cold with a chill wind blowing from the north. Ryan was expecting us, wandering around a grassy square just outside the estate with his mobile phone clamped to his ear. He finished the call as he saw us approaching.

'Ryan, this is Duncan.'

Duncan, tall and well built, the complete opposite of Ryan, shook his hand. 'Can we go somewhere private?' he asked.

'This'll do. I live here. So what kind of business you looking for?'

'How much can you do me?'

'As much as you want. If you want one eighth, that's £160.'

'OK, give me two of them.'

Ryan called over another man, a short guy with no hair and wearing a heavy trenchcoat, and whispered to him. He disappeared while Ryan led us through the estate to a children's play area and sat down on the end of a slide, blowing into his hands to keep them warm. The gofer returned with two small slabs of crack in a brown envelope and Duncan handed over the money.

After that one buy, Duncan was able to deal directly with Ryan and I moved on to other things. He made two more relatively small buys of £200 each to boost the dealer's confidence, then set him up for the big bust.

'I'm looking to expand my end of the operation, increase my level of sales,' Duncan explained.

'Yeah? How much crack do you think you can shift in a week?' Ryan asked.

'Four or five ounces.'

'You want me to give you a price for four ounces? I can do you an ounce for £1,800.'

'Do me four for seven then.'

'OK, that's cool.'

'Good. We'll do it next Thursday. I'll call later in the week to confirm.'

Some members of the back-up squad were worried that Ryan's team might be armed for this deal because of the size and value of the order, but I had never seen any evidence of a gun in all the time that I had been dealing with Ryan. Neither had Duncan, and the original informant who had known Reid for years said that, as far as he knew, that just wasn't Ryan's style.

On Thursday 14 March at 6 p.m., Duncan kept his promise and called Ryan's mobile.

'It's me, Duncan. Everything all right for later?'

'No problem, ring me when you get here.'

'I'm only just leaving so it'll be a couple of hours. But I tell you this, there's no way I'm bringing that much money on to the estate.'

'Just ring me when you get near and we will sort it.'

'I want to stay in my car. I don't want to come into the playground.'

The back-up team were positioned in an unmarked Transit van on Craven Road. Duncan, driving a Jaguar Sovereign, parked up in Shrewsbury Court and called Ryan who told him to sit and wait. Ten minutes later, two men came up behind his car and sat down on a nearby wooden bench. Duncan recognized one as the gofer who had fetched the crack for his first buy. Ryan had brought his own back-up along. A few minutes after that, Ryan appeared and tapped on the window of Duncan's car. Duncan lowered it and asked, 'Everything all right?'

'Yeah, yeah.'

'You got the stuff?'

Ryan unzipped his baggy black leather jacket and pulled out a brown envelope, ripped off the top and held it out so Duncan could see the quarter-inch-thick slabs of magnolia-coloured rock inside.

'How much is there?'

'You asked for four ounces,' replied Duncan. 'Have you got the scales?'

Duncan shook his head. 'It's OK. It looks about right. I'll get the money, it's in the boot.'

Duncan got out of his car. That was the signal and the arrest team, led by officers Jason Squibb and Paul 'Yozzer' Hughes, started to move in. At that same moment, a car flashed past on the road just beyond where Duncan was parked. Ryan was already nervous – he had wanted to do the deal in the playground and considered the road far too public. He had also been made even more suspicious when Duncan had not wanted to weigh the drugs. Ryan was taking a chance by having considerably less than four ounces in the envelope but Duncan hadn't called his bluff. He'd just looked at it and then said he was going to get the money. Ryan was convinced he was about to get ripped off. He'd been convinced of that for the past week. When the car went by he panicked for a second.

'Don't open the boot, don't open the boot,' he shouted, backing away from the car.

By this time Jason Squibb was closing in, walking as if simply making his way to a block of flats behind Ryan. But as he got within spitting distance, he flung himself at the dealer from behind and grabbed him around the neck. Ryan tried to fight him off, wriggling around like a slippery eel, stopping Squibb from getting a firm grip. Yozzer Hughes ran in from the front to assist and watched in horror as a panicking Ryan whipped out a .32 Colt automatic from the folds of his jacket.

Squibb saw the weapon and tried desperately to force Ryan's gun arm towards the ground but Ryan broke his grip, took aim and fired. Yozzer was hit in the chest two inches above his left nipple. He tumbled backwards leaving Squibb grappling with the gunman and fighting for his own life. The pair fell to the ground, Squibb on top with his left arm around Ryan's throat and his right arm holding Ryan's wrist just below the gun. They wrestled violently and Squibb felt the gun move across his body under his chin, then fire four times in quick succession. The drug dealer was trying to blow his head off. The bullets missed their target but the red-hot flare of the Colt's muzzle flash scorched Squibb's neck. The shock loosened his grip allowing Ryan, using all his strength, to lash out with the heavy automatic against the side of the under-cover's head, all but knocking him out cold.

Half the back-up team was now out of action but the two remaining officers, Dave Porter and Gordon Heyes, were closing in. Both had been less than ten yards away when Yozzer was shot and were boiling with rage and disbelief. 'People ask how you react to something like that,' Heyes said later. 'The answer is that there is no time for reaction. You are on automatic pilot. Dave and I broke into a run and pounded full-tilt for Ryan. But we were still three or four yards from him when he struggled free of Squibb.'

Standing upright alongside Squibb's dazed body, Ryan pointed the gun at the two officers running towards him and screaming abuse. He fired five shots in such quick succession that eyewitnesses thought he was using a machine gun. None of the bullets found its target.

Anyone trained in using firearms is taught the importance of bringing the gun up to eye level before shooting. Failure to do this means your chances of hitting anything more than a few feet away, even if you are pointing directly at it, are minimal. Had Ryan had more experience with a gun there is no doubt that both Porter and Heyes would have been killed.

Ryan Reid dropped the gun and legged it. He was found hiding under a nearby Transit van, clinging to the prop shaft until his strength gave out and he fell to the ground.

Amazingly, Yozzer survived but the whole operation led to significant changes in the way that the Met deployed firearms in such cases. No matter what the intelligence says about the chances of the targets being armed, they always have an armed response team ready and waiting at the scene.

'So you see,' I said to Morton, 'it doesn't mean anything if they haven't mentioned it. You've simply got to have firearms. Any job where you mix Jamaicans, drugs and money has the same potential. These people are so unpredictable. OK, so in the greater scheme of things it's not a large amount of money. But it is for them. They will take ten grand and blow it tomorrow and that is that. Villains like this will stick guns in your face over a spilt pint.'

I wanted to call the whole thing off and go home but you can't just drop the job like that. I'd never have worked undercover again and it would inevitably affect my CID career as well. We were stuck with it. Against my better judgement, we were going ahead.

So Martin called Carl to tell him he was in London and would be leaving a little later. Carl was very keen to do the deal. It was going to be a big payday for him.

Martin and I went back to the station in the early afternoon to sort out who was going to wear the Nagra. We expected the third undercover to wear it as Martin was now simply too close to the gang. If he wore the tape, he would have to disclose in court that he was an undercover officer. That in turn would mean Floyd would be exposed and therefore Del, the informant, would be in danger.

For the same reason, it wasn't really practical for me to wear the tape either, so the newest member of the undercover team seemed the obvious choice.

'I . . . er . . . don't think he can wear the tape,' said one of the senior officers, fidgeting nervously with his pen.

'Why's that?' Martin and I asked together.

'Well, he hasn't had much recent experience. In fact, we were wondering if you could give him a quick lesson in drugs prices and stuff. He's a bit out of touch.'

'How come?'

'Well, he's been on traffic duty for the last two years.'

This was beyond a joke. At every stage things just seemed to get more and more cack-handed. I hoped that I was going to wake up at any moment and discover the whole thing had been some awful nightmare.

As Martin and I sat there trying to work out the best way to proceed, this black guy marched in and, ignoring us completely, went straight over to a desk with a phone. He dialled a number then spent the next ten minutes ranting and raving about the fact that his squad car had broken down He was completely shameless, embarrassing everyone else in the room. Then he came over and introduced himself. His name was Larry, the third undercover operative.

He should have been the man to check the drugs but since he seemed to have no experience whatsoever in deals of this kind, the risk of the operation being compromised was too great to entrust him with anything of importance.

For the same reason, he couldn't wear the Nagra tape either. We wanted to keep him as far away from the plot as possible, instructing him to play the role of the money man and wait in a car around the corner. In the event of the Marshall brothers wanting to see the money first, the last thing we wanted was for him to get into any kind of conversation with them and show his lack of knowledge. We told him to flash the money through the window of the car and drive off again.

We left the station to head for the briefing. Larry got into the car he was going to be using. It was a dark orange Vauxhall Cavalier covered in bird shit and patches of rust. It didn't look as if it would hold together long enough to get to Soho Road. He drove out of the back yard of the police station, and started waving at us as we walked to our car. Anyone walking by could have seen. He just didn't have a clue. We ignored him, walked back to the Mondeo and drove over to Tally Ho Corner for the briefing.

This briefing took place in what looked like a university lecture hall. There were at least seventy people there. Operation Marine was the biggest anti-crack initiative the West Midlands police had ever launched and their greatest fear was that the very public arrest of high-profile members of the local black community would spark off a riot.

One team was assigned to block off the roads around the attack site, a uniform team was to stand by in full riot gear to deal with any public disorder, a third team would hand out specially printed leaflets to members of the public explaining that a major police operation was in progress, targeting suspected drug dealers. The rest of the officers involved would carry out simultaneous raids on two addresses connected to the Marshall gang.

The briefing was also to ensure that there would be no confusion over the signals: both hands up in the air would mean come and get us because we are in trouble, while opening the boot of the car would mean that the drugs had been seen and it was time to make the arrest. We also had to be seen by the arrest team so that they would recognize us.

We stayed little more than two minutes. The back-up officers had to discuss where they were going to be hiding and so on, information that we weren't entitled to know and didn't want to. We walked into the canteen for a cup of tea and saw Larry, our undercover traffic cop friend, tightly clutching a plastic supermarket bag to his chest.

'That the money then?' I asked.

He nodded, nervously.

'Did you make sure it's been sorted out properly?'

'What?'

'You know, make sure it's been sorted out as proper drugs money.'

'Yeah, yeah. It's fine.'

I left it for a few minutes but somehow Larry's attitude was making me uncomfortable.

'Can I have a quick look at the money, Larry? It's not that I don't believe you, I'd just like to see it for myself.'

I reached out for the bag but Larry pulled back. 'I don't think I should,' he said.

'What do you mean? Stop arsing about and hand it over.'

'I don't know. I've heard 'bout the blokes from London, Met, CID, you're all a bit light-fingered. My guvnor told me to hang on to this, make sure you two didn't take any liberties.'

'Don't be so fucking stupid.'

Martin and I wrenched the bag away from him and opened it up. And immediately our hearts sank. There was £10,000 inside all right. All in tens and twenties. And each neat £1,000 bundle was wrapped in a strip of paper stamped 'Property of West Midlands Police'. I could hardly breathe. If we'd flashed the money without having looked at it, we would have been dead in seconds.

'For fuck's sake Larry, you've got to be joking. They've got to be folded up the way that market traders do it, four twenties together then another twenty folded across the middle so that each bundle is 100 quid. It's just the way it is done. Anything else and they'll smell a rat. This stuff looks as if you've just taken it out of the bank.'

Martin and I spent the next twenty minutes sitting in the canteen, teaching a very pissed off Larry how to fold drug money and laboriously going through the ten grand. When it was all back in the bag, we went through the plan for that evening.

Since he had dealt with the gang before, Martin felt they would trust him to have the money and would show him the drugs first.

Once the drugs arrived, I would give the signal and everyone would get arrested. There was, however, a strong possibility that they would want to see the money first, especially as it was such a large amount. If that happened, Larry would be waiting round the corner in the car with the money. If they insisted on seeing it, he would drive up, flash it through the window and leave. No hanging about.

'OK,' I said. 'So we're clear on everything. You keep out of sight but if we need the money, we'll give you a call.'

'OK, fine. Let's make it Green Seven.'

I looked at Larry. Then at Martin. Then back at Larry, my face a picture of incredulity. This was another world.

'What do you mean by Green Seven?'

'That'll be the code. What you do is when they turn up, if they want to see the money, you call me up on the mobile and say "All right, Larry. Green Seven. See you in a minute."'

It was desperate. Larry was doing his best, but his lack of under-cover experience concerned me. 'I tell you what, I've got a better idea. What we'll do, if they come over and want to see the money, we'll call you up and say, "Larry, bring the fucking money over". How's that? I think it speaks for itself, gets the message across nice and clear.'

'OK. If that's what you want. So there's no Green Seven then.'

'No. Forget Green Seven. No one is going to be saying Green Seven.'

He nodded glumly, unable to conceal his disappointment.

We left the station and walked in absolute silence to the parked Mondeo. We weren't nervous, just pissed off with being messed about and desperate to get back to London.

'This whole job's a right dog's breakfast,' I said.

'Too right. But it's a hiding to nothing if we complain. Let's just get it out of the way.'

Martin made one more phone call to Carl and then we climbed into our poxy little Mondeo to leave for the buy. As I got ready to pull away, Martin began scrabbling about in the car, looking first in the glove compartment then on the floor and finally on the seat behind him.

'What's the matter? Have you lost something?'

'Shit, shit, shit!'

'What is it?'

'Oh, it's nothing really. It's just that I've gone and left my lucky hat back in London.'

13

Philip: We were half a mile from Soho Road when I pulled the Mondeo over into a quiet crescent and parked in the shadows between the lamp-posts. I reached round to the small of my back, trying to make it look as if I was scratching myself, and flicked on the Nagra: 'I am a serving police officer who for the purpose of this operation will be known as Philip. I can, should a court require, produce my warrant card. The date is Friday 28 October, the time is 1800 hours and I have just switched on the tape.'

We pulled off again and I drove right past the plot so I could have a quick look round. Although Martin had been there before, I hadn't and I wanted to suss out the lie of the land. Once the drugs arrived and we gave the attack signal, we'd have to make a quick exit. There wouldn't be time to figure a route out. I had to make sure I knew where I was going and that I wouldn't end up racing off into a dead end.

I drove along Soho Road, heading out towards West Bromwich, until we hit the high street. The road was almost four lanes wide with numerous shops along the right-hand side. On the left, there was a railing on the far edge of the pavement and then the street dropped away, down about five feet, to where a slip road ran up to a small parade of shops including the Kentucky Fried Chicken outside which the deal was to take place. I drove on past Stafford Road on the right until I reached the second set of traffic lights. I had seen enough to feel safe about my getaway so I turned back and parked the car alongside a set of telephone kiosks opposite and a little way down from the slip road.

There were loads of people around, most of them trooping down to the slip road to go in and out of the Kentucky, but no one who looked even remotely like the targets. Martin pulled out his mobile and dialled Carl's number.

'Carl? It's Martin. I'm in Soho Road. What's happening?'

I could hear Carl replying, his low, rough voice sounding small and tinny through the phone's speaker. 'Yeah, yeah. Everything's OK, I'll be over in about twenty minutes.'

'OK, we'll be in the car park down the slip road right opposite the Kentucky.'

'Right. See you there.'

I turned to Martin as I started up the car for the short drive to the slip road. 'Twenty minutes? I don't think so somehow. These guys are never going to turn up on time. They're probably only just waking up.'

Reversing up against the low wall that separated the slip road from the main road, I parked so the front of the car was facing the Kentucky. There was another car on our right and on our left there was a gap in the wall and four steps leading up to Soho Road. It was a typical cold October night, and everything was bathed in a mix of the orange glow of the street lights and the bright white light coming through the window of the fast food restaurant. There was nothing to do but wait and marvel at the size of the queue in the KFC. It looked as if virtually every man, woman and child in Handsworth must be in there.

Dozens of cars drove in and out of the car park and the line extended all the way back to the main doors. We worked out that people were taking at least half an hour to get served and yet still more people were piling in by the minute. I turned to Martin, amazed, 'I've never seen anything like it. What the fuck's the matter with these people? Don't they know how to cook their own food or something?'

Martin: There were so many people moving around the area that Philip and I were constantly scanning the street and shadows, looking out for Carl or Lenny. There's an element of tension in any undercover job but in this case it was being pushed to the extreme. The broken promises, the stupid questions, the lack of armed support, the incident with the money – nothing had been easy. To make matters worse, I was really starting to feel the effects of having got up so early. Trying to stay really alert when I was physically exhausted was draining me. I just wanted to get the job out of the way and head home for a good night's sleep.

Twenty minutes went by and there was still no sign of anyone. Every minute we sat there we felt more exposed. When the mobile rang it was a relief, a distraction. I assumed it would be Carl with another lame excuse.

'Yeah?'

'Hello. What's happening? Are they there yet?' asked a voice I didn't recognize.

'Who the hell is this?'

'It's Mick from the observation team. Have you talked to the targets? When are they going to get there?'

I was staggered. What were they going to do next? Send a couple of uniformed officers over with a cup of tea and a sandwich while we waited? I couldn't figure out what was going through the bloke's mind. If the targets had been there I could hardly have said anything. It was incredible. To make matters worse, the battery on my mobile phone was running low. I told him I'd call back and cut him off.

There was a pair of phone boxes on Soho Road, just behind our parked car. I got out and jogged back to the dimly lit booths. It had been dusk when we had arrived but now the little light that was left was rapidly fading away as night approached. One phone box was occupied and I stepped into the other. My first call was to DCI Morton.

'For fuck's sake stop calling us,' I complained. 'What do you think you're doing? You could have blown the whole job.' As I spoke, I became suddenly aware of the man in the other booth next to mine. He was wearing a tracksuit with the hood up over his head and, even though I couldn't see his mouth properly, it didn't look as though he was speaking. He was holding the phone up to his ear but I couldn't hear him saying anything. Our eyes met briefly and he turned away, self-consciously mumbling into the receiver. I dialled Carl's number.

He picked up immediately. 'Hello?'

'Look, we've been here long enough. What's going on?'

'We're sorting it out now, I'm in the place.'

'Well, we're going to be leaving soon.'

'Hold on, no, don't do that. Just a second, here, speak to someone else.'

Another man came on the phone and told me his name was Chris. 'Look man, we're sorting it, there's no problems. We're going to be there. We'll be there. Give us fifteen minutes and this thing will be done quickly and you geezers can go.'

'OK.' I returned to Philip in the Mondeo.

The guy in the phone box had unnerved me a little. He was behind us but had a clear line of sight directly to where our car was parked. I was fully immersed in my undercover role and he should have just been part of the normal Handsworth landscape, but there was something about him that didn't feel right. He'd made me feel very exposed. I told Philip about it once I'd sat back in the passenger seat and we decided to lock the car's rear doors.

And we waited. I couldn't keep on phoning Carl otherwise I could make myself vulnerable to the accusation that I was acting as an *agent provocateur*, begging him to come and sell me drugs rather than letting him make all the running. So we waited.

Philip: At 7.15 p.m. there was still no sign of the Marshalls. I decided to turn off the tape. It had been running for more than an hour, recording nothing but the ragga music in the car and the occasional exchange between Martin and myself. I didn't want to risk having it run out at a crucial moment.

It might just have been the fact that we'd had such a difficult day trying to get West Midlands to see things from our point of view, but stuck there at night on Soho Road, I began to get into a real downer about even the idea of undercover work.

'When we get back to London, I'm gonna really cut down on undercover work,' I said to Martin. 'Might even knock it on the head altogether and concentrate on my career instead. I can do without this shit.'

The thing about undercover work is that, while it is good for your general kudos, it does nothing to advance you in the police hierarchy. Studying for your sergeant's exams is a major commitment and you simply can't afford to allow yourself to be called off at a moment's notice and spend hours, days or weeks trying to infiltrate some gang or other.

My wife, Joanne, was increasingly getting fed up with my protracted absences from home, the late nights and working on my days off. She and I had sat down for a serious talk. 'I really don't know why you do it. I don't know how you can cope with all that stress,' she said. 'I wouldn't ask you to give up your job because I know how much it means to you, but I don't think I can handle knowing where you are going and what might happen to you. From now on, when you go out of that door, just don't tell me where you're going. I don't want to know.'

I was starting to miss my kid who was growing up virtually without a father. I was keen to move on to the Regional Crime Squad where I would be targeting villains of a similar calibre, just using different methods.

There were times when I wondered how I managed to cope with the stress, especially when all around me, even some of my SO10 colleagues, could not. With undercovers there was always the danger of getting sucked in. It could begin when, feeling under pressure to fit in with the villains they were hanging out with, and kidding themselves that it was acceptable, officers might smoke the odd spliff. Then when lines of coke were prepared and offered round to celebrate the forthcoming deal, they'd snort them with everyone else.

At first they would justify it to themselves. 'It's the perfect way of showing them that we're not cops. We turn up at a meeting, pick up a sample and check the gear there and then.' But to everyone else it would quickly become increasingly clear that the only reason they were keen for work was to feed their addiction, not to collar a few more dealers.

There was another story doing the rounds about an undercover being so strung out that the gangsters around him took full advantage. He arranged to buy forty kilos of cannabis resin and came away with a bag load of elephant dung. He was so out of it he didn't even notice until he got back to the station. The realization broke him and he ended up in rehab.

The stress of the job also makes SO10 officers more susceptible to corruption. As a uniform officer, the only time you see successful villains is when they are handcuffed in the back of your van. Undercover officers mingle with them all the time. They see the fast cars they drive (and drive similar models themselves), hang out with them at the best restaurants, watch how everyone around them treats them like film stars. The temptations are obvious.

During one operation I was the money man in a drugs buy and had £60,000 in an old carrier bag. The meeting was delayed for four hours. There was no point going through the hassle of trying to book the money back into SO10 for the sake of a couple of hours so I popped home to put my feet up and watch a bit of TV. I left the money on the sofa while I went upstairs to the bathroom. When my wife arrived home from work and found enough money to buy a house she almost had a heart attack. We'd always talked about the irony of working so hard for my policeman's salary and then dealing with villains who could earn in a week what I made in a year.

The final danger is 'going native', becoming too like the people that you target. In the mid-eighties Operation Own Goal targeted a group of football hooligans following Chelsea. Officers were sent out to join the notorious Headhunters gang and report back.

Hangers-on were not welcome by the Headhunters. The policemen's only hope of survival was to participate fully in everything that was going on. And be seen to participate. In the space of a few weeks, serving police officers had been implicated in a range of assaults, robberies and drug offences. When the operation finally came to court, all but a handful of the charges against the gang members were thrown out.

In 1996, following a highly critical internal report, the mechanisms for monitoring the health and well-being of members of SO10 were radically overhauled. Such officers are now subjected to regular psychological checks to ensure they can be pulled out of a job at the first sign of trouble.

But even for those who can cope, the stresses still need to be dealt with. SO10 operates an 'uncle' system whereby every new recruit to undercover work has a nominated officer they can call at any time to discuss any problems or difficulties they might be having. It's purely voluntary and unless your uncle is someone you really like and trust, not a lot of use. One of the reasons Martin and I had bonded so well was that we shared a similar attitude to undercover work. Talking to one another was our way of coping.

Martin had picked up some obscure ragga music from a local pirate station and we were playing that on the stereo at eleven. It was brutal stuff driven by thumping basslines. Every song carried the same message and was delivered in the same abrasive Jamaican rap – me got a woman, me got a gun, me shoot man down'. It was drawing attention from passers-by but we would have looked a damn sight more suspicious if the two of us had been sitting there in a car in total silence. With the music blaring we looked like a couple of drug dealers waiting to make a buy; without it, we would have looked like a couple of coppers on a stake-out.

We continued to talk, taking the piss out of the stream of people filing in and out of the Kentucky when two men crossed the front of the car, turned sharply and made their way towards my window. Both were well built and at least six feet tall, the tracksuit tops with hoods up over their heads adding to their bulk. A cigarette hung from the mouth of the man in the lighter top. He gestured towards it then tapped on the window and asked if I had a light.

I turned to Martin. 'This bloke wants a light. Do you smoke?' I knew that Martin didn't smoke, of course. I was just stalling for time. What I wanted to find out was whether these were the guys we were supposed to be meeting.

Martin picked up the subtext right away. 'No,' he replied firmly, shaking his head. 'I don't smoke.'

I turned back to the men outside and pressed the button to operate the electric window. I only meant for it to drop an inch or so but the speed of the motor took me by surprise, winding the window almost all the way down before I had a chance to stop it.

In that same instant, two pairs of hands pushed in through the gap and made a frenzied grab for the car keys.

I'd been caught completely off guard. Who were these geezers and what was their game? It took a split second before I regained my composure and went for the keys myself. One of the men had managed to get a firm grip and began twisting the key in the ignition to try to get it out. I grabbed his hand with both of mine and started prising his fingers away. But as I worked to release his grasp the other guy wrenched open the car door, activating the interior light and bathing the inside of the car in a pale yellow glow.

Everything was happening too fast. I was fighting through the chaos to fend off both of them. Keeping my right hand on the keys I moved my left to the inside door handle, desperately seeking to keep it closed, while trying to flick the window up with my thumb. I'd given up the attempt to get the first guy's hands off the keys, instead I was wrestling to turn his hand clockwise and start the engine. That would be our ticket to safety, and if I had to drag these two jerks along the road to make my getaway, then so be it.

Martin: The fright set in the second the hands came in through the window. All of a sudden I was no longer a policeman out on a job, I was concerned with self-preservation. I'd crossed over to the other side, no longer in control. I was the victim of a crime. I didn't know who these guys were or what they were after. Did they think we had drugs? Money? Or were they just after the car itself? The easiest thing in the world would have been to shout out that we were police officers but it wasn't really an option.

I was in undercover mode and to do that would have been to blow the whole operation. Instead I decided to get the back-up to kick in. I could see Philip tearing at the hand on the ignition key and I knew he was trying to get the car started. I quickly flung my door open and got out of the car to give the emergency signal. I raised both my hands high in the air, right above my head, then sat back in the car and closed the door, waiting for Philip to drive us out of there.

As I swung back into my seat, to my absolute horror, Philip got out.

There was no point in me staying in the car unless it was going to offer an escape route so I went to get out myself. But the second I opened the door another man seemed to appear from nowhere, filling the gap and blocking my escape. It was too dark to see his face, all I could make out were the whites of his eyes floating in the shadows within the hood of his tracksuit top. In his pocket I could see the outline of a gun which was pointed directly at my head. His voice, the now familiar collision between Birmingham and Jamaica, was loaded with aggression. 'Get back in the car bumba clot,' he screamed. 'Back in the car, get back in the fucking car before I kill you.'

Philip: Out of the corner of my eye I'd seen Martin give the signal then jump back in the car, waiting for me to start it, but I just couldn't get the key out of the guy's hand, especially when I was fighting to keep the door closed. I decided to make the fight fairer. I pushed back on the door and got out to face them.

The man who'd been holding the door handle was nearest. I shot my hand out and struck him in the throat with the gap between my index finger and thumb, pushing him back off balance. I turned to the other one and was just about to say to him, 'Don't be so fucking stupid. Give us the keys back,' when I heard a loud crack and simultaneously felt a searing pain go through my right calf. I knew straight away that I'd been shot, even though it felt like nothing on earth. It was if someone had taken the burning end of a cigarette and forced it all the way through my leg, in one side and out the other. All I could feel was the intense heat of the hot lead. The force of the bullet buckled my leg and sent me stumbling backwards. I could smell a mixture of gunpowder and my own burning flesh.

The guy I had pushed back on to the bonnet of an adjacent car regained his balance and came at me with heavy kicks and punches. He grabbed the collar of my leather coat and pulled me towards him, repeatedly trying to slam his knees into my face.

In the midst of the pain and confusion, I was waiting for another bullet. I couldn't bear the idea that I wouldn't even see the second shot coming. I had to get away. The guy still had hold of my collar and was pulling hard. I stretched my arms forward so that my coat slipped over my head and came off. He jumped forward, fists flailing and I grabbed on to him like a boxer in a clinch. But my injured leg couldn't support the weight of two people and as I crumpled to the ground I dragged him down with me.

We hit the asphalt hard, knocking the wind out of both of us. The gunman stepped forward and started waving his pistol and shouting at me, 'Where's the fucking money, give us the fucking money!' I just shouted back the first thing that came into my head, 'Fuck off!' I could see the gun glinting in the street lights as he loomed above me. He tried to land a couple of kicks but I was holding on to his friend for dear life, using all my strength to keep him right up against my chest. If the gunman wanted to shoot me again, he was going to have to risk putting one into his mate as well.

We were rolling around on the ground, struggling violently in the space between the Mondeo and the Fiesta parked alongside. The guy I was holding was trying to punch me but he couldn't get any leverage because he was so close. At the same time the gunman was trying to kick and stamp on my shot leg. Each time he connected, the blow felt like a lightning strike. The searing pain made me want to throw up. 'D'ya want another one?' hissed the gunman, trying to point the pistol at my head. 'Where's the fucking money?'

I still had plenty of fight left in me but I realized that, in my condition, I needed to get rid of at least one of them. I threw my left arm aimlessly in the air. 'It's over there,' I said and the gunman flicked his head in the direction I had pointed and vanished in search of the cash.

I didn't know what had happened to Martin and I couldn't see anything from where I was. He could have been in the car or anywhere. I only knew that he must have something to deal with himself otherwise he would have been there too. The guy I was fighting ripped himself away, pulling back to try to get a good punch in. I was too quick for him. I squeezed my good leg under his chest and flipped him off. And then his bottle went. I'd been shot and kicked but I still wasn't giving up easily enough. He got to his feet and ran off towards the front of the Mondeo. I struggled up on to all fours and scrabbled round to the back of the car, crouching beside the wall while I tried to get my breath back and consider my options.

Keeping the weight off my right leg to avoid the intense pain I hobbled to my feet by the rear lights for a better view. I could see people running up and down on the pavement outside the Kentucky, many of them screaming in panic. Martin was nowhere to be seen but the gunman was just a few feet away from me, close to the front of the car. His right arm was up in the air with the gun pointed off in the distance. A delicate wisp of smoke was rising from the barrel, snaking up the still air.

Then he turned round smoothly and looked towards me, his movements deliberate with malicious intent. He took his time, slowly walking closer to me and the Mondeo before stopping by the headlights, the length of a car away. He lifted his arm and pointed the gun directly at my chest. 'D'ya want another one, bumba clot?' he hissed. 'D'ya want some more? Eh bwoy? D'ya want it again?'

I felt sick inside as I realized there was nothing I could do. Martin was gone. The back-up team were nowhere around and I was all alone, literally staring death in the face. The guy had come for money and had failed to get any. I was going to have to bear the brunt of his anger. I closed my eyes for a second, hoping he would get it over with but the gunman wanted to play a game, taunting me, running off his mouth. 'I'm gonna put one in you now. I'm gonna shoot you down, bwoy.'

He kept talking, intoxicated by the power the gun gave him, but I wasn't really listening. When I opened my eyes again the only thing I was aware of was the circles in the air being drawn by the barrel of the gun. He was moving it from side to side slowly and the light kept catching against the triangular sight over the muzzle. It was coming in and out of view, totally hypnotic. For a while all

I could see was the gun and the sight, as though there was nothing else in the world. And I knew it would be the last thing I would ever see.

Martin: I clambered up to the top of the low wall and gave the signal to the back-up team again. I looked back and saw Philip staggering round the rear of the Mondeo. He was limping, obviously in pain and as he passed near a light I saw his right leg soaked dark with blood.

The man who had shot at me turned back and started walking towards Philip. He stopped eight feet away and aimed his gun directly at Philip's chest. I heard him shouting, 'D'ya want another one, bumba clot? D'ya want some more? Eh bwoy? D'ya want it again?'

And then the terrible realization. Oh Jesus, he's going to shoot Philip. He's going to fucking kill Philip.

The next fraction of a second still haunts me. I stood on the wall shaking with fear. To my right was the safety of the main road. The gunman hadn't seen me, I wasn't injured, I could easily make it across. On my left was Philip, my partner, moments away from being shot dead in cold blood.

In the blink of an eye I had to make a decision that I would have to live with for the rest of my life. I took once last glance at the main road, sucked in a deep breath, turned towards the gunman and started running.

Philip: I was still staring hard at the gun when I became aware of a flash of movement at the edge of my vision. It was Martin. I forced myself not to watch him as he sprinted closer. Instead I looked at the gunman's eyes for the first time and thought, right, you're going to get it now. He was so busy showing off with the gun, playing the macho gangster, that he hadn't even noticed. I braced myself as Martin hurtled into full view.

He powered in with both arms flying and smashed straight into the gunman who was sent sprawling on to the car. He bounced off while Martin span round with the momentum of the violent impact. The gunman tried to level the gun at Martin but he had yet to recover his balance and was too shaken to line up a better shot. He pulled the trigger too soon firing with the gun aimed downwards rather than at chest height.

Martin was spinning round when the bullet ripped into his left shin. I could see his leg deforming as the bullet entered. His trousers appeared to ripple over the bones and tissue as the bullet twisted and bucked its way through his shattering shin. His leg whipped around with a speed and force that, initially, seemed to leave the rest of his body behind, before lifting him up and dumping him heavily on the ground a few feet back. Blood began to pool around his ruined leg immediately.

The gunman was still winded and despite my injury I knew I had to act quickly, I hobbled over while he was distracted and struck him hard in the throat with my forearm. He buckled, dropping like a house of cards straight down on the road.

I just stood there for a beat, surveying the scene, trying to take it all in. I'd been shot, Martin was down on the ground holding his leg where he had been shot. The acrid smell of cordite floated in the air.

But the situation now seemed more under control. I decided the best thing to do was sit on our assailant and hold him down until the back-up team arrived. I hobbled over, dropped down on him, and sat across him with his arms under my shins. I thought, Right, he's not going anywhere, the police will be here any second and then I'll . . .

A size nine Nike trainer swung out of the darkness aimed at my face. Instinctively I flung my arm up to parry the force from the kick but I still took a heavy blow to the mouth. The guy had the jump on me but didn't stop, he just carried on running. I recognized him instantly: it was the second bloke I had been fighting with outside the car earlier, the one who had asked if I had a light. I thought he'd run off but he was obviously still around.

He still didn't have the stomach for a ruck. Rather than staying to fight he lost his nerve after kicking me and raced off not looking where he was going. He tripped over Martin who made almost comic efforts to bring him down with his good leg, and ended up on all fours, crawling away at speed, too panicked to take the time to get to his feet again.

That's when I made my big mistake. I assumed the man underneath me had dropped the gun. I was so sure of it that I didn't even bother looking for it when I sat on him. He had recovered from the forearm smash and was starting to struggle again. My only thought was to get him out of the picture, stop him causing any more trouble. I pulled my fist back ready to deliver a haymaker that would put him out of his misery.

As I wound up I felt him twist his hand and push the barrel of the gun under my left buttock. 'Oh fuck,' I thought. 'He's still got the damn thing . . .'

Knowing the second shot was coming was almost too much to bear. As I sensed his finger tighten on the trigger I shut my eyes and braced myself for what was to come. I felt the bullet enter my body just below my buttock and travel up into my pelvis then stop. The force of the shot picked me up and dumped me hard on my back. The pain was overwhelming. It was as if my insides were boiling over, and all my internal organs were slamming into each other. The shot through the leg had been bad enough but I knew I was in much bigger trouble this time.

I lay on the tarmac, totally still, waiting for the gunman to finish me off.

Martin: Philip was dead. Nothing on earth could have convinced me otherwise. I'd seen him gunned down in cold blood right in front of me and I was going to be next. My whole world caved in when I saw him take that final shot. All I could think was that I'd picked the guy up from his house that morning, the home he shared with his wife and kids, and now he was dead. And it was all down to me asking him to get involved in this fucked up shower of shit.

Somehow I managed to climb to my feet but the second I put any weight on my damaged leg I felt the bones in my shin grate and crumble. It sent darts of agony through my body that nearly knocked me out. I had no idea where the gunman was. The pain had brought tears to my eyes and everything was hazy from the smoke. I could make out a patch of bright lights across the road and started to run.

My leg was disintegrating beneath me, precious blood draining away. It was like running across a bed of nails. With every step I felt my leg getting shorter, buckling and warping under my weight. All the time I was bracing myself for the fatal bullet in the back. I was certain the gunman was behind me, getting closer and closer, taunting me as I tried to get away. I tried to run faster, pounding my smashed leg on the hard pavement, reaching down to hold and support it as I went but that just made the pain even worse.

I needed to stay focused but I felt too faint. My plan was to put a wall between me and the man with the gun. I'd run into the shop, tell the owner to call the police and an ambulance, then run through the back and hide in an alley until help came. I could only hope they would get there before I bled to death. If they didn't, then that would be justice. I felt that I didn't deserve to live, not after letting Philip die like that.

I could sense eyes boring in on me from all sides and I knew I was surrounded by the sound of frightened witnesses screaming and shouting. People were making way for me, diving for cover or running back and forth without purpose. I felt dead already, as if I'd gone to hell.

I reached the light and crashed through the doors into a small video shop, the strip lighting bright after the darkness of the street. There was a middle-aged Asian man behind the counter and an older black man in front talking to him and toking on a massive spliff.

'I've been shot, get an ambulance and the police,' I gasped.

Both men turned to me, their faces etched with disbelief. Then the older black man bolted for the door and ran out. I tried to tell him not to leave, that there was a gunman right behind me and that he was likely to get shot, but I could barely speak, my voice had been reduced to a low whisper. Fluids were draining out of my body through my perforated leg. My head was spinning and I was starting to feel dizzy. But I had to keep on.

I could see a door next to the Asian man behind the counter and

244

ran towards it. This was going to be my way out, my way to the alley behind the shop. I threw it open and dived through but found myself surrounded by brooms, buckets and smelly mops. Shit, shit, shit. It wasn't the back door after all, just a stupid fucking cupboard. Tears welled up in my eyes. My plan had fallen apart. And that was when I realized I didn't have any strength left, I just couldn't fight any more.

As I stumbled blindly backwards, sobbing with pain and despair I caught my shoulder on the corner of a display stand. I fell over it, sending dozens of videos flying, and crashed to the ground. There was nothing more I could do, no way I could find it in me to get up again. I'd done my best to get away and failed. I was utterly resigned to the fact that any second the gunman was going to come through the door and finish it.

Philip: I had my eyes shut for only a fraction of a second but it seemed longer. I was lying on my back on the road, feeling the blood seeping out of my two wounds, and thinking please, please don't shoot me again. When I opened my eyes there was no one there and for a brief moment I was alone in the darkness.

Out of nowhere a female police officer came running up to me, shocking me back to reality. 'Are you all right?' she asked.

'I've been shot,' I gasped through gritted teeth.

Two other officers arrived and they checked my wounds to see if the shot in my buttock had severed my femoral artery. If it had, I would have less than half an hour before I bled to death. Once they'd decided that it hadn't, they sat me down on my one good buttock on the passenger seat of the car, the only soft surface around.

'Where's Martin?' asked one.

My stomach rose up into my mouth at the mention of his name. I wanted to throw up. The last thing I had seen was Martin taking a bullet in the leg. Anything could have happened.

'I saw him get shot,' I said softly. 'But I don't know what happened to him afterwards. I honestly don't know.'

★

Martin: I kept my eyes fixed on the door. I could hear the shop owner dialling for an ambulance. He came over and put a pillow under my head but my gaze never wandered. When I saw a dark silhouette form behind the glass I knew it was all over. I looked away and closed my eyes. I couldn't bear to think about what was coming.

'Martin? Are you OK?'

I looked back to see a man in blue jeans and a chequered police hat whom I recognized as Simon, one of the back-up officers. I started to cry but my body was so dehydrated no tears came out.

It had taken them ages to find me. After Philip said he didn't know what had happened to me, they were worried that the Marshall gang might have shoved me in the boot of one of their cars and taken me hostage. The police had been running around in panic, especially when they found the pools of blood that I had left in the middle of the road.

Simon knelt down beside me and took my hand. I turned to him. 'Philip's dead, isn't he?'

'No, he's all right, he's OK.'

I wanted to punch the guy but I didn't have the strength. 'Don't give me any of that old shit. I've heard it all before. I've done it myself, lied to people a thousand times on their way to hospital to stop them panicking. He's fucking dead. I saw it happen.'

By then the first officer had been joined by a female constable. 'No really,' she said softly, 'he's OK. He's standing up and everything. The ambulance has just arrived for him.'

I was convinced she was lying just to comfort me. I didn't want to hear it. I turned back to Simon. 'Tell her to get out. I don't want her here. Tell her to piss off.'

It was at that moment that I became fully aware of just how much pain I was in. The fluid level in my body was reaching critical levels. I could hardly speak at all now and was gasping for breath. I could feel this massive pressure building up in my leg. It was swelling up fast and felt as if it was going to explode. I begged the policeman to take off my boots but he refused. I would have done it myself but I could barely move. An ambulanceman came rushing in and looked me over then turned to Simon. 'I don't know what to do. I'm not a paramedic, just a driver.'

'For fuck's sake put a drip in him,' yelled Simon, 'give the man some fluids.'

The ambulance driver looked down at the floor sheepishly. 'I can't. I'm not qualified to do that.'

I shut my eyes and listened to them arguing against the backdrop of an action film being played out on the shop's video monitors. I swear I could feel myself slipping away, thinking – this is it.

I remembered a case I'd dealt with during my early days in the CID in the East End. A local villain had been shot in the legs after ripping someone off on a drug deal. I went to visit him in hospital to get a statement and found him in good spirits and on the road to recovery but unwilling to talk. When I returned the following day to try to persuade him to co-operate, the doctor told me he had died during the night. Apparently he'd picked up an infection from all the filth on the bullet and there was nothing they could do. It literally killed him from the inside.

And suddenly I knew why the ambulanceman didn't want to treat me. 'I'm gonna die, ain't I?'

He looked me in the eye and smiled big and wide. 'Don't be silly. You can't die of this.'

'You stupid bastard.'

I was going into shock. By the time the paramedics arrived a few minutes later my condition was so serious that they couldn't risk moving me straight away. They put a drip in either arm and set about stabilizing my blood pressure. It took twenty minutes before they were ready to load me into the ambulance.

As they stretchered me through the doors, I called out to the shop owner. As far as I was concerned, he had saved my life. Even in my confused state, I still had the presence of mind to try to say something. I tried mumbling a joke about putting a video aside for me but my voice was too weak. 'Thanks' was all I could manage.

'Don't mention it,' came the reply. 'You take it easy.'

14

Philip: It wasn't until Martin arrived at Birmingham City Hospital and saw me lying two beds away from him in the accident and emergency ward that he finally believed I was alive. He had spent the ambulance journey trying to come to terms with my death and I had spent mine wondering what the Marshall gang had done with him. Only when I saw his face and the relief that swept over it did I know for certain that he too had made it through the ordeal.

The stale smell of old disinfectant, the crisp feel of the starched white sheets beneath me and the reassuring presence of the medical team surrounding us helped ease the tension I'd been feeling ever since the hands burst in through the car window. But any comfort the two of us experienced at being away from the streets of Handsworth was short lived.

No one at the hospital had any idea that we were police officers. As far as the emergency room staff were concerned, we were two drug dealers who'd been shot trying to buy crack. The hospital was less than a mile from Soho Road and the nurses were all too familiar with the way the drug trade had blighted the local community. With efficient professionalism they examined our wounds, checked our charts and changed the bags of plasma when our drips ran dry, but they refused to talk to us, answer any of our questions or even make eye contact.

With no way of knowing what had happened to the man who'd shot us or the rest of the Marshall gang, Martin and I had just seconds to decide how to play it. We could either tell the truth or stick with SO10 protocol and remain in our undercover roles. As the medical 'crash' team began removing our blood-soaked clothing, we decided on the latter.

'Hey, what address are you going to give?' I shouted across to

Martin, grimacing with pain as a nurse cut away at my jeans with a pair of scissors.

'The Lewisham one.'

'Right. In that case I'll use Hammersmith.'

Our conversation was confusing an already fraught situation. I could see the mind of the registrar, who was removing my jacket and shirt, racing. He was probably thinking, 'Whoever these guys are, they're not going to reveal their real identities to us or the police. They must be serious villains.' Then he recoiled in shock.

'Jesus. He's got wires coming out of him.' The buzz of activity around my bed snapped to a halt as the staff withdrew their hands and froze in sheer terror. 'See. There, and there,' said the registrar, nervously pointing at my chest and shoulders. 'God knows what it's hooked up to. Get the police, quick.'

With a jolt, I realized what had happened. He'd found the microphone wires for the Nagra which ran up my back and over my shoulders, stopping just above my nipples. I must have looked like a human bomb. 'Don't worry,' I said, weakly. 'It's just a tape recorder.'

I was trying to reassure him but all I did was puzzle him more. Nothing was making sense. He must have wondered why the hell a scumbag drug dealer would have a tape recorder stuck to his body. He took a half step back towards me and finished undoing my shirt at arm's length, revealing the band of sticky tape across my belly, then gently rolled me on to my good buttock to get access to the Nagra. I was just about to tell him to be careful cutting it off when he tore it away, taking the tape and hair with it. It was no more than I deserved, I was just a drug dealer, after all.

But it was the last straw. I was sure that, if only they could be made to realize who we really were, they would treat us differently. After another twenty minutes without painkillers the mask finally slipped. On my way to the X-ray department, wheeled by a Jamaican nurse who spent the journey quietly humming to herself, I knew I had to come clean. As the strips of fluorescent light flashed by overhead, I looked up at her and whispered, 'You don't understand, we're the good guys.'

She lowered her big brown eyes to look down at me and smiled warmly. 'My son, in the eyes of the Lord, we are all good guys.' There was no answer to that.

Martin: From the moment I hit the floor of the video shop, I'd felt this terrible pressure building up in my leg. When the nurses cut off my boots and trousers, it was easy to see why. The bullet that had zigzagged its way up my shin had come to rest under the skin at the back of my calf.

There was a grey swelling on the back of my leg the size of a grapefruit. When I examined it closely, I could actually see the bullet itself, the size of a fingertip, stretching the skin at the top of the distended region. Even as I watched it, the lump continued to grow visibly at an alarming rate, filling up with the fluids that were draining out of my dehydrating body. It didn't slow down until my calf was the diameter of my thigh.

Although Philip had been shot twice, I was judged to be in the more serious condition. The bullet itself had done a massive amount of damage but I had made matters a thousand times worse during my desperate sprint for the video shop. The 9mm round had effectively split my shin in half while the run had smashed the two separate pieces of bone together again and again, grinding and splintering them beyond repair.

The damage was so extensive that I was prepped and booked into theatre for emergency surgery later that same night. While I was waiting for my operation, Philip and I were moved out of the A&E ward and wheeled to a private room. It was long and narrow with windows all the way down one side. They backed our beds against separate walls so that we lay at 90 degrees to one another. Twin banks of machines to monitor our blood pressure and heart rate were stacked on either side of our heads and tall metal frames to hold the bags for the constant drips we required were wheeled into position.

Once we were settled in, the nurses switched on a television that sat in the opposite end of the room, by the door, just in time for the 10.30 p.m. regional news.

The top story was about the shootings. We saw dozens of West Midlands officers on their hands and knees crawling down the length of the slip road, conducting a fingertip search of the crime scene. The news crew interviewed a couple of witnesses who told of the looks of agony on our faces after we'd been shot. The newscaster announced that two men were in custody but that the third member of the gang, believed to be armed and dangerous, was still on the run.

As we listened a chill ran down my spine. The gang now had very little to lose by coming after us and killing us. But at least they didn't know we were police officers – something which would add urgency to any plans to get rid of us – nor did they know where we were.

As we continued to watch transfixed, a senior officer came on the screen and spoke directly to the camera from close to where we had been shot. 'I can confirm that both men were undercover police officers from London who had been seconded to Birmingham. They are currently in a critical but stable condition at the Birmingham City Hospital.' Philip and I stared with disbelief thinking, 'What the hell are you doing, why tell the world where we are and what we are?' The feelings of safety that had swept over us on our arrival at the hospital evaporated. We were utterly compromised.

The threat to us was real and serious enough to warrant the posting of a round-the-clock police guard outside our door. But the only real guarantee of our safety had been anonymity, for nobody to know who we were and where we'd gone. There's always a way through security if someone's determined enough. It's impossible to cover all the angles. With our bodies broken, the last thing we needed was the insecurity and fear our unexpected TV 'outing' brought with it.

Philip: When someone gets shot in the leg in a Western or an Arnold Schwarzenegger movie, they just grit their teeth, put a bandage around it and in a couple of days they are right as rain. If they get shot in the arse it's funny. They dance around like a cat on hot bricks, suck air and scream 'Ouch, that hurts', before someone pulls out the bullet with a pair of tweezers. Later, a doctor, his face sombre and serious, will say something about you being lucky it's only a 'flesh wound', and it heals right up. Not surprisingly, that's a load of Hollywood bollocks.

The only way to find out what had happened to the bullet that had been fired into my buttock was for the surgeons to open up my backside. The entry wound was about an inch across to start with but they cut a deep, ugly incision all the way down the back of my thigh around the path of the bullet, making it at least five times bigger. This was to allow them to check what damage had been done. As they worked, they pulled out scraps of jeans and shredded bits of underwear that had been dragged deep inside my body as the bullet ripped through the flesh.

It had bounced off my pelvic bone and shattered into three pieces. One fragment was found early, but as the surgeons probed deeper and deeper looking for the other bits of shrapnel, they started getting too close to major nerves and my bladder and had to halt the operation. To continue would have risked leaving me paralysed for life.

The other bullet had actually gone clean through my calf. When the nurses held my leg up to the light, they could see, even read a newspaper, through it. That sort of wound has to heal from the inside out, not from the outside in. If it's simply bandaged up, the muscles collapse and the flesh will rot. Gangrene will set in, in which case the leg has to be amputated to prevent the possibility of potentially fatal blood poisoning.

Instead, the bandage needs to be on the inside. Twice a day one of the nurses would use a thin metal rod to poke a piece of sterile gauze in one end of the wound and gently push it all the way through until it came out the other side of my leg. I was the only one who couldn't actually see it because of where the wound was. So the nurses would graphically demonstrate to me that the hole really did go all the way through by pulling on one end of the gauze and letting me watch the other end move. It seems brutal now, but at the time it was what passed for a laugh. Once the gauze was in place, a bandage was wrapped over the top.

I knew it was healing when one day their little party trick no longer worked. They took the bandages off and tried to pull out the gauze but couldn't because the flesh inside had grown so much that it had got stuck. If they had pulled on it it would have ripped out all the new muscle inside. So although it was a good sign and showed that things were moving in the right direction, I would later have to have an operation to remove the gauze. From this point on they would pack in the gauze from either side until the hole healed up completely.

In Martin's case, they had cut a long slit which ran all the way down the back of his calf and would open it up like a clam. A special tool with a cap on the end was used to pack the delicate gauze in as tightly as possible, right down to the bone. Twice a day they had to take it all out to put fresh dressings in. As it was pulled out it looked as if a magician was producing loads of handkerchiefs from his top pocket. Apparently endless streams of the stuff seemed to come out. Sometimes they could be at it for almost an hour.

After the news broadcast, the nurses realized that we were police officers, not drug dealers, and couldn't do enough for us. Whenever they had a spare moment they would come and chat, propping themselves up on the edge of our beds. Sometimes they'd come into work a few minutes early, just to have the chance to say hello, or stay behind after their shifts had ended to keep us company.

In the early days, they would pull screens around our beds when they were changing our dressings. Because this happened several times a day though, we soon got used to it and would simply carry on having conversations with one another while the nurses were at work. After a while we asked them to stop putting the screens up and we'd just watch what was going on. It wasn't always wise.

I was eating my dinner while Martin's leg was being packed. As I looked on, the insides of Martin's calf suddenly tumbled out, spilling after the gauze as it was removed. It was as if the whole of his lower leg suddenly peeled open. It was without doubt the grossest thing I had ever seen. I pushed away what remained of my meal. I'd seen some pretty shocking sights during my time in the police force but this put them all in the shade. Somehow when it's a friend of yours, it makes it that much worse.

We had to get used to it though. It's said that when you go into hospital you have to leave your dignity at the door and it's so true. My biggest problem was going to the toilet. I couldn't move either of my legs which were raised up on slings and at one point I had drips in both my arms, so using them was out of the question too. The only thing they could do was manoeuvre a bed pan into the right place underneath me and tell me when to get on with it.

The first time, the nurse left the room to give me a little privacy, then came back ten minutes later to check I'd finished. She then asked Martin if he needed to go as well. 'No thanks,' he told her. 'I did a big one outside the Kentucky in Handsworth. I don't need to go again for at least a month.'

The smell was always overpowering and would linger around for hours. After one particularly foul movement, my old friend Clive arrived from London to visit. His face puckered up in disgust before he'd even said 'hello'.

'Jesus, did some kind of animal crawl under your bed and die, Philip?' he said, keeping his distance.

'No, mate. I've just had a dump.'

'Really!' he said, theatrically rolling his eyes towards the ceiling. 'I'd never have guessed.'

Martin: I went to the operating theatre five times in the three weeks we spent in hospital. The first time was almost leisurely. I was given the anaesthetic, then wheeled down to a prep room and into theatre. The last time they had to wait until the very last moment before they could put me under. The problem was, my body had built up tolerance to the anaesthetic because I had had so much in such a short time. Given too early, the dose required to keep me under for long enough would have been enormous and way beyond the level deemed to be safe.

Although in the time that passed we slowly became more comfortable, we were still a long way from being in the clear. After the first few days I began feeling that I was on the road to recovery, but it wasn't long before I suddenly deteriorated alarmingly. One night the machine monitoring my blood pressure went mental, clicking and beeping and setting off an alarm. The doctor came rushing into the room and found that my readings had dropped sharply and my temperature had shot up through the roof. I'd developed a powerful infection in the wound. The doctor confessed that unless it was checked there was a strong chance I would lose the use of the lower part of my leg completely.

I spent two days fevered and barely conscious, so weak I couldn't even eat. I'd always known my injuries were serious, there was no doubt of that, but somehow up until that point I thought I was getting better, that I'd be able to go back to doing many of the things I had taken for granted. That night I realized for the first time that it might not be. I'd be lucky if I came out of hospital still able to walk. They had to fit a brace to my foot to stop it collapsing under its own weight for the next week until, thankfully, the muscles slowly started to recover.

I was beginning to feel more human by the middle of the second week and that coincided with an increase in the number of people coming to visit us. Our friends and families were so supportive, driving up from London just to spend a few hours with us, often a couple of times a week, and it really boosted our morale on the road to recovery. The visits also provided a welcome distraction from the concern we felt at still being in Birmingham. Just being there caused constant anxiety and continual reminders of the danger we were still in.

And these sometimes came from the most unexpected quarter. Early on Rashid, the owner of the video shop that I had run into on Soho Road, came in. Like everyone else he too had assumed initially that I was a gangster but, after discovering I was a police officer, he decided to visit me to check on my progress. As a gift, he brought a selection of videos. 'Hospital can be pretty boring,' he said with a smile, his voice a rich mixture of brummy and the subcontinent. 'These should help pass the time.'

Although the TV and video were there for our entertainment, the police officer guarding our room seemed to think he had full access to them as well. Every night, once he was sure we were asleep, he would sneak into the room and roll the TV trolley out into the corridor to watch videos of his own. It meant that when we woke up in the morning, we wouldn't be able to catch up with the news or watch anything until he remembered to bring the TV back.

As soon as we were strong enough to care, we decided to teach him a lesson. We asked the nurse to take all the cables out of the back of the video and TV and pass them to us. Then we hid them under our pillows. That night, we listened to the officer muttering under his breath as he realized he had been rumbled. After that, it never happened again.

It left us free to watch Rashid's videos and after dinner one evening, I got the nurse to put the first film on. The opening scene exploded out of the little TV's speakers as Uzis sprayed bullets around the streets of South Central LA. Each bullet hit was shown in excruciating slow motion. We managed about thirty seconds before screaming in unison for the nurse to switch it off.

We didn't dare let the second one be seen in public. *Asian Babes* did pretty much what it said on the tin. As some 90 per cent of the nurses in the hospital were Asian, we didn't watch the video much – somehow it didn't seem a very good idea. The final video was *Sister Act*, the one in which Whoopi Goldberg witnesses a murder and goes undercover in a convent. Neither Philip nor I could stand the woman.

When Rashid came back a few days later, we thanked him warmly. It had been such a kind gesture, we didn't want to hurt his feelings by telling him how inappropriate his selections had been.

After three full weeks in hospital, we were both desperate to get back to London and our families, but we were still incredibly fragile, in a great deal of pain and not really able to walk. The long journey home down the motorway was sickeningly painful. But it felt good to be getting out of Birmingham. It was the only way to leave behind the threat that remaining there posed to us. I felt safer with each passing mile.

It was decided that we should be treated by our local GPs rather than in the fully equipped hospital at the police training centre in Hendon. This may have been a decision taken to allow us to be with our families, though not surprisingly it caused its own problems. Though good doctors, they had no experience in dealing with trauma caused by gunshot wounds. The real problem was that our doctors weren't allowed to know that we had been working as undercover police officers or to be given any of the background to the shooting.

At first, when we got back to London there seemed to be genuine concern for our well-being but this soon faltered. We were caught up in an endless round of hospital appointments, physiotherapy and counselling. Neither of us was particularly mobile. We spent our days lying in bed or sitting on sofas watching TV. We were on the phone constantly and our quarterly bills would regularly top £600 as we spoke to each other and tried to get information about the events in the Midlands and about our own futures. 'Don't worry about all that stuff now,' DS Chris Taylor would say, 'just you concentrate on getting better.' But we'd been doing that now for two years.

There's no doubt that the shooting was a massive cock-up and the blame had to lie somewhere. Our problem was that we were the most obvious and problematic reminder of it to all concerned. We were being fobbed off because we were damaged goods. It was as if no one wanted to talk to us in case they were tainted through association.

Nearly three years after being shot, I got called in to see the police doctor. He spoke even before I'd had a chance to sit down. 'It looks as if we've come to the end of the road, Martin.'

'What do you mean?'

'Well, this leg of yours. I don't think it's ever going to mend fully. So I guess we have to say goodbye.'

I just sat there in stunned silence. I didn't know what to say. I had spent three years fighting back to health in the expectation that some part of my career would remain open for me, especially considering that my injuries were inflicted in the line of duty. I couldn't believe I had been so mistaken.

'Is that it then? Is that all you can say?' I said at last.

'Don't worry,' said the doctor, completely misreading my expression. 'I'll help you with the forms and all that for your medical retirement. And I want you to know that I wish you the best of luck for the future.'

Philip was medically retired on the same day.

Epilogue

Philip: From where we were sitting, my wife and I could see it all clearly: four guys, Tommy, Henry, Anthony and Jimmy, were sitting around a table playing cards while the waiter, a lanky teenager named Spider, sporting an enormous bandage on his left foot, limped to and from the bar fetching drinks.

'Hey, Spider,' yelled Tommy, 'that fucking bandage on your foot is bigger than your fucking head, you know that?'

Everyone laughed apart from Spider who threw Tommy a contemptuous look. 'Thank you, sir.'

Tommy didn't miss a beat. 'The next thing you know, he's gonna be coming in with one of those fucking walkers. Even though you got that, you could dance, huh? Give us a twirl, give us a couple of fucking steps here, Spider. You fucking bullshitter you. Tell the truth, you're looking for sympathy is that it, sweetie?'

Spider finished loading some extra ice in Anthony's glass then dragged himself back to the bar. 'Why don't you go fuck yourself, Tommy?'

A roar went up from the table as everyone but Tommy exploded in a mixture of laughter and surprise. 'I didn't fucking hear right. I can't believe what I just heard,' chuckled Jimmy, reaching into his pocket and pulling out a wad of bills. 'Here Spider, this is for you. Tommy, you gonna let him get away with that? Are you gonna let this fucking punk get away with that? What's the matter with you? What's the world coming to?'

Jimmy and the others were still laughing when, without warning, a furious Tommy pulled a silver handgun from his belt and pumped six deafening shots into Spider's chest, ripping him in half and sending his broken body sprawling back on the floor. Dead.

From where we were sitting, on the sofa in front of the television, my wife and I saw it all clearly but as that scene in the film came to an end, I noticed Joanne was staring at me, concern etched into her face.

'Are you OK?' she asked gently.

'Yeah. I'm fine. Why shouldn't I be?'

'Well, it's just that every time the guy on TV fired his gun, your leg did this.' Joanne mimicked a series of violent twitches with her own leg. I hadn't even realized it was happening.

As Martin and I have discovered, the slow and painful recovery from our physical injuries was only one part of the battle. The mental scars left by the trauma of what happened that night in Birmingham will take much longer to heal.

'To be honest Philip,' my psychologist told me a few months after the shooting, 'I'm absolutely amazed that the two of you are coping with all this so well. I know people who have been in similar situations and who've been unable to look forward. They just couldn't handle the fact that an injury had ended their career.

One of the most difficult challenges Martin and I had to face following the shooting was the court case. Clifton Sharpe, the man who had shot us, was charged with two counts of attempted murder, and possession of a firearm. Gerald Thomas, the man who along with Sharpe had tried to the grab the car keys, was also charged with the same. Eddie Barnes, the hooded man who had appeared from nowhere by Martin's door when he tried to escape from the car, was charged with conspiracy to rob, while Carl and Lenny Marshall were picked up for charges relating to the crack they had sold Martin and Floyd during the test buys.

At first the whole gang pleaded not guilty to everything. That meant Martin and I had to travel to Birmingham to give evidence in court. We both began feeling sick as the date approached and on the morning I was due to travel up, I had such severe stomach cramps I nearly called a doctor. We were put up in a hotel just a few hundred yards from the court building and watched the defendants arrive in a van with darkened windows. The area surrounding the court was dotted with armed police officers and inside the court, a special screen had been erected to prevent our faces being seen by those in the public gallery.

A few hours before we were due to give evidence, Martin and I sat in the hotel, unable to speak, numb with anticipation. And then the phone rang. The defendants had struck a deal. We would not have to give evidence after all. Sharpe was sentenced to twelve years after admitting conspiracy to rob and possessing the gun, Thomas to eight for conspiracy to rob. Eddie Barnes got five years for conspiracy while Carl and Lenny got six and four years respectively for their part in the crime.

Summing up at the trial, the judge, Mr Justice Mellor QC, said: 'Undercover police officers, I know from my experience in this city, operate at considerable peril to themselves and Martin certainly on many occasions put himself at risk in Birmingham by endeavouring to penetrate, and indeed succeeding in penetrating, some of those dealing in crack cocaine in this city. 'They both deserve commendation for their work in that regard but they deserve highly to be commended for their courage and persistence in the attack upon them when faced with an armed man who was ready to discharge the pistol into them and did, and in the way in which each of them acted, Martin in seeking to rescue Philip and Philip in seeking to overcome at least one of the robbers when he was severely injured. I will direct that they each of them be highly commended and a record be made of my remarks and passed to the appropriate authority.'

Before the shooting we were on the verge of becoming firm friends; since it, we have become almost inseparable. Despite the best intentions of those around us, they simply cannot fully empathize with our experiences and the range of emotions that was unleashed as a result. All undercover officers rely on one another for emotional support, even at the best of times. Today, Martin and I can barely do without one another. There is a deep bond between us that can never, will never be broken. I am alive today only because Martin was willing to risk his own life to save me from certain death. I remind him of that regularly. Despite my immeasurable gratitude it's a debt that can never be repaid.

Martin: It's now been more than five years since I was shot and I still suffer from regular, violent nightmares. Sometimes I am being chased by a man with a gun but I can't see his face, just the shadows inside the hood of his tracksuit. Other times I'm fighting for my life or I wake up to find someone firing a gun in my face. It's a classic symptom of post-traumatic stress syndrome. Not a single week goes by that I don't see a counsellor. I never feel completely relaxed, I'm always on edge. I can be doing something totally innocuous such as sitting in a supermarket car park, waiting for my partner to return with the shopping, and I'll start to panic and break out in a cold sweat every time someone walks by the side of the car.

I'm only too well aware that, even if you're alert and looking out for danger, it can still sneak up on you and everything can change in a heartbeat. There I was, going along with my normal life, knowing that things could change at any moment but expecting everything to remain the same and then, in the course of just one night, my whole life was turned upside down.

Even now I agonize over the choice that I made. As I stood on the wall, scared but uninjured, looking back towards Philip and the gunman, I knew I could either save my own life or try to prevent the gunman shooting Philip again. I could never regret what I did, but I have to live with the knowledge that the injuries I suffered were a direct result of my own actions.

My leg will never heal completely. The fibia was irreparably damaged by the bullet and the gap between the two severed ends has yet to close up. In the winter, cold air cuts through my scars like a scalpel. I have twinges of pain all the time but I just have to put up with them. There are only so many painkillers you can take in one day, and when you've hit the limit there's not a lot more you can do.

Philip's in the same boat. He still has two bullet fragments trapped in his pelvis and suffers from almost constant discomfort all the way down his legs. If he has a busy day – going to the shops and picking up his kids from school – it can leave him exhausted for hours.

His other leg, where he was shot in the calf, is always tight, and is still numb, five years on. He just can't feel a thing. Complaints tend to be kept between the two of us though. We both consider ourselves lucky to be alive and to have all four limbs intact – even if they're not quite top drawer any more.

Apart from the physical effects there are other worries too. Danger is all around us. On the streets of Britain today there are people who only knew us in our undercover role, people who think we are criminals like them. There are others who may have worked out that we must have been police during the extended thinking time they get at Her Majesty's pleasure. Finally, there are a group of people in Birmingham who know exactly what we were and what we look like. They would be very keen to track us down.

For that reason, our homes are, and will continue to be, fitted with panic buttons connected to our local police stations. Our names have been kept off the electoral register and the Royal Mail double-checks our post for suspicious packages.

I could never have come through all this had it not been for Philip. We are very different characters but I absolutely love him to death. I know he'll be in my life for ever, he has to be. We're so close now it's almost as if we share one life, and together we are at last starting to move on from the shooting.

Philip: For me, being in the police was a career. It meant I had an idea of where I was going and what I was doing. For fifteen years I built my entire life around it. I truly believed that I was making a difference, that I was an effective role model for people. Both Martin and I had good reports, we were well thought of by other officers and had a certain position in life.

Like the first time we met, we still tell each other stories from our days in the force, the glory days. We both miss the fast cars, the glamour and the excitement of working undercover. We were responsible for putting away some of the most prolific and dangerous villains in the country. Murderers, armed robbers, drug dealers and fraudsters are inside solely because of us. There are countless people who would have become victims of crime but for our actions. And there is a sense of satisfaction in that which will never go away.

All that is gone now and I try not to look back. There comes a time when you realize that you have to put things behind you, have to put the experiences of the past to bed once and for all. Otherwise you can spend your whole life talking about the things you've done as a way of avoiding having to focus too hard on what comes next.

There are, of course, people around us who are interested in it all. They want to know every detail of what it was like to work undercover, how it felt, what the people we were dealing with were like and how we coped with doing what we did. They want to know what it is like to stare death in the face, to be shot at point-blank range, to not know if your partner is dead or alive. In other words, they want you to take the most terrifying, traumatic experience of your entire life and re-live it in minute detail, over and over again.

Yet at the same time, talking can help. It's what we do with our counsellors. For Martin and I, writing this book has been a kind of therapy. It's a way of getting everything off our chest, locking it away and moving on.

So the next time someone asks, we'll just tell them to read the book.

Acknowledgements

Philip

I would like to thank, first of all, my parents, who have provided many forms of support, emotional, physical and spiritual.

The support from both families has been fantastic. Friends have listened and taken an active interest in my well-being. My agent and the team from Penguin who made this project happen. To all of the above, Thank you.

Martin deserves a special mention for making a split-second decision which saved my life and changed his for ever.

And finally I would like to thank my wife, who managed to keep our family going throughout the last six years.

Martin

Fo, thanks for all your love and support.

Beverly and Carol and my children, my thoughts are with you always.

Family and friends, I couldn't have made it without you.

Authors' note

While all the events described in the book happened, some details, including names and locations, have been changed.